Ensemble Machine Learning Cookbook

Over 35 practical recipes to explore ensemble machine learning techniques using Python

Dipayan Sarkar
Vijayalakshmi Natarajan

BIRMINGHAM - MUMBAI

Ensemble Machine Learning Cookbook

Commissioning Editor: Sunith Shetty
Acquisition Editor: Devika Battike
Content Development Editor: Nathanya Dias
Technical Editor: Utkarsha S. Kadam
Copy Editor: Safis Editing
Language Support Editor: Mary McGowan
Project Coordinator: Kirti Pisat
Proofreader: Safis Editing
Indexer: Priyanka Dhadke
Graphics: Jisha Chirayil
Production Coordinator: Tom Scaria

First published: January 2019

Production reference: 1300119

Published by Packt Publishing Ltd.
Livery Place
35 Livery Street
Birmingham
B3 2PB, UK.

ISBN 978-1-78913-660-9

www.packtpub.com

`mapt.io`

Mapt is an online digital library that gives you full access to over 5,000 books and videos, as well as industry leading tools to help you plan your personal development and advance your career. For more information, please visit our website.

Why subscribe?

- Spend less time learning and more time coding with practical eBooks and Videos from over 4,000 industry professionals

- Improve your learning with Skill Plans built especially for you

- Get a free eBook or video every month

- Mapt is fully searchable

- Copy and paste, print, and bookmark content

Packt.com

Did you know that Packt offers eBook versions of every book published, with PDF and ePub files available? You can upgrade to the eBook version at `www.packt.com` and as a print book customer, you are entitled to a discount on the eBook copy. Get in touch with us at `customercare@packtpub.com` for more details.

At `www.packt.com`, you can also read a collection of free technical articles, sign up for a range of free newsletters, and receive exclusive discounts and offers on Packt books and eBooks.

Foreword

Artificial Intelligence with Machine Learning alongside is currently occupying a formidable position in the analytics domain for automating strategic decisions. The unabated meteoric growth that we have been witnessing in business analytics in the last 3 to 5 years that is responsible for this new Avatar AIMLA, an acronym that stands for Artificial Intelligence and Machine Learning Algorithms.

AIMLA is the new frontier in business analytics that promises a great future in terms of attractive career opportunities for budding young students of management and managers. Andrew Ng, a luminary in this field, predicts "AI will transform every industry just like electricity transformed them 100 years back." AI will have to necessarily use machine learning algorithms for automation of decisions.

Against this backdrop, the role of this book titled *Ensemble Machine Learning Cookbook* that is being introduced into the market by Packt Publishing looms large. Personally speaking, it was indeed a pleasure reading this book. Every chapter has been so nicely organized in terms of the themes "Getting ready", "How to do it", "How it works", and "There's more". The book uses Python, the new analytic language for deriving insights from data in the most effective manner. I congratulate the two authors, Dipayan Sarkar and Vijayalakshmi Natarajan, for producing a practical, yet conceptually rigorous analytic decision-oriented book that is the need of the hour.

Conceptual clarity, cohesive content, lucid explanation, appropriate datasets for each algorithm, and analytics for insights using Python coding are the hallmarks of the book. The journey of ensemble machine learning algorithms in the book involves eight chapters starting from the preliminary background to Python and going all the way step-by-step, to Chapter 7, *Boosting Model Performance with Boosting*. The fascinating part to me has been Chapter 4, *Statistical and Machine Learning Algorithms* that is so nicely packed with multiple regression, logistic regression, Naïve Bayes, decision trees, and support vector machines that are the bedrock of supervised machine learning. Apart from the rest of the content on machine learning that was very carefully and effectively covered, what stands out is the all-important ensemble model-random forest and its implementation in Chapter 6, *When in Doubt, Use Random Forests*.

The book is compact, with about 300+ pages and does not frighten anyone by it's huge size. This new book *Ensemble Machine Learning Cookbook* will be extremely handy for both students and practitioners as a guide for not only understanding machine learning but also automating it for analytic decisions.

I wish authors Dipayan Sarkar and Vijayalakshmi Natarajan all the best.

Dr. P. K.Viswanathan

Professor (Analytics), Director, PGP-BABI and AIMLA

Great Lakes Institute of Management, Chennai

Contributors

About the authors

Dipayan Sarkar holds a Masters in economics and comes with 15+ years of experience. He has also pursued business analytics studies from Great Lakes Institute of Management. Dipayan has won international challenges in predictive modeling and takes a keen interest in the mathematics behind machine learning techniques. Before opting to become an independent consultant and a mentor in the data science and machine learning space with various organizations, universities, and educational institutions, he served in the capacity of senior data scientist with Fortune 500 companies.

This book is dedicated to my mother, Rina Sarkar, my father, Gurudas Sarkar, and my niece, PomPom.

Vijayalakshmi Natarajan holds an ME in computer science and has 4 years of industry experience. She is a data science enthusiast and a passionate trainer in the fields of data science and data visualization. She takes keen interest in deep-diving into machine learning techniques. Her specializations include machine learning techniques in the field of image processing.

This book is dedicated to my mother, Jayanthi, and my father, Natarajan.

A special thanks to Kajal Goel, Pravalika Aitipamula, Rajat Sharma, Rehan Ali Ansari, and Siddhartha Kothotya.

About the reviewers

Dr. P.K. Viswanathan has been rated as one of the top 10 and top 20 most prominent Analytics and Data Science Academicians in India in the years 2017 and 2018 respectively. In his industrial tenure, spanning 15+ years, he has held senior management positions in Ballarpur Industries and J.K. Industries. He holds degrees in MSc(Madras University), MBA(FMS, Delhi), MS(Manitoba, Canada), and PhD(Madras University). He has authored various books on Business Statistics and Marketing Research. He has published research articles in reputed journals and has presented papers in national and international conferences. He has also conducted many training programs, and is involved as a key faculty in the Management Development Programs at Great Lakes.

Vadim Smolyakov is currently pursuing his PhD at MIT in the areas of computer science and artificial intelligence. His primary research interests include Bayesian inference, deep learning, and optimization. Prior to coming to MIT, Vadim received his undergraduate degree in engineering science at the University of Toronto. He previously worked as a data scientist in the e-commerce space. Vadim is passionate about machine learning and data science, and is interested in making the field accessible to a broad audience, inspiring readers to innovate and pursue research in artificial intelligence.

Swarna Gupta holds a B.E. in computer science, and has 5 years of experience in the data science space. She is currently working with Rolls Royce in the capacity of a data scientist. Her work revolves around leveraging data science and machine learning to create value for the business. She has extensively worked on IoT-based projects in the vehicle telematics and solar manufacturing industries. Swarna also manages time from her busy schedule to be a regular pro-bono contributor to social organizations, helping them to solve specific business problems with the help of data science and machine learning. She takes a keen interest in the mathematics behind machine learning, deep learning, and artificial intelligence.

Packt is searching for authors like you

If you're interested in becoming an author for Packt, please visit `authors.packtpub.com` and apply today. We have worked with thousands of developers and tech professionals, just like you, to help them share their insight with the global tech community. You can make a general application, apply for a specific hot topic that we are recruiting an author for, or submit your own idea.

Preface

Ensemble modeling is an approach used to improve the performance of machine learning models. It combines two or more similar or dissimilar machine-learning algorithms to deliver superior powers. This book will help you to implement some popular machine-learning algorithms to cover different paradigms of ensemble machine learning, such as boosting, bagging, and stacking.

This Ensemble Machine Learning Cookbook will start by getting you acquainted with the basics of ensemble techniques and exploratory data analysis. You'll then learn to implement tasks related to statistical and machine learning algorithms to understand the ensemble of multiple heterogeneous algorithms. It'll also ensure that you don't miss out on key topics such as resampling methods. As you progress, you'll get a better understanding of bagging, boosting, stacking, and learn how to work with the Random Forest algorithm using real-world examples. The book will highlight how these ensemble methods use multiple models to improve machine learning results, compared to a single model. In the concluding chapters, you'll delve into advanced ensemble models using neural networks, **Natural Language Processing** (**NLP**), and more. You'll also be able to implement models covering fraud detection, text categorization, and sentiment analysis.

By the end of this book, you'll be able to harness ensemble techniques and the working mechanisms of machine-learning algorithms to build intelligent models using individual recipes.

Who this book is for

This book is designed for data scientists, machine learning developers, and deep learning enthusiasts who want to delve into machine learning algorithms to build powerful ensemble models. A working knowledge of Python programming and basic statistics is a must to help you grasp the concepts in the book.

What this book covers

Chapter 1, *Get Closer to Your Data*, explores a dataset and implements hands-on coding with Python for exploratory data analysis using statistical methods and visualization for the dataset.

Chapter 2, *Getting Started with Ensemble Machine Learning*, explores what ensemble learning is and how it can help in real-life scenarios. Basic ensemble techniques, including averaging, weighted averaging, and max-voting, are explained. These techniques form the basis for ensemble techniques, and an understanding of them will lay the groundwork for readers to move to more advanced stage after reading this chapter.

Chapter 3, *Resampling Methods*, introduces a handful of algorithms that will be useful when we get into an ensemble of multiple heterogeneous algorithms. This chapter uses scikit-learn to prepare all the algorithms to be used.

Chapter 4, *Statistical and Machine Learning Algorithms*, helps the readers to get to know various types of resampling methods that are used by machine-learning algorithms. Each resampling method has its advantages and disadvantages, which are explained to the readers. The readers also learn the code to be executed for each type of sampling.

Chapter 5, *Bag the Models with Bagging*, provides the readers with an understanding of what bootstrap aggregation is and how the bootstrap results can be aggregated, in a process also known as bagging.

Chapter 6, *When in Doubt, Use Random Forests*, introduces the random forest algorithm. It will introduce to readers how, and what kind of, ensemble techniques are used by Random Forest and how this helps our models avoid overfitting.

Chapter 7, *Boosting Model Performance with Boosting*, introduces boosting and discusses how it helps to improve a model performance by reducing variances and increasing accuracy. This chapter provides information such as the fact that boosting is not robust against outliers and noisy data but is flexible and can be used with a loss function.

Chapter 8, *Blend It with Stacking*, applies stacking to learn the optimal combination of base learners. This chapter will acquaint readers with stacking, which is also known as stacked generalization.

Chapter 9, *Homogeneous Ensemble Using Keras*, is a complete code walk-through on a classification case study for recognizing hand-written digits with homogeneous algorithms – in this case, multiple neural network models using Keras.

Chapter 10, *Heterogeneous Ensemble Classifiers Using H2O*, is a complete code walk-through on a classification case study for default prediction with an ensemble of multiple heterogeneous algorithms using scikit-learn.

Chapter 11, *Heterogeneous Ensemble for Text Classification Using NLP*, is a complete code walk-through on a classification case study to classify sentiment polarity using an ensemble of multiple heterogeneous algorithms. Here, NLP techniques such as semantics are used to improve the accuracy of classification. Then, the mined text information is used to employ ensemble classification techniques for sentiment analysis. In this case study, the H2O library is used for building models.

Chapter 12, *Homogeneous Ensemble for Multiclass Classification Using Keras*, is a complete code walk-through on a classification case study for multiple classification with homogeneous ensemble using data diversity with the tf.keras module from TensorFlow.

To get the most out of this book

Readers will need a working knowledge of Python programming and basic statistics to help you grasp the concepts in the book.

Download the example code files

You can download the example code files for this book from your account at `www.packt.com`. If you purchased this book elsewhere, you can visit `www.packt.com/support` and register to have the files emailed directly to you.

You can download the code files by following these steps:

1. Log in or register at `www.packt.com`.
2. Select the **SUPPORT** tab.
3. Click on **Code Downloads & Errata**.
4. Enter the name of the book in the **Search** box and follow the onscreen instructions.

Once the file is downloaded, please make sure that you unzip or extract the folder using the latest version of:

- WinRAR/7-Zip for Windows
- Zipeg/iZip/UnRarX for Mac
- 7-Zip/PeaZip for Linux

The code bundle for the book is also hosted on GitHub at `https://github.com/PacktPublishing/Ensemble-Machine-Learning-Cookbook`. In case there's an update to the code, it will be updated on the existing GitHub repository.

We also have other code bundles from our rich catalog of books and videos available at `https://github.com/PacktPublishing/`. Check them out!

Download the color images

We also provide a PDF file that has color images of the screenshots/diagrams used in this book. You can download it here: `http://www.packtpub.com/sites/default/files/downloads/9781789136609_ColorImages.pdf`.

Conventions used

There are a number of text conventions used throughout this book.

`CodeInText`: Indicates code words in text, database table names, folder names, filenames, file extensions, pathnames, dummy URLs, user input, and Twitter handles. Here is an example: "We will use the `os` package in the operating system's dependent functionality, and the `pandas` package for data manipulation."

A block of code is set as follows:

```
import os
import pandas as pd

# Set working directory as per your need
os.chdir(".../.../Chapter 1")
os.getcwd()
```

Warnings or important notes appear like this.

Tips and tricks appear like this.

Sections

In this book, you will find several headings that appear frequently (*Getting ready, How to do it..., How it works..., There's more...,* and *See also*).

To give clear instructions on how to complete a recipe, use these sections as follows:

Getting ready

This section tells you what to expect in the recipe and describes how to set up any software or any preliminary settings required for the recipe.

How to do it...

This section contains the steps required to follow the recipe.

How it works...

This section usually consists of a detailed explanation of what happened in the previous section.

There's more...

This section consists of additional information about the recipe in order to make you more knowledgeable about the recipe.

See also

This section provides helpful links to other useful information for the recipe.

Get in touch

Feedback from our readers is always welcome.

General feedback: If you have questions about any aspect of this book, mention the book title in the subject of your message and email us at customercare@packtpub.com.

Errata: Although we have taken every care to ensure the accuracy of our content, mistakes do happen. If you have found a mistake in this book, we would be grateful if you would report this to us. Please visit www.packt.com/submit-errata, selecting your book, clicking on the Errata Submission Form link, and entering the details.

Piracy: If you come across any illegal copies of our works in any form on the Internet, we would be grateful if you would provide us with the location address or website name. Please contact us at copyright@packt.com with a link to the material.

If you are interested in becoming an author: If there is a topic that you have expertise in and you are interested in either writing or contributing to a book, please visit authors.packtpub.com.

Reviews

Please leave a review. Once you have read and used this book, why not leave a review on the site that you purchased it from? Potential readers can then see and use your unbiased opinion to make purchase decisions, we at Packt can understand what you think about our products, and our authors can see your feedback on their book. Thank you!

For more information about Packt, please visit packt.com.

Table of Contents

Get Closer to Your Data 1

In this chapter, we will cover the following recipes:

- Data manipulation with Python
- Analyzing, visualizing, and treating missing values
- Exploratory data analysis

Introduction

In this book, we will cover various ensemble techniques and will learn how to ensemble multiple machine learning algorithms to enhance a model's performance. We will use pandas, NumPy, scikit-learn, and Matplotlib, all of which were built for working with Python, as we will do throughout the book. By now, you should be well aware of data manipulation and exploration.

In this chapter, we will recap how to read and manipulate data in Python, how to analyze and treat missing values, and how to explore data to gain deeper insights. We will use various Python packages, such as `numpy` and `pandas`, for data manipulation and exploration, and `seaborn` packages for data visualization. We will continue to use some or all of these libraries in the later chapters of this book as well. We will also use the Anaconda distribution for our Python coding. If you have not installed Anaconda, you need to download it from `https://www.anaconda.com/download`. At the time of writing this book, the latest version of Anaconda is 5.2, and comes with both Python 3.6 and Python 2.7. We suggest you download Anaconda for Python 3.6. We will also use the `HousePrices` dataset, which is available on GitHub.

Data manipulation with Python

In real life, it is often hard to get a complete and clean dataset formatted exactly as we need it. The data we receive often cannot be directly used in statistical or machine learning algorithms. We need to manipulate the raw data so that the processed data can be used for further analysis and modelling purposes. To begin with, we need to import the required packages, such as `pandas`, and read our dataset into Python.

Getting ready

We will use the `os` package in the operating system's dependent functionality, and the `pandas` package for data manipulation.

Let's now take a look at the data definitions to understand our variables. In the following code, we list the data definition for a few variables. The dataset and the complete data definitions are available on GitHub. Here is an abridged version of the data description file:

```
MS SubClass (Nominal): Identifies the type of dwelling involved in
the sale
Lot Frontage (Continuous): Linear feet of street connected to
property
Alley (Nominal): Type of alley access to property
Overall Qual (Ordinal): Rates the overall material and finish of
the house
Overall Cond (Ordinal): Rates the overall condition of the house
Year Built (Discrete): Original construction date
Mas Vnr Type (Nominal): Masonry veneer type
Mas Vnr Area (Continuous): Masonry veneer area in square feet
Garage Type (Nominal): Garage location
Garage Yr Blt (Discrete): Year garage was built
Garage Finish (Ordinal): Interior finish of the garage
Garage Cars (Discrete): Size of garage in car capacity
Garage Area (Continuous): Size of garage in square feet
Garage Qual (Ordinal): Garage quality
Garage Cond (Ordinal): Garage condition
...
...
SalePrice (Continuous): Sale price $$
```

We will then import the `os` and `pandas` packages and set our working directory according to our requirements, as seen in the following code block:

```
import os
import pandas as pd

# Set working directory as per your need
os.chdir(".../.../Chapter 1")
os.getcwd()
```

The next step is to download the dataset from GitHub and copy it to your working directory.

How to do it...

Now, let's perform some data manipulation steps:

1. First, we will read the data in `HousePrices.csv` from our current working directory and create our first DataFrame for manipulation. We name the DataFrame `housepricesdata`, as follows:

    ```
    housepricesdata = pd.read_csv("HousePrices.csv")
    ```

2. Let's now take a look at our DataFrame and see how it looks:

    ```
    # See first five observations from top
    housepricesdata.head(5)
    ```

    You might not be able to see all the rows; Jupyter will truncate some of the variables. In order to view all of the rows and columns for any output in Jupyter, execute the following commands:

    ```
    # Setting options to display all rows and columns
    pd.options.display.max_rows = None
    pd.options.display.max_columns = None
    ```

3. We can see the dimensions of the DataFrame with `shape`. `shape` is an attribute of the `pandas` DataFrame:

    ```
    housepricesdata.shape
    ```

With the preceding command, we can see the number of rows and columns, as follows:

```
(1460, 81)
```

Here, we can see that the DataFrame has `1460` observations and `81` columns.

4. Let's take a look at the datatypes of the variables in the DataFrame:

```
housepricesdata.dtypes
```

In the following code block, we can see the datatypes of each variable in the DataFrame:

```
Id                 int64
MSSubClass         int64
MSZoning          object
LotFrontage      float64
LotArea            int64
LotConfig         object
LandSlope         object
                   . . .
BedroomAbvGr       int64
KitchenAbvGr       int64
KitchenQual       object
TotRmsAbvGrd       int64
SaleCondition     object
SalePrice          int64
Length: 81, dtype: object
```

We're now all ready to start with our data manipulation, which we can do in many different ways. In this section, we'll look at a few ways in which we can manipulate and prepare our data for the purpose of analysis.

Let's start by summarizing our data.

5. The `describe()` function will show the statistics for the numerical variables only:

```
housepricesdata.describe()
```

We can see the output in the following screenshot:

	Id	LotFrontage	LotArea	OverallQual	OverallCond	YearBuilt	YearRemodAdd	MasVnrArea	BsmtFinSF1	BsmtFinSF2	BsmtUnfSF
count	1460.000000	1201.000000	1460.000000	1460.000000	1460.000000	1460.000000	1460.000000	1452.000000	1460.000000	1460.000000	1460.000000
mean	730.500000	70.049958	10516.828082	6.099315	5.575342	1971.267808	1984.865753	103.685262	443.639726	46.549315	567.240411
std	421.610009	24.284752	9981.264932	1.382997	1.112799	30.202904	20.645407	181.066207	456.098091	161.319273	441.866955
min	1.000000	21.000000	1300.000000	1.000000	1.000000	1872.000000	1950.000000	0.000000	0.000000	0.000000	0.000000
25%	365.750000	59.000000	7553.500000	5.000000	5.000000	1954.000000	1967.000000	0.000000	0.000000	0.000000	223.000000
50%	730.500000	69.000000	9478.500000	6.000000	5.000000	1973.000000	1994.000000	0.000000	383.500000	0.000000	477.500000
75%	1095.250000	80.000000	11601.500000	7.000000	6.000000	2000.000000	2004.000000	166.000000	712.250000	0.000000	808.000000
max	1460.000000	313.000000	215245.000000	10.000000	9.000000	2010.000000	2010.000000	1600.000000	5644.000000	1474.000000	2336.000000

6. We will remove the `id` column, as this will not be necessary for our analysis:

```
# inplace=True will overwrite the DataFrame after dropping Id
column
housepricesdata.drop(['Id'], axis=1, inplace=True)
```

7. Let's now look at the distribution of some of the object type variables, that is, the categorical variables. In the following example, we are going to look at `LotShape` and `LandContour`. We can study the other categorical variables of the dataset in the same way as shown in the following code block:

```
# Name the count column as "count"
lotshape_frequencies =
pd.crosstab(index=housepricesdata["LotShape"], columns="count")

landcountour_frequencies =
pd.crosstab(index=housepricesdata["LandContour"], columns="count")
# Name the count column as "count"

print(lotshape_frequencies)
print("\n") # to keep a blank line for display
print(landcountour_frequencies)
```

8. We will now see how to perform a conversion between datatypes. What we notice is that the data definition of variables such as `MSSubClass`, `OverallQual`, and `OverallCond` are all categorical variables. After importing the dataset, however, they appear as integers.

Prior to typecasting any variable, ensure that there are no missing values.

Here, we'll convert the variables to a categorical datatype:

```
# Using astype() to cast a pandas object to a specified datatype
housepricesdata['MSSubClass'] =
housepricesdata['MSSubClass'].astype('object')
housepricesdata['OverallQual'] =
housepricesdata['OverallQual'].astype('object')
housepricesdata['OverallCond'] =
housepricesdata['OverallCond'].astype('object')


# Check the datatype of MSSubClass after type conversion
print(housepricesdata['MSSubClass'].dtype)
print('\n') # to keep a blank line for display

# Check the distribution of the levels in MSSubClass after
conversion
# Make a crosstab with pd.crosstab()
# Name the count column as "count"
print(pd.crosstab(index=housepricesdata["MSSubClass"],
columns="count"))
```

We can see the count of observations for each category of houses, as shown in the following code block:

```
category

col_0          count
MSSubClass
20               536
30                69
40                 4
45                12
50               144
60               299
70                60
75                16
80                58
85                20
90                52
120               87
160               63
180               10
190               30
```

There are many variables that might not be very useful by themselves, but transforming them gives us a lot of interesting insights. Let's create some new, meaningful variables.

9. `YearBuilt` and `YearRemodAdd` represent the original construction date and the remodel date respectively. However, if they can be converted into age, these variables will tell us how old the buildings are and how many years it has been since they were remodeled. To do this, we create two new variables, `BuildingAge` and `RemodelAge`:

```
# Importing datetime package for date time operations
import datetime as dt

# using date time package to find the current year
current_year = int(dt.datetime.now().year)

# Subtracting the YearBuilt from current_year to find out the age
of the building
building_age = current_year - housepricesdata['YearBuilt']

# Subtracting the YearRemonAdd from current_year to find out the
age since the
# building was remodelled
remodelled_age = current_year - housepricesdata['YearRemodAdd']
```

10. Now, let's add the two variables to our dataset:

```
# Adding the two variables to the DataFrame
housepricesdata['building_age'] = building_age
housepricesdata['remodelled_age'] = remodelled_age

# Checking our DataFrame to see if the two variables got added
housepricesdata.head(5)
```

We notice that `building_age` and `remodelled_age` are now added to the DataFrame, as shown in the following screenshot:

Utilities	...	Fence	MiscFeature	MiscVal	MoSold	YrSold	SaleType	SaleCondition	SalePrice	building_age	remodelled_age
AllPub	...	NaN	NaN	0	2	2008	WD	Normal	208500	15	15
AllPub	...	NaN	NaN	0	5	2007	WD	Normal	181500	42	42
AllPub	...	NaN	NaN	0	9	2008	WD	Normal	223500	17	16
AllPub	...	NaN	NaN	0	2	2006	WD	Abnorml	140000	103	48
AllPub	...	NaN	NaN	0	12	2008	WD	Normal	250000	18	18

Variables that contain label data need to be converted into a numerical form for machine learning algorithms to use. To get around this, we will perform encoding that will transform the labels into numerical forms so that the algorithms can use them.

11. We need to identify the variables that need encoding, which include `Street`, `LotShape`, and `LandContour`. We will perform one-hot encoding, which is a representation of categorical variables as binary vectors. We will use the `pandas` package in Python to do this:

```
# We use get_dummies() function to one-hot encode LotShape
one_hot_encoded_variables =
pd.get_dummies(housepricesdata['LotShape'],prefix='LotShape')

# Print the one-hot encoded variables to see how they look like
print(one_hot_encoded_variables)
```

We can see the one-hot encoded variables that have been created in the following screenshot:

	LotShape_IR1	LotShape_IR2	LotShape_IR3	LotShape_Reg
0	0	0	0	1
1	0	0	0	1
2	1	0	0	0
3	1	0	0	0
4	1	0	0	0
5	1	0	0	0

12. Add the one-hot encoded variables to our DataFrame, as follows:

```
# Adding the new created one-hot encoded variables to our DataFrame
housepricesdata =
pd.concat([housepricesdata,one_hot_encoded_variables],axis=1)

# Let's take a look at the added one-hot encoded variables
# Scroll right to view the added variables
housepricesdata.head(5)
```

We can see the output that we get after adding the one-hot encoded variables to the DataFrame in the following screenshot:

SaleType	SaleCondition	SalePrice	building_age	remodelled_age	LotShape_IR1	LotShape_IR2	LotShape_IR3	LotShape_Reg
WD	Normal	208500	15	15	0	0	0	1
WD	Normal	181500	42	42	0	0	0	1
WD	Normal	223500	17	16	1	0	0	0
WD	Abnorml	140000	103	48	1	0	0	0
WD	Normal	250000	18	18	1	0	0	0

13. Now, let's remove the original variables since we have already created our one-hot encoded variables:

```
# Dropping the original variable after one-hot encoding the
original variable
# inplace = True option will overwrite the DataFrame

housepricesdata.drop(['LotShape'],axis=1, inplace=True)
```

How it works...

The `pandas` module is a part of the Python standard library – it is one of the key modules for data manipulation. We have also used other packages, such as `os` and `datetime`. After we set our working directory and read the CSV file into Python as a `pandas` DataFrame, we moved on to looking at a few data manipulation methods.

Step 1 to *Step 5* in the preceding section showed us how to read the data from a CSV file in Python using `pandas`, and also how to use functions such as `dtypes`.

The `pandas` package also provides methods for reading data from various file types. For example, `pandas.read_excel()` reads an Excel table into a `pandas` DataFrame; `pandas.read_json()` converts a JSON string into a`pandas` object; and `pandas.read_parquet()` loads a parquet object from a file path and returns the `pandas` DataFrame. More information on this can be found at `https://bit.ly/2yBqtvd`.

You can also read HDF5 format files in Python using the `h5py` package. The `h5py` package is a Python interface to the HDF5 binary data format. HDF® supports n-dimensional datasets, and each element in the dataset may itself be a complex object. There is no limit on the number or size of data objects in the collection. More info can be found at `https://www.hdfgroup.org/`. A sample code block looks like this:

```
import h5py

# With 'r' passed as a parameter to the h5py.File()
# the file will be read in read-only mode
data = h5py.File('File Name.h5', 'r')
```

We look at the datatypes of the variables, and use `describe()` to see the summary statistics for the numerical variables. We need to note that `describe()` works only for numerical variables and is intelligent enough to ignore non-numerical variables. In *Step 6*, we saw how to look at the count of each level for categorical variables such as `LotShape` and `LandContour`. We can use the same code to take a look at the distribution of other categorical variables.

In *Step 7*, we took a look at the distribution of the `LotShape` and `LandContour` variables using `pd.crosstab()`.

One common requirement in a crosstab is to include subtotals for the rows and the columns. We can display subtotals using the `margins` keyword. We pass `margins=True` to the `pd.crosstab()` function. We can also give a name to subtotal columns using the `margins_name` keyword. The default value for `margins_name` is `All`.

We then moved on to learning how to convert datatypes. We had a few variables that were actually categorical, but appeared to be numerical in the dataset. This is often the case in a real-life scenario, hence we need to learn how to typecast our variables. *Step 8* showed us how to convert a numerical variable, such as `MSSubClass`, into a categorical type. In *Step 8*, we converted a few variables into a categorical datatype. We then created a crosstab to visualize the frequencies of each level of categorical variables.

In *Step 9*, we created new meaningful variables from existing variables. We created the new variables, `BuildingAge` and `RemodelAge`, from `YearBuilt` and `YearRemodAdd` respectively, to represent the age of the building and the number of years that have passed since the buildings were remodeled. This method of creating new variables can provide better insights into our analysis and modeling. This process of creating new features is called **feature engineering**. In *Step 10*, we added the new variables to our DataFrame.

From there, we moved on to encoding our categorical variables. We needed to encode our categorical variables because they have named descriptions. Many machine learning algorithms cannot operate on labelled data because they require all input and output variables to be numeric. In *Step 12*, we encoded them with one-hot encoding. In *Step 11*, we learned how to use the `get_dummies()` function, which is a part of the `pandas` package, to create the one-hot encoded variables. In *Step 12*, we added the one-hot_encoded_variables to our DataFrame. And finally, in *Step 13*, we removed the original variables that are now one-hot encoded.

There's more...

The types of data manipulation required depend on your business requirements. In this first recipe, we saw a few ways to carry out data manipulation, but there is no limit to what you can do and how you can manipulate data for analysis.

We have also seen how to convert a numerical variable into a categorical variable. We can do this kind of typecasting in many ways. For example, we can convert a categorical variable into a numerical variable, if required, with the following code:

```
# Converting a categorical variable to numerical
# Using astype() to cast a pandas object to a specified datatype

# Here we typecast GarageYrBlt from float64 type to int64 type
housepricesdata['GarageYrBlt'] =
housepricesdata['GarageYrBlt'].astype('int64')
```

You can only convert the `GarageYrBlt` variable if it does not contain any missing values. The preceding code will throw an error, since `GarageYrBlt` contains missing values.

We have looked at how we can use one-hot encoding to convert categorical variables to numerical variables, and why we do this. In addition to one-hot encoding, we can perform other kinds of encoding, such as label encoding, frequency encoding, and so on. An example code for label encoding is given in the following code block:

```python
# We use sklearn.preprocessing and import LabelEncoder class
from sklearn.preprocessing import LabelEncoder

# Create instance of LabelEncoder class
lb_make = LabelEncoder()

# We create a new variable LotConfig_code to hold the new numerical labels
# We label encode LotConfig variable
housepricesdata["LotConfig_Code"] =
lb_make.fit_transform(housepricesdata["LotConfig"])

# Display the LotConfig variable and its corresponding label encoded
numerical values
housepricesdata[["LotConfig", "LotConfig_Code"]]
```

See also

- The pandas guide to type conversion functions (`https://bit.ly/2MzFwiG`)
- The pandas guide to one-hot encoding using `get_dummies()` (`https://bit.ly/2N1xjTZ`)
- The scikit-learn guide to one-hot encoding (`https://bit.ly/2wrNNLz`)
- The scikit-learn guide to label encoding (`https://bit.ly/2pDddVb`)

Analyzing, visualizing, and treating missing values

Missing values are caused by incomplete data. It is important to handle missing values effectively, as they can lead to inaccurate inferences and conclusions. In this section, we will look at how to analyze, visualize, and treat missing values.

How to do it...

Let's start by analyzing variables with missing values. Set the options in pandas to view all rows and columns, as shown in the previous section:

1. With the following syntax, we can see which variables have missing values:

```
# Check which variables have missing values

columns_with_missing_values =
housepricesdata.columns[housepricesdata.isnull().any()]
housepricesdata[columns_with_missing_values].isnull().sum()
```

This will produce the following output:

LotFrontage	259
Alley	1369
MasVnrType	8
MasVnrArea	8
BsmtQual	37
BsmtCond	37
BsmtExposure	38
BsmtFinType1	37
BsmtFinType2	38
Electrical	1
FireplaceQu	690
GarageType	81
GarageYrBlt	81
GarageFinish	81
GarageQual	81
GarageCond	81
PoolQC	1453
Fence	1179
MiscFeature	1406

2. You might also like to see the missing values in terms of percentages. To see the count and percentage of missing values, execute the following command:

```
import numpy as np
import matplotlib.pyplot as plt
%matplotlib inline

# To hold variable names
labels = []

# To hold the count of missing values for each variable
valuecount = []
```

```
# To hold the percentage of missing values for each variable
percentcount = []

for col in columns_with_missing_values:
    labels.append(col)
    valuecount.append(housepricesdata[col].isnull().sum())
    # housepricesdata.shape[0] will give the total row count
percentcount.append(housepricesdata[col].isnull().sum()/houseprices
data.shape[0])
ind = np.arange(len(labels))

fig, (ax1, ax2) = plt.subplots(1,2,figsize=(20,18))

rects = ax1.barh(ind, np.array(valuecount), color='blue')
ax1.set_yticks(ind)
ax1.set_yticklabels(labels, rotation='horizontal')
ax1.set_xlabel("Count of missing values")
ax1.set_title("Variables with missing values")

rects = ax2.barh(ind, np.array(percentcount), color='pink')
ax2.set_yticks(ind)
ax2.set_yticklabels(labels, rotation='horizontal')
ax2.set_xlabel("Percentage of missing values")
ax2.set_title("Variables with missing values")
```

It will show you the missing values in both absolute and percentage terms, as shown in the following screenshot:

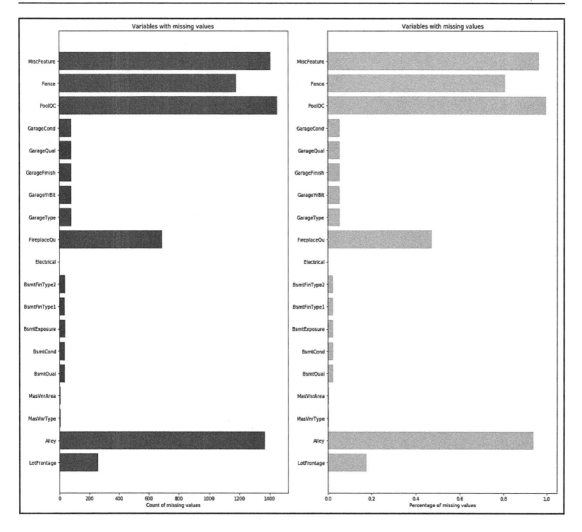

We notice that variables such as **Alley**, **PoolQC**, **Fence**, and **MiscFeature** have **80%** to **90%** of their values missing. **FireplaceQu** has **47.26%** of its values missing. A few other variables, such as **LotFrontage**, **MasVnrType**, **MasVnrArea**, **BsmtQual**, **BsmtCond**, and a few more Garage-related variables have missing values as well.

But there is a catch. Let's look at the `Alley` variable again. It shows us that it has **93.76%** missing values. Now take another look at the data description that we looked at in the preceding section. The variable description for `Alley` shows that it has three levels: *gravel*, *paved*, and *no access*. In the original dataset, `'No Access'` is codified as `NA`. When `NA` is read in Python, it is treated as **NaN**, which means that a value is missing, so we need to be careful.

3. Now, we will replace the missing values for `Alley` with a valid value, such as `'No Access'`:

    ```
    # Replacing missing values with 'No Access' in Alley variable
    housepricesdata['Alley'].fillna('No Access', inplace=True)
    ```

4. Now, let's visualize the missing values and try to see how can we treat them. The following code generates a chart that showcases the spread of missing values. Here we use the `seaborn` library to plot the charts:

    ```
    # Lets import seaborn. We will use seaborn to generate our charts
    import seaborn as sns

    # We will import matplotlib to resize our plot figure
    import matplotlib.pyplot as plt
    %matplotlib inline
    plt.figure(figsize=(20, 10))

    # cubehelix palette is a part of seaborn that produces a colormap
    cmap = sns.cubehelix_palette(light=1, as_cmap=True, reverse=True)
    sns.heatmap(housepricesdata.isnull(), cmap=cmap)
    ```

The color of the map is generated with linearly increasing brightness by the `cubehelix_palette()` function:

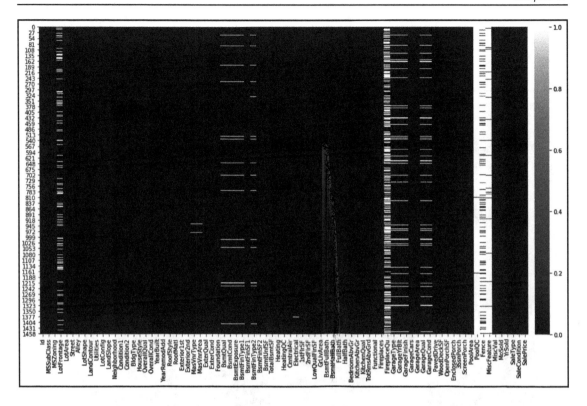

From the preceding plot, it is easier to read the spread of the missing values. The white marks on the chart indicate missing values. Notice that `Alley` no longer reports any missing values.

5. `LotFrontage` is a continuous variable and has **17.74%** of its values missing. Replace the missing values in this variable with its median as follows:

```
# Filling in the missing values in LotFrontage with its median
value
housepricesdata['LotFrontage'].fillna(housepricesdata['LotFrontage'
].median(), inplace=True)
```

6. Let's view the missing value plot once again to see if the missing values from `LotFrontage` have been imputed. Copy and execute the preceding code. The missing value plot will look as follows:

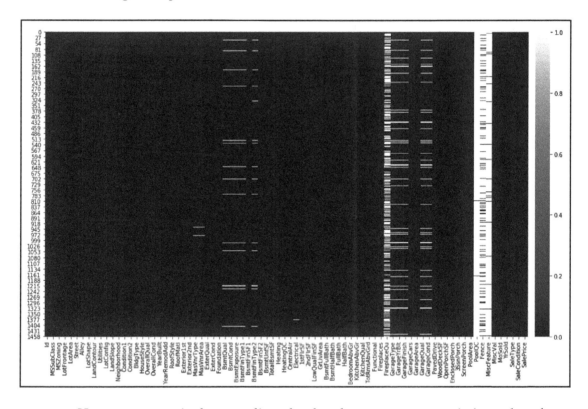

Here, we can see in the preceding plot that there are no more missing values for `Alley` or `LotFrontage`.

7. We have figured out from the data description that several variables have values that are codified as NA. Because this is read in Python as missing values, we replace all of these with their actual values, which we get to see in the data description shown in the following code block:

```
# Replacing all NA values with their original meaning
housepricesdata['BsmtQual'].fillna('No Basement', inplace=True)
housepricesdata['BsmtCond'].fillna('No Basement', inplace=True)
housepricesdata['BsmtExposure'].fillna('No Basement', inplace=True)
housepricesdata['BsmtFinType1'].fillna('No Basement', inplace=True)
housepricesdata['BsmtFinType2'].fillna('No Basement', inplace=True)

housepricesdata['GarageYrBlt'].fillna(0, inplace=True)
```

```
# For observations where GarageType is null, we replace null values
in GarageYrBlt=0
housepricesdata['GarageType'].fillna('No Garage', inplace=True)
housepricesdata['GarageFinish'].fillna('No Garage', inplace=True)
housepricesdata['GarageQual'].fillna('No Garage', inplace=True)
housepricesdata['GarageCond'].fillna('No Garage', inplace=True)


housepricesdata['PoolQC'].fillna('No Pool', inplace=True)
housepricesdata['Fence'].fillna('No Fence', inplace=True)
housepricesdata['MiscFeature'].fillna('None', inplace=True)

housepricesdata['FireplaceQu'].fillna('No Fireplace', inplace=True)
```

8. Let's take a look at the missing value plot after having treated the
   preceding variables:

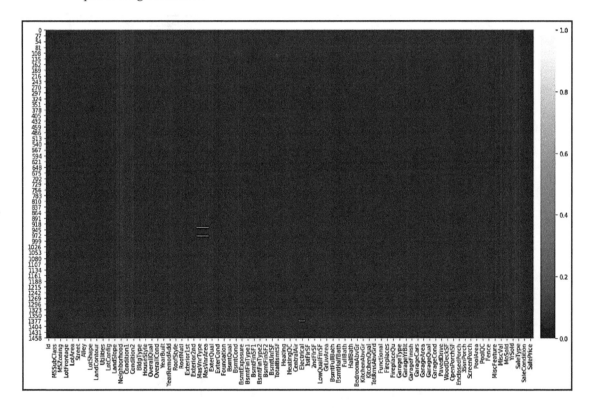

We notice from the preceding plot that there are no more missing values for the variables that we have just treated. However, we are left with a few missing values in `MasVnrType`, `MasVnrArea`, and `Electrical`.

9. Let's try to look at the distribution of `MasVnrType` by `MasVnrArea` with a crosstab:

```
# Using crosstab to generate the count of MasVnrType by type of
MasVnrArea
print(pd.crosstab(index=housepricesdata["MasVnrType"],\
                  columns=housepricesdata["MasVnrArea"],
dropna=False, margins=True))
```

The following output shows that when `MasVnrArea` is zero, we have `MasVnrType` as `None` in the majority of cases:

MasVnrArea	0.0	1.0	11.0	14.0	16.0	18.0	22.0	24.0	27.0	28.0	30.0
MasVnrType											
BrkCmn	0	0	0	0	0	0	0	0	0	0	0
BrkFace	1	0	1	1	6	2	1	0	1	1	2
None	859	2	0	0	0	0	0	0	0	0	0
Stone	1	0	0	0	1	0	0	1	0	0	0
All	861	2	1	1	7	2	1	1	1	1	2

10. We will then impute the missing values in `MasVnrType` with `None` and `MasVnrArea` with zero. This is done with the commands shown in the following code block:

```
# Filling in the missing values for MasVnrType and MasVnrArea with
None and 0 respectively
housepricesdata['MasVnrType'].fillna('None', inplace=True)
housepricesdata['MasVnrArea'].fillna(0, inplace=True)
```

We are still left with one missing value in the `Electrical` variable.

11. Let's take a look at the observation where `Electrical` has a missing value:

```
housepricesdata['MSSubClass'][housepricesdata['Electrical'].isnull(
)]
```

```
1379    80
Name: MSSubClass, dtype: int64
```

12. We see that `MSSubClass` is 80 when `Electrical` is null. Let's see the distribution of the `Electrical` type by `MSSubClass`:

```
# Using crosstab to generate the count of Electrical Type by
MSSubClass
print(pd.crosstab(index=housepricesdata["Electrical"],\
columns=housepricesdata['MSSubClass'], dropna=False, margins=True))
```

From the following output, we can see that when `MSSubClass` is 80, the majority of cases of the `Electrical` type are `SBrkr`:

MSSubClass	20	30	40	45	50	60	70	75	80	85	90	120	160	180	190
Electrical															
FuseA	31	18	2	3	20	0	8	2	0	0	5	0	0	0	5
FuseF	5	4	0	2	8	0	2	0	1	0	4	0	0	0	1
FuseP	0	1	0	0	0	0	0	0	0	0	1	0	0	0	1
Mix	0	1	0	0	0	0	0	0	0	0	0	0	0	0	0
SBrkr	500	45	2	7	116	299	50	14	56	20	42	87	63	10	23
All	536	69	4	12	144	299	60	16	58	20	52	87	63	10	30

13. Go ahead and impute the missing value in the `Electrical` variable with `SBrKr` by executing the following code:

```
housepricesdata['Electrical'].fillna('SBrkr', inplace=True)
```

14. After this, let's take a look at our missing value plot for a final time:

```
import seaborn as sns
import matplotlib.pyplot as plt
%matplotlib inline
plt.figure(figsize=(20, 10))

cmap = sns.cubehelix_palette(light=1, as_cmap=True, reverse=True)
sns.heatmap(housepricesdata.isnull(), cmap=cmap)
```

The output we get can be seen in the following chart:

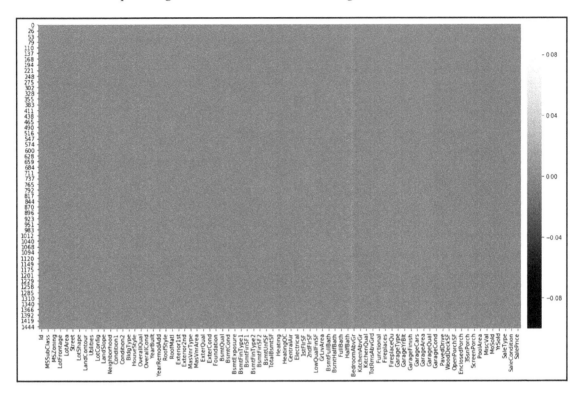

Notice that the plot has changed and now shows no missing values in our DataFrame.

How it works...

In *Step 1* and *Step 2*, we looked at the variables with missing values in absolute and percentage terms. We noticed that the `Alley` variable had more than **93%** of its values missing. However, from the data description, we figured out that the `Alley` variable had a **No Access to Alley** value, which is codified as NA in the dataset. When this value was read in Python, all instances of NA were treated as missing values. In *Step 3*, we replaced the NA in `Alley` with `No Access`.

Note that we used `%matplotlib inline` in *Step 2*. This is a magic function that renders the plot in the notebook itself.

In *Step 4*, we used the `seaborn` library to plot the missing value chart. In this chart, we identified the variables that had missing values. The missing values were denoted in white, while the presence of data was denoted in color. We noticed from the chart that `Alley` had no more missing values.

In *Step 4*, we used `cubehelix_palette()` from the `seaborn` library, which produces a color map with linearly decreasing (or increasing) brightness. The `seaborn` library also provides us with options including `light_palette()` and `dark_palette()`. `light_palette()` gives a sequential palette that blends from light to color, while `dark_palette()` produces a sequential palette that blends from dark to color.

In *Step 5*, we noticed that one of the numerical variables, `LotFrontage`, had more than **17%** of its values missing. We decided to impute the missing values with the median of this variable. We revisited the missing value chart in *Step 6* to see whether the variables were left with any missing values. We noticed that `Alley` and `LotFrontage` showed no white marks, indicating that neither of the two variables had any further missing values.

In *Step 7*, we identified a handful of variables that had data codified with `NA`. This caused the same problem we encountered previously, as Python treated them as missing values. We replaced all such codified values with actual information.

We then revisited the missing value chart in *Step 8*. We saw that almost all the variables then had no missing values, except for `MasVnrType`, `MasVnrArea`, and `Electrical`.

In *Step 9* and *10*, we filled in the missing values for the `MasVnrType` and `MasVnrArea` variables. We noticed that `MasVnrType` is `None` whenever `MasVnrArea` is `0.0`, except for some rare occasions. So, we imputed the `MasVnrType` variable with `None`, and `MasVnrArea` with `0.0` wherever those two variables had missing values. We were then only left with one variable with missing values, `Electrical`.

In *Step 11*, we looked at what type of house was missing the `Electrical` value. We noticed that `MSSubClass` denoted the dwelling type and, for the missing `Electrical` value, the `MSSubClass` was `80`, which meant it was split or multi-level. In *Step 12*, we checked the distribution of `Electrical` by the dwelling type, which was `MSSubClass`. We noticed that when `MSSubClass` equals `80`, the majority of the values of `Electrical` are `SBrkr`, which stands for standard circuit breakers and Romex. For this reason, we decided to impute the missing value in `Electrical` with `SBrkr`.

Finally, in *Step 14*, we again revisited the missing value chart and saw that there were no more missing values in the dataset.

There's more...

Using the preceding plots and missing value charts, it was easy to figure out the count, percentage, and spread of missing values in the datasets. We noticed that many variables had missing values for the same observations. However, after consulting the data description, we saw that most of the missing values were actually not missing, but since they were codified as `NA`, pandas treated them as missing values.

It is very important for data analysts to understand data descriptions and treat the missing values appropriately.

Usually, missing data is categorized into three categories:

- **Missing completely at random (MCAR)**: MCAR denotes that the missing values have nothing to do with the object being studied. In other words, data is MCAR when the probability of missing data on a variable is not related to other measured variables or to the values themselves. An example of this could be, for instance, the age of certain respondents to a survey not being recorded, purely by chance.
- **Missing at random (MAR)**: The name MAR is a little misleading here because the absence of values is not random in this case. Data is MAR if its absence is related to other observed variables, but not to the underlying values of the data itself. For example, when we collect data from customers, rich customers are less likely to disclose their income than their other counterparts, resulting in MAR data.

- **Missing not at random** (**MNAR**): Data is MNAR, also known as **non-ignorable** if it can't be classified as MCAR nor MAR. For example, perhaps some consumers don't want to share their age when it is above 40 because they would like to hide it.

There are various strategies that can be applied to impute the missing values, as listed here:

- Source the missing data
- Leave out incomplete observations
- Replace missing data with an estimate, such as a mean or a median
- Estimate the missing data from other variables in the dataset

See also

- The scikit-learn module for imputation (`https://bit.ly/2MzFwiG`)
- Multiple imputation by chained equations using the `StatsModels` library in Python (`https://bit.ly/2PYLuYy`)
- Feature imputation algorithms using fancyimpute (`https://bit.ly/2MJKfOY`)

Exploratory data analysis

We will continue from where we left off in the previous section, on analyzing and treating missing values. Data scientists spend the majority of their time doing data preparation and exploration, not model building and optimization. Now that our dataset has no missing values, we can proceed with our exploratory data analysis.

How to do it...

1. In the first section on data manipulation, we saw the summary statistics for our datasets. However, we have not looked at this since imputing the missing values.

   Let's now look at the data and its basic statistics using the following code:

   ```
   # To take a look at the top 5 rows in the dataset
   housepricesdata.head(5)

   # To display the summary statistics for all variables
   housepricesdata.describe()
   ```

2. With the preceding code, we can see the summary statistics of the variables in the earlier section.

Now let's see how many columns there are by datatype:

```
# How many columns with different datatypes are there?
housepricesdata.get_dtype_counts()
```

The following code shows us how many variables there are for each datatype. We can see that we have 3 float-type variables, 33 integer-type variables, 45 object-type variables, and 4 unsigned integers that hold the one-hot encoded values for the LotShape variable:

```
float64       3
int64        33
object       45
uint8         4
dtype: int64
```

3. Let's create two variables to hold the names of the numerical and categorical variables:

```
# Pulling out names of numerical variables by conditioning dtypes
NOT equal to object type
numerical_features = housepricesdata.dtypes[housepricesdata.dtypes
!= "object"].index
print("Number of Numerical features: ", len(numerical_features))

# Pulling out names of categorical variables by conditioning dtypes
equal to object type
categorical_features =
housepricesdata.dtypes[housepricesdata.dtypes == "object"].index
print("Number of Categorical features: ",
len(categorical_features))
```

This shows us the amount of numerical and categorical variables there are:

```
Number of Numerical features:  40
Number of Categorical features:  45
```

4. We will now use the `numerical_features` variable that we previously created to see the distributions of numerical variables. We will use the `seaborn` library to plot our charts:

> **TIP**
>
> We use the `melt()` method from pandas to reshape our DataFrame. You may want to view the reshaped data after using the `melt()` method to understand how the DataFrame is arranged.

```
melt_num_features = pd.melt(housepricesdata,
value_vars=numerical_features)

grid = sns.FacetGrid(melt_num_features, col="variable", col_wrap=5,
sharex=False, sharey=False)
grid = grid.map(sns.distplot, "value", color="blue")
```

The preceding code shows us the univariate distribution of the observations of numerical variables using distribution plots:

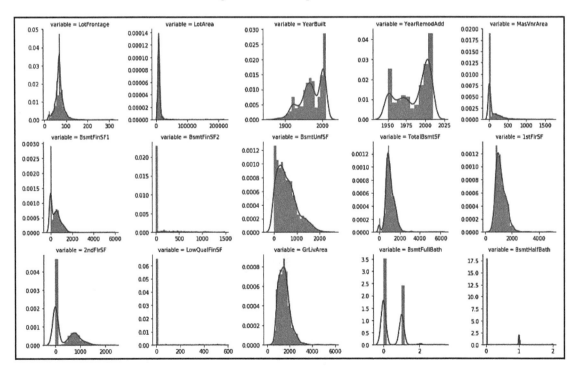

5. Now, we use the `categorical_features` variable to plot the distribution of house prices by each categorical variable:

```
melt_cat_features = pd.melt(housepricesdata, id_vars=['SalePrice'],
value_vars=categorical_features)

grid = sns.FacetGrid(melt_cat_features, col="variable", col_wrap=2,
sharex=False, sharey=False, size=6)
grid.map(sns.boxplot, "value", "SalePrice", palette="Set3")
grid.fig.subplots_adjust(wspace=1, hspace=0.25)

for ax in grid.axes.flat:
    plt.setp(ax.get_xticklabels(), rotation=90)
```

 In our dataset, we see that various attributes are present that can drive house prices. We can try to see the relationship between the attributes and the `SalesPrice` variable, which indicates the prices of the houses.

Let's see the distribution of the house sale prices by each categorical variable in the following plots:

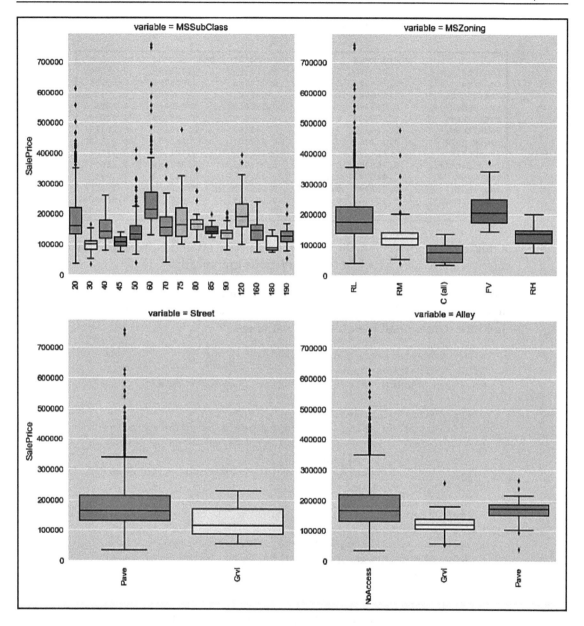

6. We will now take a look at the correlation matrix for all numerical variables using the following code:

```
# Generate a correlation matrix for all the numerical variables
corr=housepricesdata[numerical_features].corr()
print(corr)
```

This will give you the following output:

	LotFrontage	LotArea	YearBuilt	YearRemodAdd	MasVnrArea
LotFrontage	1.000000	0.304522	0.116685	0.083348	0.178469
LotArea	0.304522	1.000000	0.014228	0.013788	0.103321
YearBuilt	0.116685	0.014228	1.000000	0.592855	0.311600
YearRemodAdd	0.083348	0.013788	0.592855	1.000000	0.176529
MasVnrArea	0.178469	0.103321	0.311600	0.176529	1.000000
BsmtFinSF1	0.214367	0.214103	0.249503	0.128451	0.261256
BsmtFinSF2	0.042463	0.111170	-0.049107	-0.067759	-0.071330
BsmtUnfSF	0.124098	-0.002618	0.149040	0.181133	0.113862
TotalBsmtSF	0.363472	0.260833	0.391452	0.291066	0.360067
1stFlrSF	0.413773	0.299475	0.281986	0.240379	0.339850
2ndFlrSF	0.072388	0.050986	0.010308	0.140024	0.173800
LowQualFinSF	0.037469	0.004779	-0.183784	-0.062419	-0.068628
GrLivArea	0.368007	0.263116	0.199010	0.287389	0.388052

It might be tough to view the correlations displayed in the preceding format. You might want to take a look at the correlations graphically.

7. We can also view the correlation matrix plot for the numerical variables. In order to do this, we use the `numerical_features` variable that we created in *Step 3* to hold the names of all the numerical variables:

```
# Get correlation of numerical variables
df_numerical_features=
housepricesdata.select_dtypes(include=[np.number])

correlation= df_numerical_features.corr()
correlation["SalePrice"].sort_values(ascending=False)*100
# Correlation Heat Map (Seaborn library)
f, ax= plt.subplots(figsize=(14,14))
plt.title("Correlation of Numerical Features with Sale Price", y=1,
size=20)

# cmap - matplotlib colormap name or object - can be used to set
the color options
# vmin and vmax is used to anchor the colormap
sns.heatmap(correlation, square= True, vmin=-0.2, vmax=0.8,
cmap="YlGnBu")
```

In the preceding code, we used `select_dtypes(include=[np.number])` to create the `df_numeric_features` variable. However, in *Step 3*, we used `dtypes[housepricesdata.dtypes != "object"].index`. Note that `select_dtypes()` returns a `pandas.DataFrame`, whereas `dtypes[].index` returns a `pandas.Index` object.

We can now visualize the correlation plot as follows:

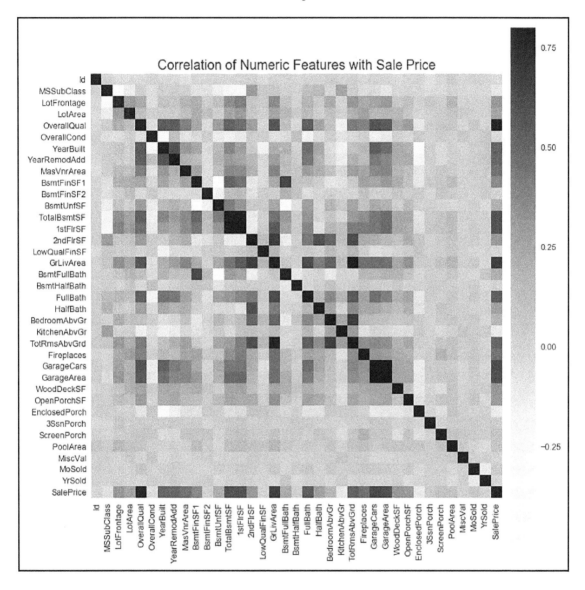

cmap is a Matplotlib color map object. There are various categories of color map, including sequential, diverging, and qualitative. Among the sequential colors, you may choose to set your cmap parameter to BuPu or YlGn. For qualitative colors, you can set it to values such as Set3, Pastel2, and so on. More information on color options can be found at https://matplotlib.org/tutorials/colors/colormaps.html.

8. You may also want to evaluate the correlation of your numerical variables with SalePrice to see how these numerical variables are related to the prices of the houses:

```
row_count = 11
col_count = 3

fig, axs = plt.subplots(row_count, col_count, figsize=(12,36))
exclude_columns = ['Id', 'SalePrice']
plot_numeric_features = [col for col in numerical_features if col
not in exclude_columns]

for eachrow in range(0, row_count):
    for eachcol in range(0, col_count):
        i = eachrow*col_count + eachcol
        if i < len(plot_numeric_features):
            sns.regplot(housepricesdata[plot_numeric_features[i]],
housepricesdata['SalePrice'], \
                ax = axs[eachrow][eachcol], color='purple',
fit_reg=False)

# tight_layout automatically adjusts subplot params so that the
subplot(s) fits in to the figure area
plt.tight_layout()
plt.show()
```

The following screenshot shows us the correlation plots. Here, we plot the correlation between each of the numerical variables and SalePrice:

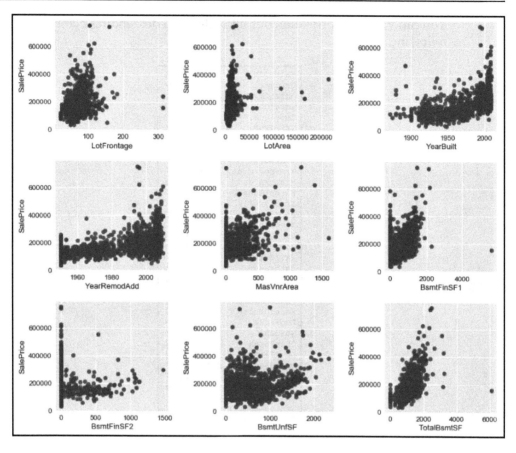

9. If you want to evaluate the correlation of your numerical variables with the sale prices of the houses numerically, you can use the following commands:

```
# See correlation between numerical variables with house prices
corr=housepricesdata.corr()["SalePrice"]

# Sort the correlation values.
# Use [::-1] to sort it in descending manner
# Use [::+1] to sort it in ascending manner
corr[np.argsort(corr)[::-1]]
```

You can view the correlation output sorted in a descending manner in the following table:

```
SalePrice          1.000000
GrLivArea          0.708624
GarageCars         0.640409
GarageArea         0.623431
TotalBsmtSF        0.613581
1stFlrSF           0.605852
FullBath           0.560664
TotRmsAbvGrd       0.533723
YearBuilt          0.522897
YearRemodAdd       0.507101
MasVnrArea         0.472614
Fireplaces         0.466929
BsmtFinSF1         0.386420
LotFrontage        0.334771
WoodDeckSF         0.324413
2ndFlrSF           0.319334
OpenPorchSF        0.315856
HalfBath           0.284108
LotArea            0.263843
BsmtFullBath       0.227122
BsmtUnfSF          0.214479
BedroomAbvGr       0.168213
ScreenPorch        0.111447
PoolArea           0.092404
MoSold             0.046432
3SsnPorch          0.044584
BsmtFinSF2        -0.011378
BsmtHalfBath      -0.016844
MiscVal           -0.021190
LowQualFinSF      -0.025606
YrSold            -0.028923
EnclosedPorch     -0.128578
KitchenAbvGr      -0.135907
```

How it works...

In *Step 1*, we started by reading and describing our data. This step provided us with summary statistics for our dataset. We looked at the number of variables for each datatype in *Step 2*.

In *Step 3*, we created two variables, namely, `numerical_features` and `categorical_features`, to hold the names of numerical and categorical variables respectively. We used these two variables in the steps when we worked with numerical and categorical features separately.

In *Step* 4 and *Step* 5, we used the `seaborn` library to plot our charts. We also introduced the `melt()` function from pandas, which can be used to reshape our DataFrame and feed it to the `FacetGrid()` function of the `seaborn` library. Here, we showed how you can paint the distribution plots for all the numerical variables in one single go. We also showed you how to use the same `FacetGrid()` function to plot the distribution of `SalesPrice` by each categorical variable.

We generated the correlation matrix in *Step 6* using the `corr()` function of the DataFrame object. However, we noticed that with too many variables, the display does not make it easy for you to identify the correlations. In *Step 7*, we plotted the correlation matrix heatmap by using the `heatmap()` function from the `seaborn` library.

 The `corr()` function computes the pairwise correlation of variables, excluding the missing values. The `pearson` method is used as the default for computing the correlation. You can also use the `kendall` or `spearman` methods, depending on your requirements. More information can be found at `https://bit.ly/2CdXr8n`.

In *Step 8*, we saw how the numerical variables correlated with the sale prices of houses using a scatter plot matrix. We generated the scatter plot matrix using the `regplot()` function from the `seaborn` library. Note that we used a parameter, `fit_reg=False`, to remove the regression line from the scatter plots.

In *Step 9*, we repeated *Step 8* to see the relationship of the numerical variables with the sale prices of the houses in a numerical format, instead of scatter plots. We also sorted the output in descending order by passing a `[::-1]` argument to the `corr()` function.

There's more...

We have seen a few ways to explore data, both statistically and visually. There are quite a few libraries in Python that you can use to visualize your data. One of the most widely used of these is `ggplot`. Before we look at a few commands, let's learn how `ggplot` works.

There are seven layers of grammatical elements in `ggplot`, out of which, first three layers are mandatory:

- Data
- Aesthetics
- Geometrics

- Facets
- Statistics
- Coordinates
- Theme

You will often start by providing a dataset to `ggplot()`. Then, you provide an aesthetic mapping with the `aes()` function to map the variables to the x and y axes. With `aes()`, you can also set the color, size, shape, and position of the charts. You then add the type of geometric shape you want with functions such as `geom_point()` or `geom_histogram()`. You can also add various options, such as plotting statistical summaries, faceting, visual themes, and coordinate systems.

The following code is an extension to what we have used already in this chapter, so we will directly delve into the `ggplot` code here:

```
f = pd.melt(housepricesdata, id_vars=['SalePrice'],value_vars=
numerical_features[0:9])
ggplot(f,aes('value', 'SalePrice')) + geom_point(color='orange') +
facet_wrap('variable',scales='free')
```

The preceding code generates the following chart:

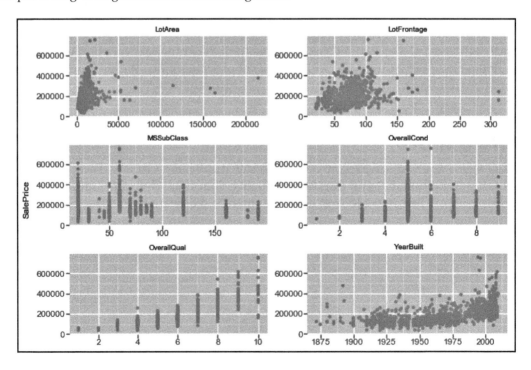

Similarly, in order to view the density plot for the numerical variables, we can execute the following code:

```
f_1 = pd.melt(housepricesdata, value_vars=numerical_features[0:9])
ggplot(f_1, aes('value')) + geom_density(color="red") +
facet_wrap('variable',scales='free')
```

The plot shows us the univariate density plot for each of our numerical variables. The `geom_density()` computes and draws a kernel density estimate, which is a smoothed version of the histogram:

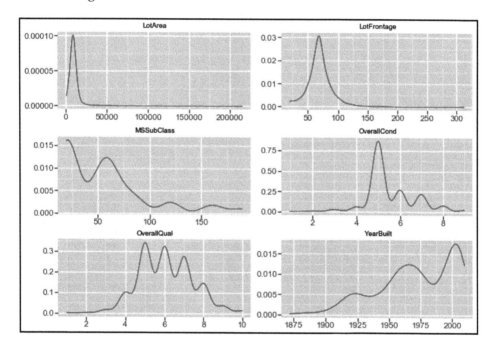

See also

The guide to the `seaborn` library (https://bit.ly/2iU2aRU)

Getting Started with Ensemble Machine Learning

2

In this chapter, we'll cover the following recipes:

- Max-voting
- Averaging
- Weighted averaging

Introduction to ensemble machine learning

Simply speaking, ensemble machine learning refers to a technique that integrates output from multiple learners and is applied to a dataset to make a prediction. These multiple learners are usually referred to as base learners. When multiple base models are used to extract predictions that are combined into one single prediction, that prediction is likely to provide better accuracy than individual base learners.

Ensemble models are known for providing an advantage over single models in terms of performance. They can be applied to both regression and classification problems. You can either decide to build ensemble models with algorithms from the same family or opt to pick them from different families. If multiple models are built on the same dataset using neural networks only, then that ensemble would be called a **homogeneous ensemble model**. If multiple models are built using different algorithms, such as **support vector machines** (**SVMs**), neural networks, and random forests, then the ensemble model would be called a **heterogeneous ensemble model**.

The construction of an ensemble model requires two steps:

1. Base learners are learners that are designed and fit on training data
2. The base learners are combined to form a single prediction model by using specific ensembling techniques such as max-voting, averaging, and weighted averaging

The following diagram shows the structure of the ensemble model:

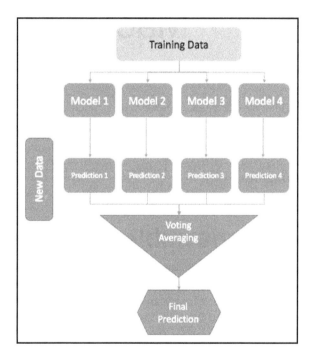

However, to get an ensemble model that performs well, the base learners themselves should be as accurate as possible. A common way to measure the performance of a model is to evaluate its generalization error. A generalization error is a term to measure how accurately a model is able to make a prediction, based on a new dataset that the model hasn't seen.

To perform well, the ensemble models require a sufficient amount of data. Ensemble techniques prove to be more useful when you have large and non-linear datasets.

An ensemble model may overfit if too many models are included, although this isn't very common.

Irrespective of how well you fine-tune your models, there's always the risk of high bias or high variance. Even the best model can fail if the bias and variance aren't taken into account while training the model. Both bias and variance represent a kind of error in the predictions. In fact, the total error is comprised of bias-related error, variance-related error, and unavoidable noise-related error (or irreducible error). The noise-related error is mainly due to noise in the training data and can't be removed. However, the errors due to bias and variance can be reduced.

The total error can be expressed as follows:

```
Total Error = Bias ^ 2 + Variance + Irreducible Error
```

A measure such as **mean square error** (**MSE**) captures all of these errors for a continuous target variable and can be represented as follows:

$$MSE = E[(Y - \hat{f}(x))^2]$$

In this formula, E stands for the expected mean, Y represents the actual target values and $\hat{f}(x)$ is the predicted values for the target variable. It can be broken down into its components such as bias, variance and noise as shown in the following formula:

$$MSE = \underbrace{[E[\hat{f}(x)] - f(x)]^2}_{\text{Bias}} + \underbrace{E[(\hat{f}(x) - E[\hat{f}(x)])^2]}_{\text{Variance}} + \underbrace{\varepsilon}_{\text{Noise}}$$

While bias refers to how close is the ground truth to the expected value of our estimate, the variance, on the other hand, measures the deviation from the expected estimator value. Estimators with small MSE is what is desirable. In order to minimize the MSE error, we would like to be centered (0-bias) at ground truth and have a low deviation (low variance) from the ground truth (correct) value. In other words, we'd like to be confident (low variance, low uncertainty, more peaked distribution) about the value of our estimate. High bias degrades the performance of the algorithm on the training dataset and leads to underfitting. High variance, on the other hand, is characterized by low training errors and high validation errors. Having high variance reduces the performance of the learners on unseen data, leading to overfitting.

Ensemble models can reduce bias and/or variance in the models.

Max-voting

Max-voting, which is generally used for classification problems, is one of the simplest ways of combining predictions from multiple machine learning algorithms.

In max-voting, each base model makes a prediction and votes for each sample. Only the sample class with the highest votes is included in the final predictive class.

For example, let's say we have an online survey, in which consumers answer a question in a five-level Likert scale. We can assume that a few consumers will provide a rating of five, while others will provide a rating of four, and so on. If a majority, say more than 50% of the consumers, provide a rating of four, then the final rating is taken as four. In this example, taking the final rating as four is similar to taking a mode for all of the ratings.

Getting ready

In the following steps we will download the following packages:

To start with, import the os and pandas packages and set your working directory according to your requirements:

```
# import required packages
import os
import pandas as pd

# Set working directory as per your need
os.chdir(".../.../Chapter 2")
os.getcwd()
```

Download the Cryotherapy.csv dataset from GitHub and copy it to your working directory. Read the dataset:

```
df_cryotherapydata = pd.read_csv("Cryotherapy.csv")
```

Take a look at the data with the following code:

```
df_cryotherapydata.head(5)
```

We can see that the data has been read properly and has the `Result_of_Treatment` class variable. We then move on to creating models with `Result_of_Treatment` as the response variable.

How to do it...

You can create a voting ensemble model for a classification problem using the `VotingClassifier` class from Python's `scikit-learn` library. The following steps showcase an example of how to combine the predictions of the decision tree, SVMs, and logistic regression models for a classification problem:

1. Import the required libraries for building the decision tree, SVM, and logistic regression models. We also import `VotingClassifier` for max-voting:

```
# Import required libraries
from sklearn.tree import DecisionTreeClassifier
from sklearn.svm import SVC
from sklearn.linear_model import LogisticRegression
from sklearn.ensemble import VotingClassifier
```

2. We then move on to building our feature set and creating our train and test datasets:

```
# We create train & test sample from our dataset
from sklearn.cross_validation import train_test_split

# create feature & response sets
feature_columns = ['sex', 'age', 'Time', 'Number_of_Warts', 'Type',
'Area']
X = df_cryotherapydata[feature_columns]
Y = df_cryotherapydata['Result_of_Treatment']

# Create train & test sets
X_train, X_test, Y_train, Y_test = \
train_test_split(X, Y, test_size=0.20, random_state=1)
```

3. We build our models with the decision tree, SVM, and logistic regression algorithms:

    ```
    # create the sub models
    estimators = []

    dt_model = DecisionTreeClassifier(random_state=1)
    estimators.append(('DecisionTree', dt_model))

    svm_model = SVC(random_state=1)
    estimators.append(('SupportVector', svm_model))

    logit_model = LogisticRegression(random_state=1)
    estimators.append(('Logistic Regression', logit_model))
    ```

4. We build individual models with each of the classifiers we've chosen:

    ```
    from sklearn.metrics import accuracy_score

    for each_estimator in (dt_model, svm_model, logit_model):
        each_estimator.fit(X_train, Y_train)
        Y_pred = each_estimator.predict(X_test)
        print(each_estimator.__class__.__name__, accuracy_score(Y_test,
    Y_pred))
    ```

    We can then see the accuracy score of each of the individual base learners:

    ```
    DecisionTreeClassifier 0.833333333333
    SVC 0.944444444444
    LogisticRegression 0.777777777778
    ```

5. We proceed to ensemble our models and use `VotingClassifier` to score the accuracy of the ensemble model:

    ```
    #Using VotingClassifier() to build ensemble model with Hard
    Voting
    ensemble_model = VotingClassifier(estimators=estimators,
    voting='hard')

    ensemble_model.fit(X_train,Y_train)
    predicted_labels = ensemble_model.predict(X_test)

    print("Classifier Accuracy using Hard Voting: ",
    accuracy_score(Y_test, predicted_labels))
    ```

We can see the accuracy score of the ensemble model using `Hard Voting`:

```
Classifier Accuracy using Hard Voting:   0.944444444444
```

How it works...

`VotingClassifier` implements two types of voting—**hard** and **soft** voting. In hard voting, the final class label is predicted as the class label that has been predicted most frequently by the classification models. In other words, the predictions from all classifiers are aggregated to predict the class that gets the most votes. In simple terms, it takes the mode of the predicted class labels.

In hard voting for the class labels, $\hat{y}$ is the prediction based on the majority voting of each classifier C_i, where *i=1.....n* observations, we have the following:

$$\hat{y} = mode\{C_1(x), C_2(x), \ldots, C_n(x)\}$$

As shown in the previous section, we have three models, one from the decision tree, one from the SVMs, and one from logistic regression. Let's say that the models classify a training observation as class 1, class 0, and class 1 respectively. Then with majority voting, we have the following:

$$\hat{y} = mode\{1, 0, 1\} = 1$$

In this case, we would classify the observation as class 1.

In the preceding section, in *Step 1*, we imported the required libraries to build our models. In *Step 2*, we created our feature set. We also split our data to create the training and testing samples. In *Step 3*, we trained three models with the decision tree, SVMs, and logistic regression respectively. In *Step 4*, we looked at the accuracy score of each of the base learners, while in *Step 5*, we ensembled the models using `VotingClassifier()` and looked at the accuracy score of the ensemble model.

There's more...

Many classifiers can estimate class probabilities. In this case, the class labels are predicted by averaging the class probabilities. This is called **soft voting** and is recommended for an ensemble of well-tuned classifiers.

In the `scikit-learn` library, many classification algorithms have the `predict_proba()` method to predict the class probabilities. To perform the ensemble with soft voting, simply replace `voting='hard'` with `voting='soft'` in `VotingClassifier()`.

The following code creates an ensemble using soft voting:

```
# create the sub models
estimators = []

dt_model = DecisionTreeClassifier(random_state=1)
estimators.append(('DecisionTree', dt_model))

svm_model = SVC(random_state=1, probability=True)
estimators.append(('SupportVector', svm_model))

logit_model = LogisticRegression(random_state=1)
estimators.append(('Logistic Regression', logit_model))

for each_estimator in (dt_model, svm_model, logit_model):
    each_estimator.fit(X_train, Y_train)
    Y_pred = each_estimator.predict(X_test)
    print(each_estimator.__class__.__name__, accuracy_score(Y_test,
Y_pred))

# Using VotingClassifier() to build ensemble model with Soft Voting
ensemble_model = VotingClassifier(estimators=estimators, voting='soft')
ensemble_model.fit(X_train,Y_train)
predicted_labels = ensemble_model.predict(X_test)
print("Classifier Accuracy using Soft Voting: ", accuracy_score(Y_test,
predicted_labels))
```

We get to see the accuracy from individual learners and the ensemble learner using soft voting:

```
DecisionTreeClassifier 0.833333333333
SVC 0.944444444444
LogisticRegression 0.777777777778
Classifier Accuracy using Soft Voting:  0.888888888889
```

The `SVC` class can't estimate class probabilities by default, so we've set its probability hyper-parameter to `True` in the preceding code. With `probability=True`, `SVC` will be able to estimate class probabilities.

Averaging

Averaging is usually used for regression problems or can be used while estimating the probabilities in classification tasks. Predictions are extracted from multiple models and an average of the predictions are used to make the final prediction.

Getting ready

Let us get ready to build multiple learners and see how to implement averaging:

Download the `whitewines.csv` dataset from GitHub and copy it to your working directory, and let's read the dataset:

```
df_winedata = pd.read_csv("whitewines.csv")
```

Let's take a look at the data with the following code:

```
df_winedata.head(5)
```

In the following screenshot, we can see that the data has been read properly:

	fixed acidity	volatile acidity	citric acid	residual sugar	chlorides	free sulfur dioxide	total sulfur dioxide	density	pH	sulphates	alcohol	quality
0	6.7	0.62	0.24	1.10	0.039	6.0	62.0	0.99340	3.41	0.32	10.400000	5
1	5.7	0.22	0.20	16.00	0.044	41.0	113.0	0.99862	3.22	0.46	8.900000	6
2	5.9	0.19	0.26	7.40	0.034	33.0	123.0	0.99500	3.49	0.42	10.100000	6
3	5.3	0.47	0.10	1.30	0.036	11.0	74.0	0.99082	3.48	0.54	11.200000	4
4	6.4	0.29	0.21	9.65	0.041	36.0	119.0	0.99334	2.99	0.34	10.933333	6

How to do it...

We have a dataset that is based on the properties of wines. Using this dataset, we'll build multiple regression models with the quality as our response variable. With multiple learners, we extract multiple predictions. The averaging technique would take the average of all of the predicted values for each training sample:

1. Import the required libraries:

```
# Import required libraries
from sklearn.linear_model import LinearRegression
from sklearn.tree import DecisionTreeRegressor
from sklearn.svm import SVR
```

2. Create the response and feature sets:

```
# Create feature and response variable set
from sklearn.cross_validation import train_test_split

# create feature & response variables
feature_columns = ['fixed acidity', 'volatile acidity', 'citric
acid', 'residual sugar','chlorides', 'free sulfur dioxide', 'total
sulfur dioxide','density', 'pH', 'sulphates', 'alcohol']
X = df_winedata[feature_columns]
Y = df_winedata['quality']
```

3. Split the data into training and testing sets:

```
# Create train & test sets
X_train, X_test, Y_train, Y_test = \
train_test_split(X, Y, test_size=0.20, random_state=1)
```

4. Build the base regression learners using linear regression, SVR, and a decision tree:

```
# Build base learners
linreg_model = LinearRegression()
svr_model = SVR()
regressiontree_model = DecisionTreeRegressor()

# Fitting the model
linreg_model.fit(X_train, Y_train)
svr_model.fit(X_train, Y_train)
regressiontree_model.fit(X_train, Y_train)
```

5. Use the base learners to make a prediction based on the test data:

```
linreg_predictions = linreg_model.predict(X_test)
svr_predictions = svr_model.predict(X_test)
regtree_predictions = regressiontree_model.predict(X_test)
```

6. Add the predictions and divide by the number of base learners:

```
# We divide the summation of the predictions by 3 i.e. number of
base learners
average_predictions=(linreg_predictions + svr_predictions +
regtree_predictions)/3
```

How it works...

In *Step 1*, we imported the required packages. In *Step 2*, we separated the feature set and the response variable from our dataset. We split our dataset into training and testing samples in *Step 3*.

Note that our response variable is continuous in nature. For this reason, we built our regression base learners in *Step 4* using linear regression, SVR, and a decision tree. In *Step 5*, we passed our test dataset to the predict() function to predict our response variable. And finally, in *Step 6*, we added all of the predictions together and divided them by the number of base learners, which is three in our example.

Weighted averaging

Like averaging, weighted averaging is also used for regression tasks. Alternatively, it can be used while estimating probabilities in classification problems. Base learners are assigned different weights, which represent the importance of each model in the prediction.

 A weight-averaged model should always be at least as good as your best model.

Getting ready

Download the wisc_bc_data.csv dataset from GitHub and copy it to your working directory. Let's read the dataset:

```
df_cancerdata = pd.read_csv("wisc_bc_data.csv")
```

Take a look at the data with the following code:

```
df_cancerdata.head(5)
```

We can see that the data has been read properly:

	id	diagnosis	radius_mean	texture_mean	perimeter_mean	area_mean	smoothness_mean	compactness_mean
0	87139402	B	12.32	12.39	78.85	464.1	0.10280	0.06981
1	8910251	B	10.60	18.95	69.28	346.4	0.09688	0.11470
2	905520	B	11.04	16.83	70.92	373.2	0.10770	0.07804
3	868871	B	11.28	13.39	73.00	384.8	0.11640	0.11360
4	9012568	B	15.19	13.21	97.65	711.8	0.07963	0.06934

How to do it...

Here, we have a dataset based on the properties of cancerous tumors. Using this dataset, we'll build multiple classification models with `diagnosis` as our response variable. The diagnosis variable has the values, B and M, which indicate whether the tumor is benign or malignant. With multiple learners, we extract multiple predictions. The weighted averaging technique takes the average of all of the predicted values for each training sample.

In this example, we consider the predicted probabilities as the output and use the `predict_proba()` function of the scikit-learn algorithms to predict the class probabilities:

1. Import the required libraries:

```
# Import required libraries
from sklearn.tree import DecisionTreeClassifier
from sklearn.svm import SVC
from sklearn.linear_model import LogisticRegression
```

2. Create the response and feature sets:

```
# Create feature and response variable set
# We create train & test sample from our dataset
from sklearn.cross_validation import train_test_split

# create feature & response variables
X = df_cancerdata.iloc[:,2:32]
Y = df_cancerdata['diagnosis']
```

We retrieved the feature columns using the `iloc()` function of the `pandas` DataFrame, which is purely integer-location based indexing for selection by position. The `iloc()` function takes row and column selection as its parameter, in the form: `data.iloc(<row selection>, <column selection>)`. The row and column selection can either be an integer list or a slice of rows and columns. For example, it might look as follows: `df_cancerdata.iloc(2:100, 2:30)`.

3. We'll then split our data into training and testing sets:

```
# Create train & test sets
X_train, X_test, Y_train, Y_test = \
train_test_split(X, Y, test_size=0.20, random_state=1)
```

4. Build the base classifier models:

```
# create the sub models
estimators = []

dt_model = DecisionTreeClassifier()
estimators.append(('DecisionTree', dt_model))

svm_model = SVC(probability=True)
estimators.append(('SupportVector', svm_model))

logit_model = LogisticRegression()
estimators.append(('Logistic Regression', logit_model))
```

5. Fit the models on the test data:

```
dt_model.fit(X_train, Y_train)
svm_model.fit(X_train, Y_train)
logit_model.fit(X_train, Y_train)
```

6. Use the `predict_proba()` function to predict the class probabilities:

```
dt_predictions = dt_model.predict_proba(X_test)
svm_predictions = svm_model.predict_proba(X_test)
logit_predictions = logit_model.predict_proba(X_test)
```

7. Assign different weights to each of the models to get our final predictions:

```
weighted_average_predictions=(dt_predictions * 0.3 +
svm_predictions * 0.4 + logit_predictions * 0.3)
```

How it works...

In *Step 1*, we imported the libraries that are required to build our models. In *Step 2*, we created the response and feature sets. We retrieved our feature set using the `iloc()` function of the `pandas` DataFrame. In *Step 3*, we split our dataset into training and testing sets. In *Step 4*, we built our base classifiers. Kindly note that we passed `probability=True` to our `SVC` function to allow `SVC()` to return class probabilities. In the `SVC` class, the default is `probability=False`.

In *Step 5*, we fitted our model to the training data. We used the `predict_proba()` function in *Step 6* to predict the class probabilities for our test observations.

Finally, in *Step 7*, we assigned different weights to each of our models to estimate the weighted average predictions. The question that comes up is how to choose the weights. One way is to sample the weights uniformly and to make sure they normalize to one and validate on the test set and repeat keeping track of weights that provide the highest accuracy. This is an example of a random search.

See also

The following are the scikit reference links:

- Scikit guide to ensemble methods (https://bit.ly/2oVNogs)
- Scikit guide to `VotingClassifier` (https://bit.ly/2oW0avo)

Resampling Methods

3

In this chapter, we will be introduced to the fundamental concept of sampling. We'll also learn about resampling and why it's important.

Sampling is the process of selecting a subset of observations from the population with the purpose of estimating some parameters about the whole population. Resampling methods, on the other hand, are used to improve the estimates of the population parameters.

In this chapter, we will cover the following recipes:

- Introduction to sampling
- k-fold and leave-one-out cross-validation
- Bootstrap sampling

Introduction to sampling

Sampling techniques can be broadly classified into non-probability sampling techniques and probability sampling techniques. Non-probability sampling techniques are based on the judgement of the user, whereas in probability sampling, the observations are selected by chance.

Probability sampling most often includes **simple random sampling (SRS)**, stratified sampling, and systematic sampling:

- **SRS**: In SRS, each observation in the population has an equal probability of being chosen for the sample.
- **Stratified sampling**: In stratified sampling, the population data is divided into separate groups, called **strata**. A probability sample is then drawn from each group.

- **Systematic sampling**: In this method, a sample is drawn from the population by choosing observations at regular intervals.

 If the sample is too small or too large, it may lead to incorrect findings. For this reason, it's important that we've got the right sample size. A well-designed sample can help identify the biasing factors that can skew the accuracy and reliability of the expected outcome.

Errors might be introduced to our samples for a variety of reasons. An error might occur due to random sampling, for example, which is known as a **sampling error**, or because the method of drawing observations causes the samples to be skewed, which is known as **sample bias**.

Getting ready

In Chapter 1, *Get Closer to your Data,* we manipulated and prepared the data from the HousePrices.csv file and dealt with the missing values. In this example, we're going to use the final dataset to demonstrate these sampling and resampling techniques.

You can get the prepared dataset from the GitHub.

We'll import the required libraries. We'll read the data and take a look at the dimensions of our dataset:

```
# import os for operating system dependent functionalities
import os

# import other required libraries
import pandas as pd
from sklearn.model_selection import train_test_split

# Set your working directory according to your requirement
os.chdir(".../Chapter 3/Resampling Methods")
os.getcwd()
```

Let's read our data. We'll prefix the DataFrame name with df_ to make it easier to understand:

```
df_housingdata = pd.read_csv("Final_HousePrices.csv")
```

In the next section, we'll look at how to use `train_test_split()` from `sklean.model_selection` to split our data into random training and testing subsets.

How to do it...

Now that we have read our dataset, let's look at how to do the sampling:

1. We check the dimensions of our DataFrame, as follows:

    ```
    df_housingdata.shape
    ```

    We can see the dimension of our DataFrame:

    > **(1460, 80)**

2. We then look to see if our DataFrame has any missing values:

    ```
    df_housingdata.isnull().sum()
    ```

    We notice that there are no missing values in `df_housingdata`

3. We separate the predictor and response variable into two different DataFrames, as follows:

    ```
    # create feature & response variables
    X = df_housingdata.iloc[:,0:79]
    Y = df_housingdata['SalePrice']
    ```

4. We split both our predictor and our response datasets into training and testing subsets using `train_test_split()`:

    ```
    # Create train & test sets
    X_train, X_test, Y_train, Y_test = train_test_split(X, Y,
    train_size=0.7, test_size=0.3)
    ```

5. We can find the number of observations and columns in each subset as follows:

    ```
    print(X_train.shape)
    print(Y_train.shape)
    print(X_test.shape)
    print(Y_test.shape)
    ```

We can see that 70% of the data has been allocated to the training dataset and 30% has been allocated to the testing dataset:

```
(1021, 80)
(1021,)
(438, 80)
(438,)
```

How it works...

In *Step 1* and *Step 2*, we looked at the dimensions of our DataFrame and found that our dataset had no missing values. In *Step 3*, we separated out the features and the response variable. In *Step 4*, we used the `train_test_split()` function from `sklearn.model_selection` to split our data and create the training and testing subsets. Notice that we passed two parameters, `train_size` and `test_size`, and set the values to `0.7` and `0.3`, respectively. `train_size` and `test_size` can take values between 0.0 and 1.0, which represent the proportion of the dataset allocated to each. If an integer value is provided, the number represents the absolute number of observations.

 We can choose not to provide either of the two parameters, that is `train_size` or `test_size`. If we set the value of the `train_size` to `None` or if we do not provide it at all, the value is automatically set to complement the test size. Similarly, if `test_size` is unspecified or we set its value to `None`, the value is automatically set to complement the train size.

In *Step 5*, we looked at the shape of the subsets that were created by the `train_test_split()` function.

There's more...

In this example, we're going to use a dataset in which we measure a dichotomous categorical target variable. It's important to understand that the distribution of both classes of our target variable is similar in both the training and testing subsets:

1. We start by reading our dataset and looking at its dimensions:

```
df_creditcarddata = pd.read_csv("creditcarddefault.csv")
df_creditcarddata.shape
```

We have 30,000 observations with 25 variables. The last variable, the default payment next month, is our target variable, which has values that are either *0* or *1*.

2. We separate our data into a feature set and the response variable and split it into training and testing subsets using the following code:

```
# create feature & response set
X = df_creditcarddata.iloc[:,0:24]
Y = df_creditcarddata['default payment next month']

# Create train & test sets
X_train, X_test, Y_train, Y_test = train_test_split(X, Y,
train_size=0.7, test_size=0.3, stratify=Y)
```

Note that, this time, we've used a parameter, `stratify`, in our `train_test_split()` function. The `stratify` parameter makes a split so that the proportion of values in the sample that's produced is equal to the proportion of values in the variable that's provided to it. Also note that we've assigned the response variable, `Y`, to the `stratify` parameter.

We can now see the distribution of our dichotomous class in our target variable for both the training and testing subsets:

```
print(pd.value_counts(Y_train.values)*100/Y_train.shape)
print(pd.value_counts(Y_test.values)*100/Y_test.shape)
```

In the following output, we can see that the distributions of both the classes are the same in both subsets:

```
0     77.88
1     22.12
dtype: float64
0     77.88
1     22.12
dtype: float64
```

 We can also pass another parameter, `shuffle`, to `train_test_split()`. This takes a Boolean value, `True` or `False`, to indicate whether or not to shuffle the data before splitting it. If `shuffle=False`, then `stratify` must be `None`.

See also

- The scikit-learn guide to `sklearn.model_selection`: `https://bit.ly/2px08Ii`

k-fold and leave-one-out cross-validation

Machine learning models often face the problem of generalization when they're applied to unseen data to make predictions. To avoid this problem, the model isn't trained using the complete dataset. Instead, the dataset is split into training and testing subsets. The model is trained on the training data and evaluated on the testing set, which it doesn't see during the training process. This is the fundamental idea behind cross-validation.

The simplest kind of cross-validation is the holdout method, which we saw in the previous recipe, *Introduction to sampling*. In the holdout method, when we split our data into training and testing subsets, there's a possibility that the testing set isn't that similar to the training set because of the high dimensionality of the data. This can lead to instability in the outcome. For this reason, it's very important that we sample our data efficiently. We can solve this problem using other cross-validation methods such as **leave-one-out cross-validation (LOOCV)** or **k-fold cross-validation (k-fold CV)**.

k-fold CV is a widely used approach that's used for estimating test errors. The original dataset with N observations is divided into K subsets and the holdout method is repeated K times. In each iteration, $K-1$ subsets are used as the training set and the rest are used as the testing set. The error is calculated as follows:

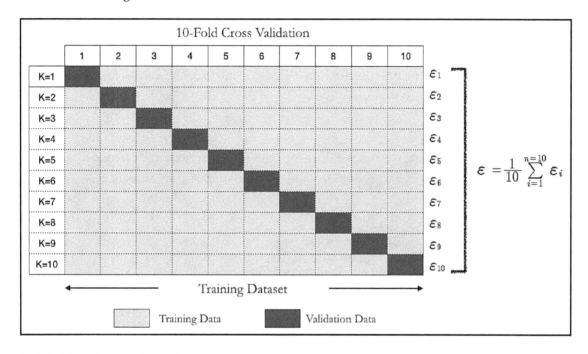

In LOOCV, the number of subsets K is equal to the number of observations in the dataset, N. LOOCV uses one observation from the original dataset as the validation set and the remaining $N-1$ observations as the training set. This is iterated N times, so that each observation in the sample is used as the validation data in each iteration. This is the same as k-fold CV, in which K equals N, the number of data points in the set. LOOCV usually takes a lot of computational power because of the large number of iterations required.

In LOOCV, the estimates from each fold are highly correlated and their average can have a high level of variance.

Estimating the test error is based on a single observation and is represented as $MSE = (\bar{y}-\hat{y})^2$. We can compute the average of the MSEs for all the folds as follows:

$$CV_n = \frac{1}{n} \sum_{i=1}^{n} MSE_i$$

This calculation is no different from the calculation involved in k-fold CV. We'll use scikit-learn libraries to see how techniques such as k-fold CV and LOOCV can be implemented.

Getting ready

In the following code block, we can see how we can import the required libraries:

```
import pandas as pd

from sklearn.model_selection import train_test_split
from sklearn.linear_model import LinearRegression
from sklearn.metrics import mean_squared_error, r2_score
from sklearn.model_selection import KFold
import matplotlib.pyplot as plt
```

We read our data and split the features and the response variable:

```
# Let's read our data.
df_autodata = pd.read_csv("autompg.csv")

# Fill NAs with the median value
df_autodata['horsepower'].fillna(df_autodata['horsepower'].median()
, inplace=True)

# Drop carname variable
df_autodata.drop(['carname'], axis=1, inplace=True)

X = df_autodata.iloc[:,1:8]
Y = df_autodata.iloc[:,0]
X=np.array(X)
Y=np.array(Y)
```

How to do it...

The k-folds cross-validator provides us with the train and test indices to split the data into training and testing subsets:

1. We'll split the dataset into *K* consecutive folds (without shuffling by default) with *K=10*:

```
kfoldcv = KFold(n_splits=10)
kf_ytests = []
kf_predictedvalues = []
mean_mse = 0.0

for train_index, test_index in kfoldcv.split(X):
    X_train, X_test = X[train_index], X[test_index]
    Y_train, Y_test = Y[train_index], Y[test_index]
    model = LinearRegression()
    model.fit(X_train, Y_train)
    Y_pred = model.predict(X_test)
    # there is only one y-test and y-pred per iteration over the
kfoldcv.split,
    # so we append them to the respective lists.
    kf_ytests += list(Y_test)
    kf_predictedvalues += list(Y_pred)
    mse = mean_squared_error(kf_ytests, kf_predictedvalues)
    r2score = r2_score(kf_ytests, kf_predictedvalues)
    print("R^2: {:.2f}, MSE: {:.2f}".format(r2score, mse))
    mean_mse += mse
```

2. We can look at our coefficient of determination using `r2_score()` and the mean squared error using `mse()`:

```
print("Average CV Score :" ,mean_mse/10)
```

The results of the preceding code are as follows:

```
R^2: 0.68, MSE: 8.96
R^2: 0.73, MSE: 9.10
R^2: 0.69, MSE: 9.90
R^2: 0.72, MSE: 9.47
R^2: 0.75, MSE: 8.50
R^2: 0.77, MSE: 8.32
R^2: 0.75, MSE: 9.83
R^2: 0.77, MSE: 10.13
R^2: 0.78, MSE: 12.59
R^2: 0.79, MSE: 12.85
Average CV Score : 9.962852981837424
```

3. We plot the predicted values against the actual values of the response variable:

```
## Let us plot the model
plt.scatter(kf_ytests, kf_predictedvalues)
plt.xlabel('Reported mpg')
plt.ylabel('Predicted mpg')
```

The plot generated by the preceding code is as follows:

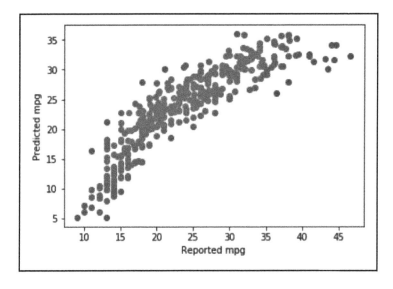

How it works...

In *Step 1*, the k-fold cross validator splits the dataset into *K* consecutive folds with *K*=10. The k-fold cross-validator provides us with the train and test indices and then splits the data into training and testing subsets. In *Step 2*, we looked at the coefficient of determination using r2_score() and the mean squared error using mse(). The coefficient of determination and the mean squared error are 79% and 12.85, respectively. In *Step 3*, we plotted the predicted values against the actual values of the response variable, mpg.

There's more...

We'll now do the same exercise with LOOCV by using LeaveOneOut from sklearn.model_selection:

1. We'll read our data once again and split it into the features and response sets:

```
# Let's read our data.
df_autodata = pd.read_csv("autompg.csv")

# Fill NAs with the median value
df_autodata['horsepower'].fillna(df_autodata['horsepower'].median()
, inplace=True)

# Drop carname variable
df_autodata.drop(['carname'], axis=1, inplace=True)

X = df_autodata.iloc[:,1:8]
Y = df_autodata.iloc[:,0]
X=np.array(X)
Y=np.array(Y)
```

2. We use LOOCV to build our models:

```
from sklearn.model_selection import LeaveOneOut
loocv = LeaveOneOut()

loo_ytests = []
loo_predictedvalues = []
mean_mse = 0.0

for train_index, test_index in loocv.split(X):
    # the below requires arrays. So we converted the dataframes to
arrays
    X_train, X_test = X[train_index], X[test_index]
    Y_train, Y_test = Y[train_index], Y[test_index]
```

```
model = LinearRegression()
model.fit(X_train, Y_train)
Y_pred = model.predict(X_test)
# there is only one y-test and y-pred per iteration over the
loo.split,
# so we append them to the respective lists.
loo_ytests += list(Y_test)
loo_predictedvalues += list(Y_pred)
mse = mean_squared_error(loo_ytests, loo_predictedvalues)
r2score = r2_score(loo_ytests, loo_predictedvalues)
print("R^2: {:.2f}, MSE: {:.2f}".format(r2score, mse))
mean_mse += mse
```

3. We can look at our coefficient of determination using `r2_score()` and the mean squared error using `mse()`:

```
print("Average CV Score :" ,mean_mse/X.shape[0])
```

We can take a look at the coefficient of determination, and the mean squared error for the LOOCV results:

```
R^2: 0.81, MSE: 11.11
R^2: 0.81, MSE: 11.09
R^2: 0.81, MSE: 11.06
R^2: 0.81, MSE: 11.04
R^2: 0.82, MSE: 11.02
R^2: 0.82, MSE: 11.03
R^2: 0.82, MSE: 11.02
R^2: 0.82, MSE: 11.00
R^2: 0.81, MSE: 11.23
R^2: 0.81, MSE: 11.24
R^2: 0.81, MSE: 11.32
R^2: 0.81, MSE: 11.29
R^2: 0.81, MSE: 11.33
R^2: 0.81, MSE: 11.31
R^2: 0.81, MSE: 11.28
R^2: 0.81, MSE: 11.50
R^2: 0.81, MSE: 11.47
R^2: 0.81, MSE: 11.45
R^2: 0.81, MSE: 11.43
Average CV Score : 8.401498720470839
```

4. We can plot the predicted values against the actual values of the response variable:

```
## Let us plot the model
plt.scatter(kf_ytests, kf_predictedvalues)
plt.xlabel('Reported mpg')
plt.ylabel('Predicted mpg')
```

The plot that is generated by the preceding code gives us the following output:

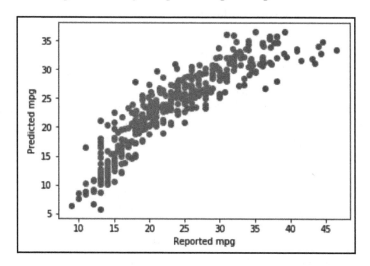

In LOOCV, there is no randomness in the splitting method, so it'll always provide you with the same result.

The stratified k-fold CV method is often used in classification problems. This is a variation of the k-fold CV method that returns stratified folds. Each set contains a similar percentage of samples of each target class as the original dataset. `startifiedShuffleSplit` is a variation of shuffle splits, which creates splits by maintaining the same percentage for every target class.

See also

- The scikit-learn guide to other methods of cross-validation: `https://bit.ly/2px08Ii`

Bootstrapping

Bootstrapping is based on the jackknife method, which was proposed by Quenouille in 1949, and then refined by Tukey in 1958. The jackknife method is used for testing hypotheses and estimating confidence intervals. It's obtained by calculating the estimate after leaving out each observation and then computing the average of these calculations. With a sample of size *N*, the jackknife estimate can be found by aggregating the estimates of every *N-1* sized sub-sample. It's similar to bootstrap samples, but while the bootstrap method is sampling with replacement, the jackknife method samples the data without replacement.

Bootstrapping is a powerful, non-parametric resampling technique that's used to assess the uncertainty in the estimator. In bootstrapping, a large number of samples with the same size are drawn repeatedly from an original sample. This allows a given observation to be included in more than one sample, which is known as **sampling with replacement**. In the bootstrap method, *n* samples are created from the original data by sampling with replacement. Each sample is of identical size. The larger *n*, the closer the set of samples will be to the ideal bootstrap sample.

> *"The essence of bootstrapping is the idea that in the absence of any other knowledge about a population, the distribution of values found in a random sample of size n from the population is the best guide to the distribution in the population. Therefore to approximate what would happen if the population was resampled, it's sensible to resample the sample. In other words, the infinite population that consists of the n observed sample values, each with probability 1/n, is used to model the unknown real population."*

> *–Bryan F. J. Manly*

A diagrammatic representation of a bootstrap sample would look as follows:

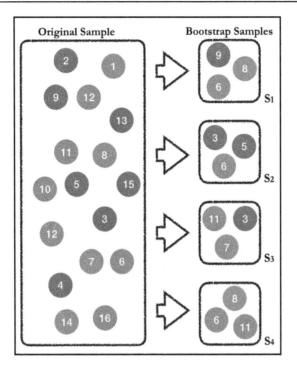

As we can see in the preceding diagram, some of the data points in the **S1** subset also appear in **S2** and **S4**.

Let's say that we have n bootstrap samples from our original sample. $\hat{\theta}_i$ denotes the estimates of the n bootstrap samples where $i=1,2,3...,n$. If $\hat{\theta}$ denotes the estimate of the parameter for the original sample, the standard error for $\hat{\theta}$ is given as follows:

$$SE(\hat{\theta}) = \sqrt{\frac{1}{n-1}\sum_{i=1}^{n}(\hat{\theta}_i - \bar{\theta})^2}$$

$\bar{\theta}$ is given as follows:

$$\bar{\theta} = (\frac{1}{n})\sum_{i=1}^{n}\hat{\theta}_i$$

$\bar{\theta}$ is the mean of the estimates across the n bootstrap samples.

Getting ready

We need to import the required libraries as usual. This time, we will use the `resample` class from `sklean.utils`, which we've not used previously:

```
import pandas as pd
import numpy as np

from sklearn.model_selection import train_test_split
from sklearn.linear_model import SGDRegressor
from sklearn.metrics import mean_squared_error, r2_score
import matplotlib.pyplot as plt

from sklearn.utils import resample
```

We load our data and fill in the missing values with the median for the `horsepower` variable. We also drop the `carname` variable:

```
# Let's read our data. We prefix the data frame name with "df_" for
easier understanding.
df_autodata = pd.read_csv("autompg.csv")
df_autodata['horsepower'].fillna(df_autodata['horsepower'].median()
, inplace=True)
df_autodata.drop(['carname'], axis=1, inplace=True)
```

How to do it...

Now that we have read our data, let's see how we can perform bootstrap sampling:

1. We write a custom function, `create_bootstrap_oob()`, which takes a DataFrame as a parameter and uses the `resample()` function from `sklearn.utils` to create a bootstrap sample with 100 observations:

```
# This custom function takes a dataframe as an argument
def create_bootstrap_oob(df):
    global df_OOB
    global df_bootstrap_sample
    # creating the bootstrap sample
    df_bootstrap_sample = resample(df, replace=True, n_samples=100)
    # creating the OOB sample
    bootstrap_sample_index = tuple(df_bootstrap_sample.index)
    bootstrap_df = df.index.isin(bootstrap_sample_index)
    df_OOB = df[~bootstrap_df]
```

2. We loop through 50 iterations and call the custom function by passing the `df_autodata` DataFrame. We capture the mean of the `mpg` variable for each bootstrap sample, which we'll measure against the mean of the `mpg` variable in our original DataFrame, which is `df_autodata`:

```
iteration=50
bootstap_statistics=list()
originalsample_statistics=list()

for i in range(iteration):
    # Call custom function create_bootstrap_oob(). Pass df_autodata
    create_bootstrap_oob(df_autodata)
    # Capture mean value of mpg variable for all bootstrap samples
    bootstap_statistics.append(df_bootstrap_sample.iloc[:,0].mean())
    originalsample_statistics.append(df_autodata['mpg'].mean())
```

3. We plot the mean of the `mpg` variable for each iteration, for which a separate bootstrap sample has been considered. We capture the mean of the `mpg` variable for each bootstrap sample in each iteration:

```
import matplotlib.pyplot as plt
f, ax= plt.subplots(figsize=(6,6))

plt.plot(bootstap_statistics, 'c--', label='Bootstrap Sample
Statistic')
plt.plot(originalsample_statistics, 'grey', label='Original Sample
Statistic')
plt.xlabel('Iterations')
plt.ylabel('Statistic (Mean of mpg)')
plt.legend(loc=4)
plt.show()
```

We finally plot the mean of the `mpg` variable against each iteration, which can be seen in the following image:

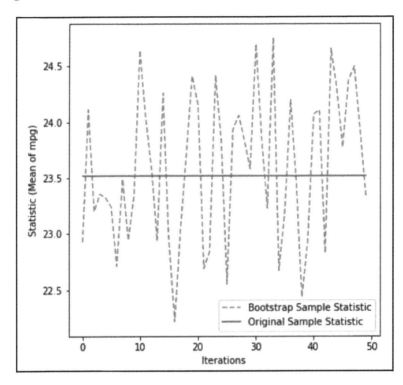

How it works...

In *Step 1*, we created a custom function, `create_bootstrap_oob( )`, and used the `resample()` function from `sklearn.utils` to create a bootstrap sample with 100 observations. The `create_bootstrap_oob( )` custom function took a DataFrame as an input parameter and created both bootstrap and **Out-Of-the-Bag** (**OOB**) samples.

We mentioned that bootstrap sampling is sampling with replacement. This means that any given observation can appear more than once in a single sample.

In *Step 2*, we looped through the 50 iterations and called the `create_bootstrap_oob(` `)` custom function by passing `df_autoframe`. We captured the mean of the `mpg` variable for each bootstrap sample. In *Step 3*, we considered a separate bootstrap sample for each iteration. We captured the mean of the `mpg` variable against each iteration and then plotted the mean of the `mpg` variable for each iteration.

See also

- The scikit-learn guide to `sklearn.cross_validation.Bootstrap`: https://bit.ly/2RC5MYv

4
Statistical and Machine Learning Algorithms

In this chapter, we will cover the following recipes:

- Multiple linear regression
- Logistic regression
- Naive Bayes
- Decision trees
- Support vector machines

Technical requirements

The technical requirements for this chapter remain the same as those we detailed in Chapter 1, *Get Closer to Your Data*.

Visit the GitHub repository to get the dataset and the code. These are arranged by chapter and by the name of the topic. For the linear regression dataset and code, for example, visit .../Chapter 3/Linear regression.

Multiple linear regression

Multiple linear regression is a technique used to train a linear model, that assumes that there are linear relationships between multiple predictor variables (x) and a continuous target variable (y). The general equation for a multiple linear regression with m predictor variables is as follows:

$$\hat{y} = \beta_0 + \beta_1 x_1 + \beta_2 x_2 + \ldots + \beta_m x_m + \epsilon$$

$$= \beta_0 + \sum_{i=1}^{m} \beta_i x_i + \epsilon$$

Training a linear regression model involves estimating the values of the coefficients for each of the predictor variables denoted by the letter β. In the preceding equation, ϵ denotes an error term, which is normally distributed, and has zero mean and constant variance. This is represented as follows:

$$\epsilon \sim N(0, \sigma^2)$$

Various techniques can be used to build a linear regression model. The most frequently used is the **ordinary least square** (**OLS**) estimate. The OLS method is used to produce a linear regression line that seeks to minimize the sum of the squared error. The error is the distance from an actual data point to the regression line. The sum of the squared error measures the aggregate of the squared difference between the training instances, which are each of our data points, and the values predicted by the regression line. This can be represented as follows:

$$Error = \sum_{i=1}^{n} (y_i - \hat{y}_i)^2$$

In the preceding equation, y is the actual training instance and $\hat{y}$ is the value predicted by the regression line.

In the context of machine learning, gradient descent is a common technique that can be used to optimize the coefficients of predictor variables by minimizing the training error of the model through multiple iterations. Gradient descent starts by initializing the coefficients to zero. Then, the coefficients are updated with the intention of minimizing the error. Updating the coefficients is an iterative process and is performed until a minimum squared error is achieved.

In the gradient descent technique, a hyperparameter called the **learning rate**, denoted by α is provided to the algorithm. This parameter determines how fast the algorithm moves toward the optimal value of the coefficients. If α is very large, the algorithm might skip the optimal solution. If it is too small, however, the algorithm might have too many iterations to converge to the optimum coefficient values. For this reason, it is important to use the right value for α.

In this recipe, we will use the gradient descent method to train our linear regression model.

Getting ready

In Chapter 1, *Get Closer To Your Data*, we took the HousePrices.csv file and looked at how to manipulate and prepare our data. We also analyzed and treated the missing values in the dataset. We will now use this final dataset for our model-building exercise, using linear regression:

In the following code block, we will start by importing the required libraries:

```
# import os for operating system dependent functionalities
import os

# import other required libraries
import pandas as pd
import numpy as np
import seaborn as sns
import matplotlib.pyplot as plt
```

We set our working directory with the os.chdir() command:

```
# Set your working directory according to your requirement
os.chdir("...../Chapter 4/Linear Regression")
os.getcwd()
```

Let's read our data. We prefix the DataFrame name with `df_` so that we can understand it easily:

```
df_housingdata = pd.read_csv("Final_HousePrices.csv")
```

How to do it...

Let's move on to building our model. We will start by identifying our numerical and categorical variables. We study the correlations using the correlation matrix and the correlation plots.

1. First, we'll take a look at the variables and the variable types:

```
# See the variables and their data types
df_housingdata.dtypes
```

2. We'll then look at the correlation matrix. The `corr()` method computes the pairwise correlation of columns:

```
# We pass 'pearson' as the method for calculating our correlation
df_housingdata.corr(method='pearson')
```

3. Besides this, we'd also like to study the correlation between the predictor variables and the response variable:

```
# we store the correlation matrix output in a variable
pearson = df_housingdata.corr(method='pearson')

# assume target attr is the last, then remove corr with itself
corr_with_target = pearson.iloc[-1][:-1]

# attributes sorted from the most predictive
corr_with_target.sort_values(ascending=False)
```

 We may also want to sort our correlation by absolute values. In order to do this, we can use the following command:
```
corr_with_target[abs(corr_with_target).argsort()[::-1]]
```

4. We can look at the correlation plot using the `heatmap()` function from the seaborn package:

```
f, ax = plt.subplots(figsize=(11, 11))

# Generate a mask for the upper triangle
# np.zeros_like - Return an array of zeros with the same shape and
type as a given array
# In this case we pass the correlation matrix
# we create a variable "mask" which is a 14 X 14 numpy array

mask = np.zeros_like(pearson, dtype=np.bool)
tt = np.triu_indices_from(mask)

# We create a tuple with triu_indices_from() by passing the "mask"
array
# k is used to offset diagonal
# with k=0, we offset all diagnoals
# If we put k=13, means we offset 14-13=1 diagonal

# triu_indices_from() Return the indices for the upper-triangle of
arr.
mask[np.triu_indices_from(mask, k=0)] = True

# First 2 param - anchor hues for negative and positive extents of
the map.
# 3rd param - Anchor saturation for both extents of the map
# If true, return a matplotlib colormap object rather than a list
of colors.

cmap = sns.diverging_palette(10, 129, s=50, as_cmap=True)

# Adjust size of the legend bar with cbar_kws={"shrink": 0.5}
# cmap="YlGnBu" gives the color from Yellow-Green-Blue palette

sns.heatmap(pearson, mask=mask, cmap="YlGnBu", vmax=.3, center=0,
            square=True, linewidths=.1, cbar_kws={"shrink": 0.5})
```

The following screenshot is the correlation plot. Note that we have removed the upper triangle of the heatmap using the `np.zeros_like()` and `np.triu_indices_from()` functions:

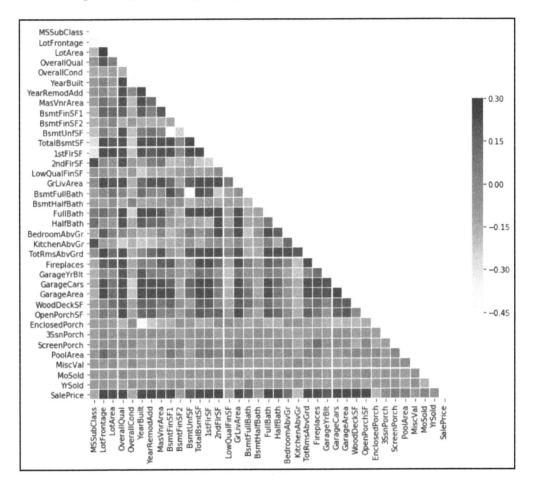

Let's explore our data by visualizing other variables.

5. We can look at the distribution of our target variable, `SalePrice`, using a histogram with a kernel density estimator as follows:

```
# Setting the plot size
plt.figure(figsize=(8, 8))

sns.distplot(df_housingdata['SalePrice'], bins=50, kde=True)
```

The following screenshot gives us the distribution plot for the `SalePrice` variable:

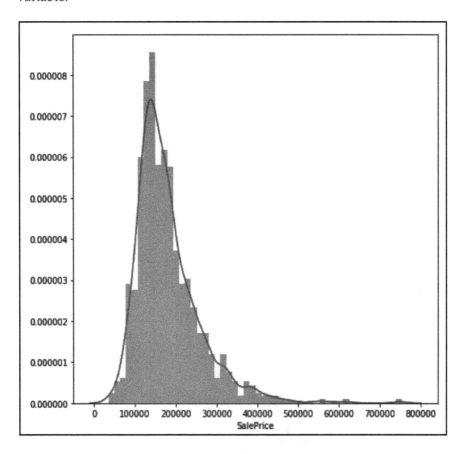

In statistics, **kernel density estimation** (**KDE**) is a non-parametric way to estimate the probability density function of a random variable. Kernel density estimation is a fundamental data smoothing problem where inferences about the population are based on a finite data sample. KDE is a technique that provides you with a smooth curve given a set of data. It can be handy if you want to visualize the shape of some data, as a kind of continuous replacement for the discrete values plotted in a histogram.

6. We can also use `JointGrid()` from our `seaborn` package to plot a combination of plots:

```
from scipy import stats
g = sns.JointGrid(df_housingdata['YearBuilt'],
df_housingdata['SalePrice'])
g = g.plot(sns.regplot, sns.distplot)
g = g.annotate(stats.pearsonr)
```

With the preceding code, we are able to plot the scatter plot for **GarageArea** and **SalePrice**, while also plotting the histogram for each of these variables on each axis:

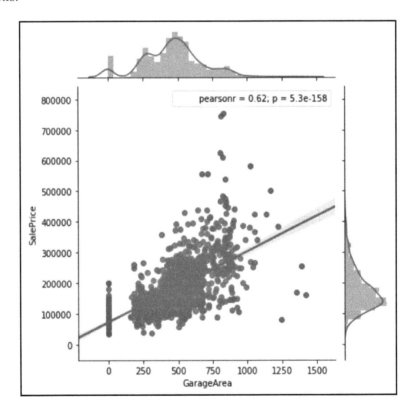

7. Let's now scale our numeric variables using min-max normalization. To do this, we first need to select only the numeric variables from our dataset:

```
# create a variable to hold the names of the data types viz int16,
in32 and so on
num_cols = ['int16', 'int32', 'int64', 'float16', 'float32',
'float64']

# Filter out variables with numeric data types
df_numcols_only = df_housingdata.select_dtypes(include=num_cols)
```

8. We will now apply the min-max scaling to our numeric variables:

```
# Importing MinMaxScaler and initializing it
from sklearn.preprocessing import MinMaxScaler
min_max=MinMaxScaler()

# Scaling down the numeric variables
# We exclude SalePrice using iloc() on df_numcols_only DataFrame
df_housingdata_numcols=pd.DataFrame(min_max.fit_transform(df_numcol
s_only.iloc[:,0:36]),
columns=df_numcols_only.iloc[:,0:36].columns.tolist())
```

In the following table, we can see that our numeric variables have been scaled down:

	MSSubClass	LotFrontage	LotArea	OverallQual	OverallCond	YearBuilt	YearRemodAdd	MasVnrArea	BsmtFinSF1
0	0.235294	0.150685	0.033420	0.666667	0.500	0.949275	0.883333	0.12250	0.125089
1	0.000000	0.202055	0.038795	0.555556	0.875	0.753623	0.433333	0.00000	0.173281
2	0.235294	0.160959	0.046507	0.666667	0.500	0.934783	0.866667	0.10125	0.086109
3	0.294118	0.133562	0.038561	0.666667	0.500	0.311594	0.333333	0.00000	0.038271
4	0.235294	0.215753	0.060576	0.777778	0.500	0.927536	0.833333	0.21875	0.116052

9. Now, we will perform one-hot encoding on our categorical variables:

```
# We exclude all numeric columns
df_housingdata_catcol =
df_housingdata.select_dtypes(exclude=num_cols)

# Steps to one-hot encoding:
# We iterate through each categorical column name
# Create encoded variables for each categorical columns
# Concatenate the encoded variables to the DataFrame
# Remove the original categorical variable
for col in df_housingdata_catcol.columns.values:
```

```
    one_hot_encoded_variables =
pd.get_dummies(df_housingdata_catcol[col],prefix=col)
    df_housingdata_catcol =
pd.concat([df_housingdata_catcol,one_hot_encoded_variables],axis=1)
    df_housingdata_catcol.drop([col],axis=1, inplace=True)
```

10. We have now created a DataFrame with only numeric variables that have been scaled. We have also created a DataFrame with only categorical variables that have been encoded. Let's combine the two DataFrames into a single DataFrame:

```
df_housedata = pd.concat([df_housingdata_numcols,
df_housingdata_catcol], axis=1)
```

11. We can then concatenate the `SalePrice` variable to our `df_housedata` DataFrame:

```
# Concatenate SalePrice to the final DataFrame
df_housedata_final = pd.concat([df_housedata,
df_numcols_only.iloc[:,36]], axis=1)
```

12. We can create our training and testing datasets using the `train_test_split` class from `sklearn.model_selection`:

```
# Create feature and response variable set
# We create train & test sample from our dataset
from sklearn.model_selection import train_test_split

# create feature & response variables
X = df_housedata_final.iloc[:,0:302]
Y = df_housedata_final['SalePrice']

# Create train & test sets
X_train, X_test, Y_train, Y_test = \
train_test_split(X, Y, test_size=0.30, random_state=1)
```

13. We can now use `SGDRegressor()` to build a linear model. We fit this linear model by minimizing the regularized empirical loss with SGD:

```
import numpy as np
from sklearn.linear_model import SGDRegressor

lin_model = SGDRegressor()

# We fit our model with train data
lin_model.fit(X_train, Y_train)

# We use predict() to predict our values
```

```
lin_model_predictions = lin_model.predict(X_test)

# We check the coefficient of determination with score()
print(lin_model.score(X_test, Y_test))

# We can also check the coefficient of determination with
r2_score() from sklearn.metrics
from sklearn.metrics import r2_score
print(r2_score(Y_test, lin_model_predictions))
```

By running the preceding code, we find out that the coefficient of determination is roughly 0.81.

Note that `r2_score()` takes two arguments. The first argument should be the true values, not the predicted values, otherwise, it would return an incorrect result.

14. We check the **root mean square error** (**RMSE**) on the test data:

```
from sklearn.metrics import mean_squared_error
mse = mean_squared_error(Y_test, lin_model_predictions)
rmse = np.sqrt(mse)
print(rmse)
```

Running the preceding code provides output to the effect that the RMSE equals 36459.44.

15. We now plot the actual and predicted values using `matplotlib.pyplot`:

```
plt.figure(figsize=(8, 8))
plt.scatter(Y_test, lin_model_predictions)
plt.xlabel('Actual Median value of house prices ($1000s)')
plt.ylabel('Predicted Median value of house prices ($1000s)')
plt.tight_layout()
```

The resulting plot with our actual values and the predicted values will look as follows:

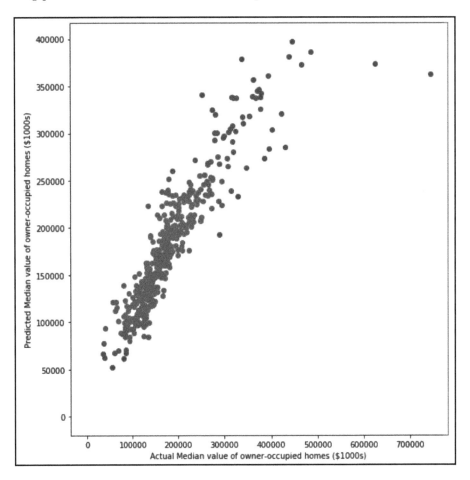

Because the chart shows most values in approximately a 45-degree diagonal line, our predicted values are quite close to the actual values, apart from a few.

How it works...

In *Step 1*, we looked at the variable types. We saw that the dataset had both numeric and non-numeric variables. In *Step 2*, we used the `Pearson` method to calculate the pairwise correlation among all the numeric variables. After that, in *Step 3*, we saw how all of the predictor variables are related to the target variable. We also looked at how to sort correlation coefficients by their absolute values.

In *Step 4*, we painted a heatmap to visualize the correlation between the variables. Then, we introduced two functions from the NumPy library: `zeros_like()` and `triu_indices_from()`. The `zeros_like()` function takes the correlation matrix as an input and returns an array of zeros with the same shape and type as the given array. `triu_indices_from()` returns the indices for the upper triangle of the array. We used these two functions to mask the upper triangular part of the correlation plot. We called the `heatmap()` function from the `seaborn` library to paint a correlation heat map and passed our correlation matrix to it. We also set the color of the matrix using `cmap="YlGnBu"` and the size of the legend bar using `cbar_kws={"shrink": 0.5}`.

 `numpy.tril_indices_from()` returns the indices for the lower triangle of the array.

In *Step 5*, we looked at the distribution of the target variable, `SalePrice`. In *Step 6*, we used `JointGrid()` from the `seaborn` library to show how it is possible to plot a scatter plot for two numeric variables with a regression line, along with plotting the distribution of both variables on the axis in the same chart. In *Steps 7* and *8*, we selected only the numeric variables and scaled the variables using min-max normalization. This scales the values to a numeric range of data between 0 and 1. This is also called feature scaling, and is performed using the following formula:

$$z = \frac{x - x_{min}}{x_{max} - x_{min}}$$

In *Step 9*, *Step 10*, and *Step 11*, we performed one-hot encoding on the categorical variables and added the encoded variables to the DataFrame. We also dropped the original categorical variables. In *Step 12*, we split our dataset into a training set and a testing set. In *Step 13*, we built our linear regression model using `SGDRegressor()` and printed the coefficient of determination. Finally, in *Step 14*, we plotted the predicted and actual values to see how well our model performed.

There's more...

Consider a linear regression model, given the following hypothesis function:

$$h(x) = \beta_0 + \beta_1 x_1$$

In this case, the cost function for β is the **mean squared error (MSE)**.

The formula is as follows:

$$f(\beta) = \frac{1}{m}(h_\beta(x^{(i)}) - y^{(i)})^2$$

In this formula, m represents the number of training instances. $x^{(i)}$ and $y^{(i)}$ are the input vector and the target vector for the ith training instance respectively, while β represents the parameters or coefficients for each input variable. $h_\beta(x^{(i)})$ is the predicted value for the ith training instance using the β parameters. The MSE is always non-negative and the closer it gets to zero, the better.

The MSE is higher when the model performs poorly on the training data. The objective of the learning algorithm, therefore, is to find the value of β such that the MSE is minimized. This can be represented as follows:

$$\min_\beta f(\beta)$$

The stochastic gradient descent method finds the values of β that minimize the cost function. In order to minimize the cost function, it keeps changing the β parameters by calculating the slope of the derivative of the cost function. It starts by initializing the β parameters to zero. The β parameters are updated at each step of the gradient descent:

$$update \; \beta_i \; for \; i = (0...n) \; \{\beta_i := \beta_i - \alpha\frac{\delta}{\delta\beta_i}f(\beta_0, \beta_1\}$$

The number of updates required for the algorithm to converge will increase with the increase in the training data. However, as the training data gets larger and larger, it is quite possible for the algorithm to converge much before every instance in the training data is learnt. In other words, the increase in the training data size need not increase the training time needed to train the best possible model where the test error is at its least.

Every training instance will modify β. The algorithm averages these β values to calculate the final β.

α is the learning rate, which tells the algorithm how rapidly to move toward the minimum. A large α might miss the minimum error, while a small α might take a longer time for the algorithm to run.

In the preceding section, we used a `SGDRegressor()` function, but we opted for the default values of the hyperparameters. We are now going to change α to 0.0000001 and the `max_iter` value to 2000:

```
lin_model = SGDRegressor(alpha=0.0000001, max_iter=2000)
```

 `max_iter` is an integer value that tells the algorithm the maximum number of passes it can make over the training data. This is also known as the number of epochs.

In our case, the preceding code gives the result that the RMSE drops from 36,459 to 31,222 and the coefficient of determination improved from 0.81 to 0.86. These results will vary for every iteration.

See also

- The scikit-learn documentation on regression metrics: https://bit.ly/2D6Wn8s
- The scikit-learn guide to density estimation: https://bit.ly/2RlnlMj

Logistic regression

In the previous section, we noted that linear regression is a good choice when the target variable is continuous. We're now going to move on to look at a binomial logistic regression model, which can predict the probability that an observation falls into one of two categories of a dichotomous target variable based on one or more predictor variables. A binomial logistic regression is often referred to as logistic regression.

Logistic regression is similar to linear regression, except that the dependent variable is measured on a dichotomous scale. Logistic regression allows us to model a relationship between multiple predictor variables and a dichotomous target variable. However, unlike linear regression, in the case of logistic regression, the linear function is used as an input to another function, such as σ:

$$h_\beta(x) = \sigma(\beta^T x) \; where \; 0 \le h_\beta \le 1$$

Here, σ is the sigmoid or logistic function. The sigmoid function is given as follows:

$$\frac{1}{1 + e^{-z}} \; where \; z = \beta^T x$$

The following graph represents a sigmoid curve in which the values of the y-axis lie between 0 and 1. It crosses the axis at 0.5. :

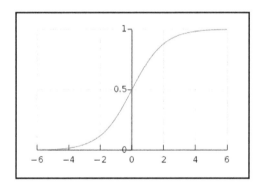

The output, which lies between 0 and 1, is the probability of the positive class. We can interpret the output of our hypothesis function as positive if the value returned is ≥ 0.5. Otherwise, we interpret it as negative.

In the case of logistic regression, we use a cost function known as cross-entropy. This takes the following form for binary classification:

$$cost(h_\beta(x), y) = -y. \, log(h_\beta(x)) - (1 - y) \, log(1 - h_\beta(x))$$

For *y=1* and *y=0*, we get the following results:

$$cost(h_\beta(x), y) = -y. \, log(h_\beta(x)) \; if \; y = 1$$
$$cost(h_\beta(x), y) = -(1 - y) \, log(1 - h_\beta(x)) \; if \; y = 0$$

Cross-entropy increases as the predicted probability diverges from the actual label. A higher divergence results in a higher cross-entropy value. In the case of linear regression, we saw that we can minimize the cost using gradient descent. In the case of logistic regression, we can also use gradient descent to update the coefficients and minimize the cost function.

In this recipe, we will use the `SGDClassfier()` implementation of scikit-learn. `SGDClassifier()` implements regularized linear models with stochastic gradient descent, which, for large datasets, is much faster than gradient descent. This is because gradient descent considers the whole training dataset, while stochastic gradient descent only considers one random point while updating the weights.

 By default, `SGDClassifier` might not perform as well as logistic regression. It is likely to require hyperparameter tuning.

Getting ready

In this section, we're going to use a dataset that contains information on default payments, demographics, credit data, payment history, and bill statements of credit card clients in Taiwan from April 2005 to September 2005. This dataset is taken from the UCI ML repository and is available at GitHub:

We will start by importing the required libraries:

```
# import os for operating system dependent functionalities
import os

# import other required libraries
import pandas as pd
from sklearn.preprocessing import StandardScaler
from sklearn.model_selection import train_test_split
from sklearn.linear_model import SGDClassifier
from sklearn.metrics import roc_curve
from sklearn.metrics import auc
import matplotlib.pyplot as plt
```

We set our working directory with the `os.chdir()` command:

```
# Set your working directory according to your requirement
os.chdir(".../Chapter 4/Logistic Regression")
os.getcwd()
```

Let's read our data. We will prefix the name of the DataFrame with `df_` to make it easier to read:

```
df_creditdata = pd.read_csv("UCI_Credit_Card.csv")
```

We will now move on to look at building our model using `SGDClassifier()`.

How to do it...

Let's start by looking at the variables and data types:

1. First, we're going to take a look at our dataset using the `read_csv()` function:

```
print(df_creditdata.shape)
print(df_creditdata.head())
```

2. We will take a look at the datatypes using `dtypes`:

```
df_creditdata.dtypes
```

3. We will drop the ID column as we do not need this here:

```
df_creditdata.drop(["ID"],axis=1,inplace=True)
```

4. In the previous section, we saw how to explore correlations among the variables. We will skip this here, but readers are advised to check for correlation as multicollinearity might have an impact on the model.

5. However, we will check if there are any null values, as follows:

```
df_creditdata.isnull().sum()
```

6. We will then separate the predictor and response variables. We will also split our training and testing data:

```
# split features & response variable
X = df_creditdata.iloc[:,0:23]
Y = df_creditdata['default.payment.next.month']

# Create train & test sets
X_train, X_test, Y_train, Y_test = train_test_split(X, Y,
test_size=0.30, random_state=1)
```

7. We standardize our predictor variables using `StandardScaler()`:

```
scaler = StandardScaler().fit(X_train)
X_train = scaler.transform(X_train)
X_test = scaler.transform(X_test)
```

8. We then move our model using `SGDClassifier()`:

```
# We create an instance of SGDClassifier()
logistic_model = SGDClassifier(alpha=0.000001, loss='log',
max_iter=100000, penalty='l2')

# We fit our model to the data
fitted_model = logistic_model.fit(X_train, Y_train)

# We use predict_proba() to predict the probabilities
predictedvalues = fitted_model.predict_proba(X_test)

# We print the probabilities to take a glance
predictedvalues
```

9. We separate out the probabilities of one class. In this case, we will look at class 1:

```
# We take the predicted values of class 1
Y_predicted = predictedvalues[:, 1]

# We check to see if the right values have been considered from the
predicted values
print(Y_predicted)
```

10. We check the accuracy of our model on the training data:

```
# Check for accuracy
logistic_model.score(X_test,Y_test)
```

11. We can then see the **area under curve** (**AUC**) value of the **receiver operating characteristic** (**ROC**) curve:

```
# We use roc_curve() to generate fpr & tpr values
fpr, tpr, thresholds = roc_curve(Y_test, Y_predicted)

# we pass the fpr & tpr values to auc() to calculate the area under
curve
roc_auc = auc(fpr, tpr)
print(roc_auc)
```

12. We plot our ROC curve as follows:

```
plt.figure()
plt.plot(fpr,tpr, color='orange', lw=2, label='ROC curve (area under
curve = %0.2f)' % roc_auc)
plt.plot([0, 1], [0, 1], color='darkgrey', lw=2, linestyle='--')
plt.xlim([0.0, 1.0])
plt.ylim([0.0, 1.0])
plt.xlabel('False Positive Rate (1-Specificity)')
plt.ylabel('True Positive Rate (Sensitivity)')
plt.title('ROC Curve')
plt.legend(loc="upper left")
plt.show()
```

The following graph shows the ROC curve with the AUC value annotated on it:

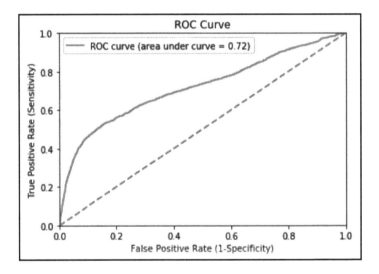

The model can be improved by tuning the hyperparameters. It can also be improved through feature selection.

How it works...

In *Step 1*, we looked at the dimensions of our dataset. In *Step 2*, we took a glimpse at the datatypes of the variables and noticed that all our variables were numeric in nature. In *Step 3*, we dropped the ID column since it is of no use for our exercise. We skipped looking at the correlations between the variables, but it is recommended that the reader adds this step in order to fully understand and analyze the data.

In *Step 4*, we moved on to check whether we had any missing values in our dataset. We noticed that our dataset had no missing values in this case. In *Step 5*, we separated the predictor and response variable and also split our dataset into a training dataset, which was 70% of the data, and a testing dataset, which was 30% of the data. In *Step 6*, we used `StandardScaler()` from `sklearn.metrics` to standardize our predictor variables in both the training and testing datasets.

After that, in *Step 7*, we used `SGDClassifier()` from `sklearn.linear_model` to build our logistic regression model using the stochastic gradient descent method. We set our hyperparameters, such as alpha, loss, `max_iter`, and penalty. We set `loss='log'` in order to use the SGDClassifier for logistic regression. We used `predict_proba()` to predict the probabilities for our test observations, which provided us with the probabilities of both classes for all the test observations.

> With `loss` set to `hinge`, `SGDClassifier()` provides a linear SVM. (We will cover SVMs in the upcoming section). The loss can be set to other values, such as `squared_hinge`, which is the same as `hinge` but is quadratically penalized.

In *Steps 8* and *9*, we filtered out the probabilities for class 1 and looked at our model score. In *Steps 10* and *11*, we looked at the AUC value and plotted our ROC curve. We will explore more about hyperparameter tuning for each technique in upcoming sections.

See also

- You might have noticed that, in *Step 7*, we used a hyperparameter penalty of `12`. The penalty is the regularization term and `12` is the default value. The hyperparameter penalty can also be set to `11`; however, that may lead to a sparse solution, pushing most coefficients to zero. More information about this topic can be found at the following link: `https://bit.ly/2RjbSwM`
- The scikit-learn guide to classification metrics: `https://bit.ly/2NUJ12C`

Naive Bayes

The **Naive Bayes algorithm** is a probabilistic learning method. It is known as **Naive** because it assumes that all events in this word are independent, which is actually quite rare. However, in spite of this assumption, the Naive Bayesian algorithm has proven over time to provide great performance in terms of its prediction accuracy.

The Bayesian probability theory is based on the principle that the estimated likelihood of an event or a potential outcome should be based on the evidence at hand across multiple trials. Bayes' theorem provides a way to calculate the probability of a given class, given some knowledge about prior observations.

This can be written as follows:

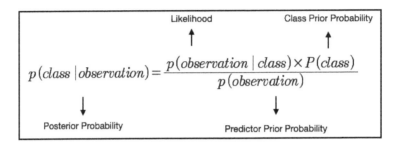

The different elements of this theorem can be explained as follows:

- **p(class | observation)**: This is the probability that the class holds given the observation.
- **P(observation)**: This is the prior probability that the training data is observed.
- **p(class)**: This is the prior probability of the class.
- **p(observation | class)**: This is the probability of the observations given that the class holds.

In other words, if H is the space for the possible hypothesis, the most probable hypothesis, class$\in$H, is the one that maximizes *p(class | observation)*.

Given a new observation with attributes $(a_1, a_2, a_3, \ldots, a_n)$, the Bayes algorithm classifies it as the most probable value:

$$class_{map} = \underset{class \in H}{argmax} \ P(class | a_1, a_2, a_3.., a_n) = argmax \ P(a_1, a_2, a_3 \ldots, a_n | class) \ P(class)$$

Given the conditional independence assumption, we have the following:

$$p(a_1, a_2, a_3 \ldots, a_n | class) = p(a_1 | class). \ p(a_2 | class). \ p(a_3 | class). \ldots. p(a_n | class)$$

The prediction of the Naive Bayesian Classifier is as follows:

$$class_{NB} = \underset{class \in H}{argmax}\ P(class) \prod_{i=1}^{n} P(a_1, a_2, a_3 \ldots, a_n | class)$$

Getting ready

A Naive Bayes classifier is one of the most basic algorithms that can be applied in text classification problems.

In this recipe, we will use the `spam.csv` file, which can be downloaded from the GitHub.

This `spam.csv` dataset has two columns. One column holds messages and the other column holds the message type, which states whether it is a spam message or a ham message. We will apply the Naive Bayes technique to predict whether a message is likely to be spam or ham.

We will start by importing the required libraries:

```
# import os for operating system dependent functionalities
import os
import pandas as pd
import numpy as np
import matplotlib.pyplot as plt
import seaborn as sns

from sklearn.model_selection import train_test_split
from sklearn.feature_extraction.text import CountVectorizer
from sklearn.naive_bayes import MultinomialNB
```

We set your working directory with the `os.chdir()` command:

```
os.chdir(".../Chapter 4/Naive Bayes")
os.getcwd()
```

Let's read our data. As we did in the previous sections, we will prefix the name of the DataFrame with `df_` so that we can read it easily:

```
df_messages = pd.read_csv('spam.csv', encoding='latin-1', \
                          sep=',', names=['labels','message'])
```

How to do it...

Let's now move on to look at how to build our model.

1. After reading the data, we use the `head()` function to take a look it:

    ```
    df_messages.head(3)
    ```

    In the following screenshot, we can see that there are two columns: **labels** and **message**. The output is as follows:

	labels	message
0	ham	Go until jurong point, crazy.. Available only ...
1	ham	Ok lar... Joking wif u oni...
2	spam	Free entry in 2 a wkly comp to win FA Cup fina...

2. We then use the `describe()` function to look at a few metrics in each of the columns:

    ```
    df_messages.describe()
    ```

    This gives us the following metrics:

	labels	message
count	5572	5572
unique	2	5169
top	ham	Sorry, I'll call later
freq	4825	30

 For the object datatype, the result of `describe()` will provide `metrics`, `count`, `unique`, `top`, and `freq`. `top` refers to the most common value, while `freq` is the frequency of this value.

3. We can also take a look at the metrics by message type, as follows:

    ```
    df_messages.groupby('labels').describe()
    ```

With the preceding command, we see the count, number of unique values, and frequency for each class of the target variable:

	message			
	count	**unique**	**top**	**freq**
labels				
ham	4825	4516	Sorry, I'll call later	30
spam	747	653	Please call our customer service representativ...	4

4. To analyze our dataset even further, let's take a look at the word count and the character count for each message:

```
df_messages['word_count'] = df_messages['message'].apply(lambda x:
len(str(x).split(" ")))
df_messages['character_count'] = df_messages['message'].str.len()

df_messages[['message','word_count', 'character_count']].head()
```

 The lambda function is used to create small, anonymous functions in Python. A lambda function can take any number of arguments, but can only have one expression. This function is passed as a parameter to other functions, such as map, apply, reduce, or filter.

The output of the preceding code will look as follows:

	message	word_count	character_count
0	Go until jurong point, crazy.. Available only ...	20	111
1	Ok lar... Joking wif u oni...	6	29
2	Free entry in 2 a wkly comp to win FA Cup fina...	28	155
3	U dun say so early hor... U c already then say...	11	49
4	Nah I don't think he goes to usf, he lives aro...	13	61

5. In this case, labels is our target variable. We have two classes: spam and ham. We can see the distribution of spam and ham messages using a bar plot:

```
labels_count =
pd.DataFrame(df_messages.groupby('labels')['message'].count())
labels_count.reset_index(inplace = True)
plt.figure(figsize=(4,4))
sns.barplot(labels_count['labels'], labels_count['message'])
```

```
plt.ylabel('Frequency', fontsize=12)
plt.xlabel('Labels', fontsize=12)
plt.show()
```

The following is the output of the preceding code:

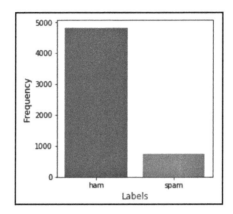

6. In the following code block, we will label spam as 1, and ham as 0:

```
# create a variable that holds a key-value pair for ham and spam
class_labels = {"ham":0,"spam":1}

# use the class_labels variable with map()
df_messages['labels']=df_messages['labels'].map(class_labels)
df_messages.head()
```

Notice that, in the following screenshot, under the labels variable, all ham and spam messages are now labelled as 0 and 1 respectively:

	labels	message	word_count	character_count
0	0	Go until jurong point, crazy.. Available only ...	20	111
1	0	Ok lar... Joking wif u oni...	6	29
2	1	Free entry in 2 a wkly comp to win FA Cup fina...	28	155
3	0	U dun say so early hor... U c already then say...	11	49
4	0	Nah I don't think he goes to usf, he lives aro...	13	61

7. We will now split our data into training and testing samples:

```
# Split your data into train & test set
X_train, X_test, Y_train, Y_test =
train_test_split(df_messages['message'],\
df_messages['labels'],test_s=0.2,random_state=1)
```

8. We need to convert the collection of messages to a matrix of token counts. This can be done using `CountVectorizer()`:

```
# Creating an instance of the CountVectorizer class
# If 'english', a built-in stop word list for English is used.
# There are known issues with 'english' and you should consider an
alternative
vectorizer = CountVectorizer(lowercase=True, stop_words='english',
analyzer='word')

# Learn a vocabulary from one or more message using the
fit_transform() function
vect_train = vectorizer.fit_transform(X_train)
```

9. We proceed to build our model with the Naive Bayes algorithm:

```
# Create an instance of MultinomialNB()
model_nb = MultinomialNB()

# Fit your data to the model
model_nb.fit(vect_train,Y_train)

# Use predict() to predict target class
predict_train = model_nb.predict(vect_train)
```

10. We load the required libraries for the evaluation metrics, as follows:

```
from sklearn.metrics import accuracy_score
from sklearn.metrics import precision_score
from sklearn.metrics import recall_score
from sklearn.metrics import f1_score
```

11. We now check our accuracy by evaluating the model with the training data:

```
# Calculate Train Accuracy
print('Accuracy score: {}'.format(accuracy_score(Y_train,
predict_train)))

# Calculate other metrics on your train results
print('Precision score: {}'.format(precision_score(Y_train,
predict_train)))
```

```
print('Recall score: {}'.format(recall_score(Y_train,
predict_train)))
print('F1 score: {}'.format(f1_score(Y_train, predict_train)))
```

The output of this is as follows:

```
Accuracy score: 0.9937177473636976
Precision score: 0.9728813559322034
Recall score: 0.9795221843003413
F1 score: 0.976190476190476
```

12. Now we check the accuracy of our test data by evaluating the model with the unseen test data:

```
# We apply the model into our test data
vect_test = vectorizer.transform(X_test)
prediction = model_nb.predict(vect_test)

# Calculate Test Accuracy
print('Accuracy score: {}'.format(accuracy_score(Y_test,
prediction)))

# Calculate other metrics on your test data
print('Precision score: {}'.format(precision_score(Y_test,
prediction)))
print('Recall score: {}'.format(recall_score(Y_test, prediction)))
print('F1 score: {}'.format(f1_score(Y_test, prediction)))
```

With the preceding code block, we print performance metrics as follows:

```
Accuracy score: 0.9829596412556054
Precision score: 0.961038961038961
Recall score: 0.9192546583850931
F1 score: 0.9396825396825396
```

These results may vary with different samples and hyperparameters.

How it works...

In *Step 1,* we looked at our dataset. In *Step 2* and *Step 3,* we looked at the statistics for the ham and spam class labels. In *Step 4,* we extended our analysis by looking at the word count and the character count for each of the messages in our dataset. In *Step 5,* we saw the distribution of our target variables (ham and spam), while in *Step 6* we encoded our class labels for the target variable with the numbers 1 and 0. In *Step 7,* we split our dataset into training and testing samples. In *Step 8,* we used `CountVectorizer()` from `sklearn.feature_extraction.text` to convert the collection of messages to a matrix of token counts.

> If you do not provide a dictionary in advance and do not use an analyzer that does some kind of feature selection, then the number of features will be equal to the vocabulary size found by analyzing the data. For more information on this, see the following: `https://bit.ly/1pBh3T1`.

In *Step 9* and *Step 10,* we built our model and imported the required classes from `sklearn.metrics` to measure the various scores respectively. In *Step 11* and *12,* we checked the accuracy of our training and testing datasets.

There's more...

The Naive Bayes algorithm comes in multiple variations. These include the Multivariate Bernoulli Naive Bayes, Multinomial Naive Bayes, and Gaussian Multinomial Naive Bayes algorithms. These variations can be applied to solve different problems.

- **Multivariate Bernoulli Naive Bayes**: This algorithm is used when the feature vectors provide a binary representation of whether a word or feature occurs in the document or not. Every token in the feature vector of a document is associated with either the 1 or 0 values. 1 represents a token in which the word occurs, and 0 represents a token in which the word does not occur. The Multivariate Bernoulli Naive Bayes algorithm can be used in situations in which the absence of a particular word matters, such as in the detection of spam content.

- **Multinomial Naive Bayes**: This is used when multiple occurrences of words are to be considered in classification problems. In this variation, text documents are characterized by the frequency of the term, instead of binary values. Frequency is a discrete count that refers to how many times a given word or token appears in a document. The Multinomial Naive Bayes algorithm can be used for topic modeling, which is a method for finding a group of words that best represent the key information in a corpus of documents.
- **Gaussian Multinomial Naive Bayes**: In scenarios where we have continuous features, one way to deal with continuous data in Naive Bayes classifications is to discretize the features. Alternatively, we can apply the Gaussian Multinomial Naive Bayes algorithm. This assumes the features follow a normal distribution and uses a Gaussian kernel to calculate the class probabilities.

See also

- In scikit-learn, `CountVectorizer()` counts the number of times a word shows up in the document and uses that value as its weight. You can also use `TfidfVectorizer()`, where the weight assigned to each token depends on both its frequency in a document and how often the term recurs in the entire corpus. You can find more on `TfidfVectorizer` at the following link: `https://bit.ly/2sJCoVN`.
- The scikit-learn documentation on the Naive Bayes classifier for multivariate Bernoulli models: `https://bit.ly/2y3fASv`.
- The scikit-learn documentation on the Naive Bayes classifier for multinomial models: `https://bit.ly/2P4Ohic`.

Decision trees

Decision trees, a non-parametric supervised learning method, are popular algorithms used for predictive modeling. The most well-known decision tree algorithms include the **iterative dichotomizer** (**ID3**), C4.5, CART, and C5.0. ID3 is only applicable for categorical features. C4.5 is an improvement on ID3 and has the ability to handle missing values and continuous attributes. The tree-growing process involves finding the best split at each node using the information gain. However, the C4.5 algorithm converts a continuous attribute into a dichotomous categorical attribute by splitting at a suitable threshold value that can produce maximum information gain.

Leo Breiman, a distinguished statistician, introduced a decision tree algorithm called the **Classification and Regression Tree (CART)**. CART, unlike ID3 and C4.5, can produce decision trees that can be used for both classification and regression problems. This algorithm also forms the basis for the important random forest algorithm.

Decision trees are built using recursive partitioning, which splits the data into subsets based on several dichotomous independent attributes. This recursive process may split the data multiple times until the splitting process terminates after a particular stopping criterion is reached. The best split is the one that maximizes a splitting criterion. For classification learning, the techniques used as the splitting criterion are entropy and information gain, the Gini index, and the gain ratio. For regression tasks, however, standard deviation reduction is used.

The C4.5 and C5.0 algorithms use entropy (also known as **Shannon entropy**) and information gain to identify the optimal attributes and decide on the splitting criterion. Entropy is a probabilistic measure of uncertainty or randomness.

Mathematically, entropy can be expressed as follows:

$$Entropy = \sum_{i=1}^{n} -p_i log_2 (p_i)$$

In the case of a two-class attribute, entropy can range from 0 to 1. For an n-class attribute, entropy can take values between 0 to $log_2 (n)$. For a homogeneous variable, where there is just a single class, the entropy would be zero because the probability of that class being zero is 1 and $log_2 (1) = 0$.

To use entropy to identify the most identified attributes at which to split, the algorithm calculates the change in homogeneity that would result from the split at each possible attribute. This change is known as information gain. Constructing a decision tree is all about finding the attribute that returns the highest information gain. This information gain is based on the decrease in entropy after a dataset is split at an attribute.

Information gain is calculated as the difference between the entropy before the split and the entropy after the split:

$$Information\ Gain = Entropy(S_{Before\ Split}) - Entropy(S_{After\ Split})$$

The higher the information gain, the better a feature is. Information gain is calculated for all features. The algorithm chooses the feature with the highest information gain to create the root node. The information gain is calculated at each node to select the best feature for that node.

 Information gain is also known as Kullback-Leibler divergence. This measures the difference between two probability distributions over the same variable. Put simply, if you have two probability distributions, the KL divergence measures the similarity of the two distributions. If the KL divergence is 0, the two distributions are equal.

The Gini index is a measure of the degree of impurity and can also be used to identify the optimal attributes for the splitting criterion. It is calculated as follows:

$$Gini = 1 - \sum_{i=1}^{n} p_i^2$$

In the preceding formula, p is the probability of a training instance belonging to a particular class. With regards to the Gini index, the lower the impurity, the better it is.

Getting ready

To build our model with q decision tree algorithm, we will use the `backorders.csv` file, which can be downloaded from the following GitHub.

This dataset has 23 columns. The target variable is `went_on_backorder`. This identifies whether a product has gone on back order. The other 22 variables are the predictor variables. A description of the data is provided in the code that comes with this book:

We will start by importing the required libraries:

```
# import os for operating system dependent functionalities
import os

# import other required libraries
import pandas as pd
import numpy as np
from sklearn.preprocessing import StandardScaler
from sklearn.model_selection import train_test_split
from sklearn.metrics import accuracy_score
from sklearn.metrics import confusion_matrix, roc_curve, auc
import itertools
from sklearn import tree
```

```
import seaborn as sns
import matplotlib.pyplot as plt
```

We set our working directory with the os.chdir() command:

```
# Set your working directory according to your requirement
os.chdir("..../Chapter 4/Decision Tree")

# Check Working Directory
os.getcwd()
```

Let's read our data. As we have done previously, we are going to prefix the name of the DataFrame with df_ to make it easier to understand:

```
df_backorder = pd.read_csv("BackOrders.csv")
```

How to do it...

Let's now move on to building our model:

1. First, we want to look at the dimensions of the dataset and the data using the shape and head() functions. We also take a look at the statistics of the numeric variables using describe():

```
df_backorder.shape
df_backorder.head()
df_backorder.describe()
```

If you get your output in scientific notation, you can change to view it in standard form instead by executing the following command:
pd.options.display.float_format = '{:.2f}'.format

2. With dtypes, we get to see the data types of each of the variables:

```
df_backorder.dtypes
```

3. We can see that sku is an identifier and will be of no use to us for our model-building exercise. We will, therefore, drop sku from our DataFrame as follows:

```
df_backorder.drop('sku', axis=1, inplace=True)
```

4. We can check whether there are any missing values with the `isnull().sum()` command:

```
df_backorder.isnull().sum()
```

We take a look at the following screenshot:

national_inv	0
lead_time	3403
in_transit_qty	0
forecast_3_month	0
forecast_6_month	0

5. Since the number of missing values in the `lead_time` variable is about 5%, we will remove all the observations where `lead_time` is missing for our initial analysis:

```
df_backorder = df_backorder.dropna(axis=0)
```

6. We now need to encode our categorical variables. We select only the categorical variables and call `pd.get_dummies()` to dummy-code the non-numeric variables:

```
non_numeric_attributes =
df_backorder.select_dtypes(include=['object']).columns
df_backorder = pd.get_dummies(columns=non_numeric_attributes,
data=df_backorder, prefix=non_numeric_attributes,
prefix_sep="_",drop_first=True)
df_backorder.dtypes
```

With the preceding code, we get to see the datatypes. We notice that dummy-coded variables are all of the unsigned integer (`uint8`) type:

potential_issue_Yes	uint8
deck_risk_Yes	uint8
oe_constraint_Yes	uint8
ppap_risk_Yes	uint8
stop_auto_buy_Yes	uint8
rev_stop_Yes	uint8
went_on_backorder_Yes	uint8

7. We will then look at our target variable distribution as follows:

```
# Target variable distribution
pd.value_counts(df_backorder['went_on_backorder_Yes'].values)
```

We can see that our data has a fairly balanced distribution, with approximately 81% of the observations belonging to class 0 and 19% belonging to class 1:

```
0      47217
1      10969
dtype: int64
```

8. We will now split our data into training and testing datasets:

```
#Performing train test split on the data
X, Y =
df_backorder.loc[:,df_backorder.columns!='went_on_backorder_Yes'].va
lues, df_backorder.loc[:,'went_on_backorder_Yes'].values

# Split our dataset into train & test set
X_train, X_test, Y_train, Y_test = train_test_split(X, Y,
test_size=0.2, random_state=1)
```

9. We will build our first model with `DecisionTreeClassifier()`:

```
# Create an instance of DecisionTreeClassifier()
classifier = tree.DecisionTreeClassifier(random_state=1)

# Fit our model to the data
model_DT_Gini = classifier.fit(X_train, Y_train)
model_DT_Gini
```

With `model_DT_Gini`, we can see the default values of the hyperparameters that have been used:

```
DecisionTreeClassifier(class_weight=None, criterion='gini', max_depth=None,
        max_features=None, max_leaf_nodes=None,
        min_impurity_decrease=0.0, min_impurity_split=None,
        min_samples_leaf=1, min_samples_split=2,
        min_weight_fraction_leaf=0.0, presort=False, random_state=None,
        splitter='best')
```

10. We can use the model to predict our class labels using both our training and our testing datasets:

```
# Predict with our test data
test_predictedvalues = model_DT_Gini.predict(X_test)

# Check accuracy
acc = accuracy_score(Y_test, test_predictedvalues)
print("Accuracy is", acc)

# Check TP, TN, FP, FN
tn, fp, fn, tp = confusion_matrix(Y_test,
test_predictedvalues).ravel()
print("TN:",tn, " FP:",fp, " FN:",fn, " TP:",tp)
```

This gives us the accuracy along with the count of **True Negative (TN)**, **False Positive (FP)**, **False Negative (FN)**, and **True Positive (TP)** values:

```
Accuracy is 0.901409257562
TN: 13200  FP: 950  FN: 771  TP: 2535
```

11. We will now use a `plot_confusion_matrix` function to plot our confusion matrix. This function is taken from `http://scikit-learn.org` and is readily available there, so we won't show this function here. It is, however, provided with the code in the book for your reference:

```
target_names = [ 'No', 'Yes']

#Pass Actual & Predicted values to confusion_matrix()
cm = confusion_matrix(Y_test, test_predictedvalues)

plt.figure()
plot_confusion_matrix(cm, classes=target_names, normalize=False)
plt.show()
```

We can then see the amount of TNs, FPs, FNs, and TPs in our confusion matrix plot:

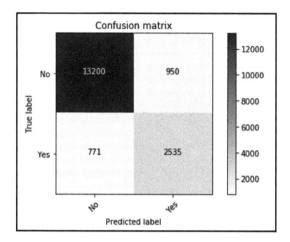

12. We can change the hyperparameters to tune our model. We can also perform a grid search to find the hyperparameter values that supply optimum results. We can use the following code to set the hyperparameter values:

```
# set the parameters for grid search
grid_search_parameters = {"criterion": ["gini", "entropy"],
            "min_samples_split": [2],
            "max_depth": [None, 2, 3],
            "min_samples_leaf": [1, 5],
            "max_leaf_nodes": [None],
            }
```

13. We will use `GridSearchCV()` to grid search the parameters:

```
from sklearn.model_selection import GridSearchCV

# Create an instance of DecisionTreeClassifier()
classifier = tree.DecisionTreeClassifier()

# Use GridSearchCV(), pass the values you have set for grid search
model_DT_Grid = GridSearchCV(classifier, grid_search_parameters,
cv=10)
model_DT_Grid.fit(X_train, Y_train)
```

14. After running the preceding command, we can see the best parameter values among those provided using `best_params_`:

```
model_DT_Grid.best_params_
```

15. You can use the model that is selected using the `GridSearchCV()` function:

```
test_predictedvalues = model_DT_Grid.predict(X_test)

cc = accuracy_score(Y_test, test_predictedvalues)
print("Accuracy is", acc)

tn, fp, fn, tp = confusion_matrix(Y_test,
test_predictedvalues).ravel()
print("TN:",tn, " FP:",fp, " FN:",fn, " TP:",tp)

cm = confusion_matrix(Y_test, test_predictedvalues)

plt.figure()
plot_confusion_matrix(cm, classes=target_names, normalize=False)
plt.show()
```

16. In order to see the metrics per-label, we can also use the `classification_report`, as follows:

```
from sklearn.metrics import classification_report

target_names = [ 'No', 'Yes']
print(classification_report(Y_test, test_predictedvalues,
target_names=target_names))
```

This step gives us the following output:

	precision	recall	f1-score	support
No	0.89	0.95	0.92	9439
Yes	0.70	0.48	0.56	2199
avg / total	0.85	0.86	0.85	11638

These results will vary depending on the samples used and the hyperparameter tuning.

How it works...

In *Step 1*, we took a look at the dimensions of our dataset. We also saw the statistics of our numerical variables. In *Step 2*, we looked at the datatypes of each of our variables. In *Step 3*, we dropped the `sku` attribute, because it is an identifier that will be of no use to us for our model. In *Step 4*, we checked for missing values and noticed that the `lead_time` attribute had 3,403 missing values, which is roughly 5% of the total number of observations. In *Step 5*, we dropped the observations for which the `lead_time` had missing values. Note that there are various strategies to impute missing values, but we haven't considered these in this exercise.

In *Step 6*, we used `get_dummies()` from the pandas library with `drop_first=True` as one of the parameters to perform a k-1 dummy coding on the categorical variables. In *Step 7*, we took a look at the distribution of our target variable. We see the class labels, 0 and 1, are in the ratio of 19%-81% approximately, which is not very well balanced. However, we had enough observations for both classes to proceed to our next steps. In *Step 8*, we separated our predictor and response variables. We also split our dataset to create a training dataset and a testing dataset. In *Step 9*, we used a `DecisionTreeClassifier()` to build our model. We noted the default hyperparameters values and noticed that, by default, `DecisionTreeClassifier()` uses the Gini impurity measure as the splitting criterion.

In *Step 10*, we used the model to predict our test sample. We took a note of the overall accuracy and the amount of TP, TN, FP, and FN values that we achieved. In *Step 11*, we used `plot_confusion_matrix()` to plot these values in the form of a confusion matrix. Please note that `plot_confusion_matrix()` is readily available at `https://bit.ly/2MdyDU9` and is also provided with the book in the code folder for this chapter.

We then looked at changing the hyperparameter values to fine-tune our model. We performed a grid search to find the optimum hyperparameter values. In *Step 12*, we defined the combination of values for our hyperparameters that we want to apply to our grid search algorithm. In *Step 13* and *14*, we used `GridSearchCV()` to look for the optimum hyperparameters. In *Step 15*, we used the model returned by the grid search to predict our test observations. Finally, in *Step 16*, we used `classification_report()` from `sklearn.metrics` to generate various scores including `precision`, `recall`, `f1-score`, and `support`.

There's more...

Sometimes, a model can classify training data perfectly but faces difficulty when working with new data. This problem is known as **overfitting**. The model fails to generalize to the new test data.

We allow a recursive splitting process to repeat until we terminate the leaf node because we cannot split the data further. This model would fit the training data perfectly but leads to poor performance. For this reason, tree-based models are susceptible to overfitting. To overcome this, we need to control the depth of our decision tree.

There are multiple ways to avoid overfitting. One method is to terminate the growth before a perfect classification of the training data is made. The following approaches can be adopted to implement this stopping method:

- Stop when a tree reaches the maximum number of levels
- Stop when a subset contains fewer than a defined number of training instances
- Stop when the minimum information gain is reached

Another method is to allow the data to overfit, and then to prune the tree after it is constructed. This involves eliminating nodes that are not clearly relevant, which also minimizes the size of the decision tree.

See also

- The scikit-learn documentation on the decision tree classifier: `https://bit.ly/1Ymrzjw`
- The scikit-learn documentation on the decision tree regressor: `https://bit.ly/2xMNSua`

Support vector machines

A **support vector machine** (**SVM**) is a popular machine learning algorithm for supervised learning. It can be used for both classification and regression problems. In classification learning, SVM performs classifications by finding an optimal separating hyperplane that differentiates two classes of observations. If the data is linearly separable and one-dimensional, we may have a point that separates the data. In two-dimensional space, the data can be separated by a straight line, while a plane separates data in three-dimensional space. When we have more than three dimensions, this is called a hyperplane.

For a linear SVM, a dataset X with n feature vectors is represented as follows:

$$X = \{x_1, x_2, x_3, \ldots, x_n\} \; where \; x_i \in \mathbb{R}^m$$

A bipolar target variable Y is written as follows:

$$Y = \{y_1, y_2, y_3, \ldots, y_m\} \; where \; y_i \in \{-1, +1\}$$

The hyperplane is given by the following:

$$w^T . x + b = 0 \; where \; w^t = \{w_1, w_2, w_3, \ldots, w_n\}^T$$

For an SVM, the two classes are represented as -1 and +1 instead of 1 and 0. The hyperplane can, therefore, be written as follows:

$$f(x) = sign(w^T . x + b)$$

To classify the data, we have the following two rules:

$$w^T . x + b > 0 \; for \; y_i = +1$$
$$w^T . x + b < 0 \; for \; y_i = -1$$

However, it's quite possible that there are a lot of hyperplanes that correctly classify the training data. There might be infinite solutions of w and b that hold for the preceding rules. An algorithm such as a perceptron learning algorithm will just find any linear classifier. SVM, however, finds the optimal hyperplane, which is at a maximum distance from any data point. The further the data points lie from the hyperplane, the more confident we are that they have been correctly classified. We would therefore like the data points to be as far away from the hyperplane as possible, while still being able to classify them correctly. The best hyperplane is the one that has the maximum margin between the two classes. This is known as the maximum-margin hyperplane.

It's possible for SVM to choose the most important vectors that define the separation hyperplane from the training data. These are the data points that lie closest to the hyperplane and are known as support vectors. Support vectors are the data points that are hardest to classify. At the same time, these represent high-quality data. If you remove all the other data points and use only the support vectors, you can get back the exact decision hyperplane and the margin using the same SVM model. The number of data points does not really matter, just the support vectors.

We normalize the weights w and b so that the support vectors satisfy the following condition:

$$|w^T . x + b| = 1$$

As a result, the classification rules change to the following:

$$w^T . x + b \geq +1 \ for \ y_i = +1$$
$$w^T . x + b \leq -1 \ for \ y_i = -1$$

The preceding equations can be combined and represented as follows:

$$y_i(w^T . x + b) \geq 1 \ for \ y_i = +1 \ or \ -1$$

The initial SVM algorithms could only be used in the case of linearly separable data. These are known as hard-margin SVMs. However, hard-margin SVMs can work only when the data is completely linearly separable and if doesn't have any noise. In the case of noise or outliers, a hard-margin SVM might fail.

Vladimir Vapnik proposed soft-margin SVMs to deal with data that is non-linearly separable by using slack variables. Slack variables allows for errors to be made while fitting the model to the training dataset. In hard-margin classification, we will get a decision boundary with a small margin. In soft-margin classification, we will get a decision boundary with a larger margin:

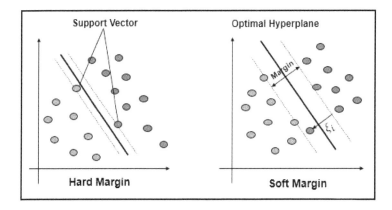

SVMs can also perform non-linear classification extremely well using something called a kernel trick. This refers to transformations in which the predictor variables are implicitly mapped to a higher-dimensional feature space. Popular kernel types include the following:

- Linear kernels
- Polynomial kernels
- Radial basis function (RBF) kernels
- Sigmoid kernels

Different kernel functions are available for various decision functions. We can add kernel functions together to achieve even more complex planes.

Getting ready

In this chapter, we are going to use the `bank.csv` file, which is based on bank marketing data and which you can download from GitHub. This data is related to a Portuguese bank's direct marketing campaigns that took place over phone calls. The goal is to predict whether the client will subscribe to a term deposit:

We will start by importing the required libraries:

```
# import os for operating system dependent functionalities
import os

# import other required libraries
import pandas as pd
import numpy as np
from sklearn.svm import SVC
from sklearn.metrics import accuracy_score, confusion_matrix,
roc_curve, auc
from sklearn.model_selection import train_test_split
```

We set our working directory with the `os.chdir()` command:

```
# Set your working directory according to your requirement
os.chdir("...../Chapter 4/Support Vector Machine")
os.getcwd()
```

Let's read our data. We will again prefix the name of the DataFrame with `df_` to make it easier to understand:

```
df_bankdata = pd.read_csv("bank.csv")
```

How to do it...

In this section, we're going to look at checking null values, standardizing numeric values, and one-hot-encoding categorical variables:

1. With the following command, we can see we that we have ten categorical variables and seven numerical variables in the dataset:

   ```
   df_bankdata.dtypes
   ```

2. With the following command, we notice there are no missing values, so we can proceed with our next steps:

   ```
   df_bankdata.isnull().sum()
   ```

3. We can check the class balance in our target variable as follows:

   ```
   print("Total number of class labels:
   {}".format(df_bankdata.shape[0]))
   print("Number of people opted for Term Deposit:
   {}".format(df_bankdata[df_bankdata.y == 'yes'].shape[0]))
   print("Number of people not opted for Term Deposit:
   {}".format(df_bankdata[df_bankdata.y == 'no'].shape[0]))
   ```

4. We can convert our target class to the binary values 1 and 0 with the following command:

   ```
   df_bankdata['y'] = (df_bankdata['y']=='yes').astype(int)
   ```

5. We can now perform one-hot encoding on our categorical variables. We only select variables that are categorical in nature. In the following code, we use `category_column_names` to provide the names of the non-numeric variables:

   ```
   # Using select_dtypes() to select only the non-numerical type
   variable
   column_type = ['object']
   df_bank_data_category_cols = df_bankdata.select_dtypes(column_type)

   # This will give you the names of the non-numerical variables
   category_column_names =
   df_bank_data_category_cols.columns.values.tolist()
   category_column_names
   ```

6. We run a loop over each of the non-numerical variables to perform one-hot encoding on them and add them back to the DataFrame. We will also delete the original non-numerical variables after performing one-hot encoding:

```
for each_col in category_column_names:
    dummy_var = pd.get_dummies(df_bank_data_category_cols[each_col],
prefix=each_col)
    df_joindata = df_bankdata.join(dummy_var)
    df_joindata.drop([each_col], axis=1, inplace=True)
    df_bankdata = df_joindata
```

7. We separate the predictor and response variables as follows:

```
# Separate features & response variable
X=df_bankdata.iloc[:, :-1]
Y=df_bankdata['y']
```

8. We also split our data into training and testing datasets:

```
X_train, X_test, Y_train, Y_test = train_test_split(X, Y,
test_size=0.2, random_state=1)
```

9. We then build our first model using SVC with the default kernel, **radial basis function (RBF)**:

```
# Note, you need not pass kernel='rbf' to the SVC() because its the
default
svc_model = SVC(kernel='rbf')
svc_model.fit(X_train, Y_train)
```

10. We check our training and testing accuracy via the SVC model built with the RBF kernel:

```
train_predictedvalues=svc_model.predict(X_train)
test_predictedvalues=svc_model.predict(X_test)

print('Train Accuracy Score:')
print(metrics.accuracy_score(Y_train,train_predictedvalues))

print('Test Accuracy Score:')
print(metrics.accuracy_score(Y_test,test_predictedvalues))
```

We get the following output:

```
Train Accuracy Score:
0.99889380531
Test Accuracy Score:
0.872928176796
```

11. We can rebuild our SVC model with a polynomial kernel as follows:

```
svc_model =SVC(kernel='poly')
svc_model.fit(X_train, Y_train)

train_predictedvalues=svc_model.predict(X_train)
test_predictedvalues=svc_model.predict(X_test)

print('Train Accuracy Score:')
print(metrics.accuracy_score(Y_train,train_predictedvalues))

print('Test Accuracy Score:')
print(metrics.accuracy_score(Y_test,test_predictedvalues))
```

We get the following output with the polynomial kernel:

```
Train Accuracy Score:
0.998340707965
Test Accuracy Score:
0.993370165746
```

12. We can also build an SVC model with the linear kernel. Instead of `kernel='ploy'`, we can replace this with `kernel='linear'` in the preceding code:

```
svc_model =SVC(kernel='linear')
```

With the linear kernel, we get the following accuracy:

```
Train Accuracy Score:
0.997234513274
Test Accuracy Score:
0.994475138122
```

Our results will vary depending on the different types of kernel and other hyperparameter values used.

How it works...

In *Step 1*, we looked at the data types of our variables. We noticed that we have ten categories and seven numerical variables. In *Step 2*, we checked for missing values and saw that there were no missing values in our dataset. In *Step 3*, we checked the class balance of our target variable and found out that it has the values of yes and no. In *Step 4*, we converted our target variable to 1 and 0 to represent yes and no respectively. In *Steps 5* and *6*, we performed one-hot encoding on the non-numerical variables.

In *Step 7*, we separate the predictor and response variables and in *Step 8*, we split our dataset into training and testing datasets. After that, in *Step 9*, we used SVC() from sklearn.svm with the default RBF kernel to build our model. We applied it to our training and testing data to predict the class. In *Step 10*, we checked the accuracy of our training and testing data. In *Step 11*, we changed our hyperparameter to set the kernel to polynomial. We noticed that training accuracy remained more or less the same, but the test accuracy improved.

With the polynomial kernel, the default degree is 3. You can change the polynomial degree to a higher degree and note of the change in the model's performance.

In *Step 12*, we changed the kernel to linear to see if the results improved compared to the polynomial kernel. We did not, however, see any significant improvement.

There's more...

In this exercise, we have seen how to use various kernels in our code. Kernel functions must be symmetrical. Preferably, they should have a positive (semi) definite gram matrix. A gram matrix is the matrix of all the possible inner products of V, where V is the set of m vectors. For convenience, we consider positive semi-definite and positive-definite functions indifferently. In practice, a positive definiteness of kernel matrices ensures that kernel algorithms converge to a unique solution.

A **linear kernel** is the simplest of all kernels available. It works well with text classification problems.

A linear kernel is presented as follows:

$$K(x, y) = x^T y + c$$

Here, **c** is the constant term.

A **polynomial kernel** has two parameters: a constant and the degree. A polynomial kernel with no constant and a degree of 1 is simply a linear kernel. As the degree of the polynomial kernel increases, the decision function becomes more complex. With higher degrees, it is possible to get good training accuracy, but the model might fail to generalize to unseen data, leading to overfitting. The polynomial kernel is represented as follows:

$$K(x, y) = (\alpha x^T y + c)^d$$

Here, α is the slope, d is the degree of the kernel, and c is the constant term.

The **radial basis function kernel (RBF)**, also known as the Gaussian kernel, is a more complicated kernel and can outperform polynomial kernels. The RBF kernel is given as follows:

$$K(x, y) = exp(-\gamma ||x - y||^2)$$

The γ parameter can be tuned to increase the performance of the kernel. This is important: with an over-estimated γ, the kernel can lose its non-linear power and behave more linearly. On the other hand, if γ is underestimated, the decision function can be highly sensitive to noise in the training data.

Not all kernels are strictly positive-definite. The sigmoid kernel function, though is quite widely used, is not positive-definite. The sigmoid function is given as follows:

$$K(x, y) = tanh(\alpha x^T y + c)$$

Here, α is the slope and **c** is the constant term. Note that an SVM with a sigmoid kernel is the same as a two-layer perceptron neural network.

Adding a kernel trick to an SVM model can give us new models. How do we choose which kernel to use? The first approach is to try out the RBF kernel, since it works pretty well most of the time. However, it is a good idea to use other kernels and validate your results. Using the right kernel with the right dataset can help you build the best SVM models.

See also

- More on the positive definite matrix can be found here: https://bit.ly/2NnGeLK.
- Positive definite kernels are a generalization of the positive definite matrix. You can find out more about this here: https://bit.ly/2NlsIs1.

- The scikit-learn documentation on support vector regression: https://bit.ly/2OFZ8ix.

5
Bag the Models with Bagging

In this chapter, we discuss the following recipes:

- Bootstrap aggregation
- Ensemble meta-estimators
- Bagging regressors

Introduction

The combination of classifiers can help reduce misclassification errors substantially. Many studies have proved such ensembling methods can significantly reduce the variance of the prediction model. Several techniques have been proposed to achieve a variance reduction. For example, in many cases, bootstrap aggregating (bagging) classification trees have been shown to have higher accuracy than a single classification tree. Bagging can be applied to tree-based algorithms to enhance the accuracy of the predictions, although it can be used with methods other than tree-based methods as well.

Bootstrap aggregation

Bootstrap aggregation, also known as **bagging**, is a powerful ensemble method that was proposed by Leo Breiman in 1994 to prevent overfitting. The concept behind bagging is to combine the predictions of several base learners to create a more accurate output.

Breiman showed that bagging can successfully achieve the desired result in **unstable** learning algorithms where small changes to the training data can lead to large variations in the predictions. Breiman demonstrated that algorithms such as neural networks and decision trees are examples of **unstable** learning algorithms. Bootstrap aggregation is effective on small datasets.

The general procedure for bagging helps to reduce variance for those algorithms have high variance. Bagging also supports the classification and regression problem. The following diagram shows how the bootstrap aggregation flow works:

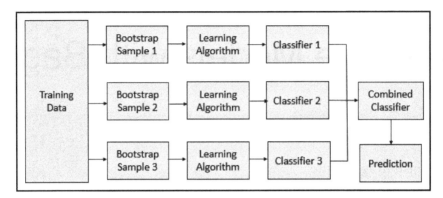

Using bootstrapping with a training dataset X, we generate N bootstrap samples X1, X2,......, XN.

For each bootstrap sample, we train a classifier, $b_i(x)$. The combined classifier will average the outputs from all these individual classifiers as follows:

$$b(x) = \frac{1}{N} \sum_{i=1}^{N} b_i(x)$$

In the preceding formula, N represents the number of samples.

In a bagging classifier, voting is used to make a final prediction. The pseudo-code for the bagging classifier proposed by Breiman is as follows:

$Bagging\,(S = ((x_1,y_1),....,(x_n,y_n)))$
1 *for* $t \leftarrow 1\,to\,T$ *do*
2      $S_t \leftarrow Bootstrap(S) \triangleright i.i.d.\,Sampling\,with\,replacement\,from\,S.$
3        $h_t \leftarrow TrainClassifier(S_t)$
4 *return* $h_s = x \rightarrow MajorityVote((h_1(x),.......,(h_T(x)))$

In the case of the bagging regressor, the final prediction is the average of the predictions of the models that are built over each bootstrap sample. The following pseudo-code describes the bagging regressor:

$$Bagging\,(S = ((x_1, y_1), ..., (x_m, y_m)))$$

1 *for* $t \leftarrow 1\,to\,T\,do$

2     $S_t \leftarrow Bootstrap(S) \triangleright i.i.d.\,Sampling\,with\,replacement\,from\,S.$

3      $h_t \leftarrow TrainRegression\,(s_t)$

4 *return* $h_s = x \rightarrow Mean\,((h_1(x), ..., (h_T(x)))$

Getting ready

We start by importing the required libraries and reading our file. We suppress any warnings using the `warnings.filterwarnings()` function from the `warnings` library:

```
import warnings
warnings.filterwarnings('ignore')

import os
import pandas as pd
import numpy as np

from sklearn.model_selection import train_test_split
from sklearn.linear_model import SGDRegressor
from sklearn.metrics import mean_squared_error, r2_score
from sklearn.utils import resample

import matplotlib.pyplot as plt
```

We have now set our working folder. Download the `autompg.csv` file from the GitHub and copy the file into your working folder as follows:

```
os.chdir('.../.../Chapter 5')
os.getcwd()
```

We read our data with `read_csv()` and prefix the name of the data frame with `df_` so that it is easier to understand:

```
df_autodata = pd.read_csv("autompg.csv")
```

We check whether the dataset has any missing values as follows:

```
# The below syntax returns the column names which has any missing
value
columns_with_missing_values=df_autodata.columns[df_autodata.isnull(
).any()]
```

```
# We pass the column names with missing values to the dataframe to
count the number
# of missing values
df_autodata[columns_with_missing_values].isnull().sum()
```

We notice that the `horsepower` variable has six missing values. We can fill in the missing values using the median of the `horsepower` variable's existing values with the following code:

```
df_autodata['horsepower'].fillna(df_autodata['horsepower'].median()
, inplace=True)
```

We notice that the `carname` variable is an identifier and is not useful in our model-building exercise, so we can drop it as follows:

```
df_autodata.drop(['carname'], axis=1, inplace=True)
```

We can look at the data with the `dataframe.head()` command:

```
df_autodata.head()
```

How to do it...

In this section, we will see how to build a model using bootstrap samples:

1. We start by creating the bootstrap samples. In Chapter 3, *Resampling Methods,* we wrote a custom function, `create_bootstrap_oob()`, to create both bootstrap and **out-of-bag** (**OOB**) samples.

   In the following code block, we see how to create bootstrap and OOB samples:

   ```
   def create_bootstrap_oob(df):
       global df_OOB
       global df_bootstrap_sample
       # creating the bootstrap sample
       df_bootstrap_sample = resample(df, replace=True, n_samples=100)
       # creating the OOB sample
       bootstrap_sample_index = tuple(df_bootstrap_sample.index)
       bootstrap_df = df.index.isin(bootstrap_sample_index)
       df_OOB = df[~bootstrap_df]
   ```

2. We build models using the bootstrap samples and average the cost function across all the models. We use the `SGDRegressor()` on each bootstrap sample. In the following code block, we reuse our previously written custom function, `create_bootstrap_oob()`, to create the bootstrap and OOB error samples:

```
iteration=50
mse_each_iterations = list()
lm=SGDRegressor()
total_mse=0
average_mse= list()

for i in range(iteration):
    create_bootstrap_oob(df_autodata)

    # Bootstrap sample features set
    X_BS = df_bootstrap_sample.iloc[:,1:8]

    # bootstrap sample response variable
    Y_BS = df_bootstrap_sample.iloc[:,0]

    X_OOB = df_OOB.iloc[:,1:8] #OOB sample features
    Y_OOB = df_OOB.iloc[:,0] #OOB sample response variable
    # fit your model with bootstrap sample
    lm=SGDRegressor()
    lm.fit(X_BS, Y_BS)
    # test your model on out-of-bag sample
    predictedvalues = lm.predict(X_OOB)
    # capture MSE for the predicted values against OOB actuals
    mse = mean_squared_error(Y_OOB, predictedvalues)
    # create a list of mse values
    mse_each_iterations.append(mse)
```

3. We are now going to plot the MSE for each model built:

```
import matplotlib.pyplot as plt
f, ax= plt.subplots(figsize=(8,6))

plt.plot(mse_each_iterations, 'c--', label='MSE by Iteration')

plt.xlabel('Iterations')
plt.ylabel('Mean Squared Error')
plt.legend(loc=1)
plt.show()
```

The plot will look as follows:

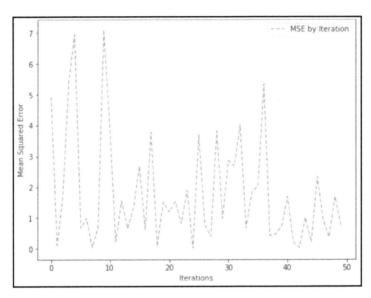

How it works...

In *Step 1*, we executed our custom function code to create the `create_bootstrap_oob()` function that creates the bootstrap and OOB samples for us. In *Step 2*, we executed the following steps:

1. We decided to make 50 iterations, so we set the `iteration` variable to `50`.
2. The `create_bootstrap_oob()` function returned two DataFrame objects, `df_bootstrap_sample` and `df_OOB`, in each iteration.
3. We used `df_bootstrap_sample` and `df_OOB` as our bootstrap and OOB samples respectively.
4. We split both the `df_bootstrap_sample` and the `df_OOB` samples into feature sets and response variables.
5. We fit the `SGDRegressor()` to our bootstrap sample to build our model.
6. We passed the OOB sample to the model to predict our values.

7. We compared the predicted values against the response variable in the OOB sample.
8. We calculated the MSE for each iteration.

In *Step 3*, we created a plot to show the MSE for each iteration up to the fiftieth iteration. This result may vary because of randomness.

See also

- *Bagging Predictors* by Leo Breiman, September 1994

Ensemble meta-estimators

The bagging classifier and the bagging regressor are ensemble meta-estimators that fit the base classifier and regressor models respectively on random subsets of the original dataset. The predictions from each model are combined to create the final prediction. These kinds of meta-estimators induce randomization into the model-building process and aggregate the outcome. The aggregation averages over the iterations for a numerical target variable and performs a plurality vote in order to reach a categorical outcome.

Bagging classifiers

Bagging classifiers train each classifier model on a random subset of the original training set and aggregate the predictions, then perform a plurality voting for a categorical outcome. In the following recipe, we are going to look at an implementation of a bagging classifier with bootstrap samples.

How to do it...

1. We import `BaggingClassifier` and `DecisionTreeClassifier` from the `scikit-learn` library. We also import the other required libraries as follows:

```
from sklearn.ensemble import BaggingClassifier
from sklearn.tree import DecisionTreeClassifier
from sklearn.model_selection import train_test_split
```

2. Next, we read out the data and take a look at the dimensions:

```
df_winedata = pd.read_csv('winedata.csv')
df_winedata.shape
```

3. We separate our features and the response set. We also split our data into training and testing subsets.

```
X = df_winedata.iloc[:,1:14]
Y = df_winedata.iloc[:,0]

X_train, X_test, Y_train, Y_test = train_test_split(X, Y,
random_state=1)
```

4. We create an instance of the `DecisionTreeClassifier` class and pass it to the `BaggingClassifier()`:

```
dt_model = DecisionTreeClassifier(criterion='entropy')
bag_dt_model = BaggingClassifier(dt_model, max_features=1.0,
n_estimators=5, \
                                random_state=1, bootstrap=True)
```

Note that in the preceding code block, we have declared `bootstrap=True`. This is the default value and indicates that samples are drawn with replacement.

5. We fit our model to the training data as follows:

```
bag_dt_model.fit(X_train, Y_train)
```

6. We can see the score after passing the test data to the model:

```
bag_dt_model.score(X_test, Y_test)
```

7. We use the `predict` function to predict the response variable as follows:

```
predictedvalues = bag_dt_model.predict(X_test)
```

8. We will now use a code to plot the confusion matrix. Note that this code has been taken from `scikit-learn.org`. We execute the following code to create the `plot_confusion_matrix()` function:

```
# code from
#
http://scikit-learn.org/stable/auto_examples/model_selection/plot_c
onfusion_matrix.html
```

```
def plot_confusion_matrix(cm, classes,
                            normalize=False,
                            title='Confusion matrix',
                            cmap=plt.cm.Blues):
    """
    This function prints and plots the confusion matrix.
    """
    plt.imshow(cm, interpolation='nearest', cmap=cmap)
    plt.title(title)
    plt.colorbar()
    tick_marks = np.arange(len(classes))
    plt.xticks(tick_marks, classes, rotation=45)
    plt.yticks(tick_marks, classes)

    thresh = cm.max() / 2.
    for i, j in itertools.product(range(cm.shape[0]),
range(cm.shape[1])):
        plt.text(j, i, cm[i, j],
                    horizontalalignment="center",
                    color="white" if cm[i, j] > thresh else "black")

    plt.tight_layout()
    plt.ylabel('Actuals')
    plt.xlabel('Predicted')
```

9. We use the preceding `plot_confusion_matrix()` function to plot our confusion matrix:

```
# This variable holds the class labels of our target variable
target_names = [ '1', '2', '3']

import itertools
from sklearn.metrics import confusion_matrix

# Constructing the Confusion Matrix
cm = confusion_matrix(Y_test, predictedvalues)

# Plotting the confusion matrix
plt.figure(figsize=(3,3))
plot_confusion_matrix(cm, classes=target_names, normalize=False)
plt.show()
```

The confusion matrix plot looks as follows:

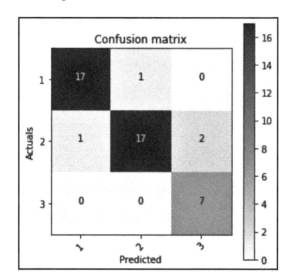

How it works...

In *Step 1*, we imported the required libraries to build our decision tree classifier model using the bagging classifier. In *Step 2*, we read our dataset, which was `winedata.csv`. In *Step 3*, we separated our feature set and the target variable. We also split our data into training and testing subsets. In *Step 4*, we created a decision tree classifier model and passed it to the `BaggingClassifier()`. In the `DecisionTreeClassifier()`, the default value for the `criterion` parameter was `gini`, but we changed it to `entropy`. We then passed our decision tree model to the `BaggingClassfier()`. In the `BaggingClassfier()`, we have parameters including `n_estimators` and `bootstrap`. `n_estimators` is the number of base estimators in the ensemble and has a default value of `10`. The `bootstrap` parameter indicates whether samples are drawn with replacement or not and is set to `True` by default.

In *Step 5* and *Step 6*, we fitted our model to the training data and looked at the score of the test set. In *Step 7*, we called the `predict()` method and passed the test feature set. In *Step 8*, we added the code for the `plot_confusion_matrix()` from `http://scikit-learn.org`, which takes the confusion matrix as one of its input parameters and plots the confusion matrix. In *Step 9*, we called the `plot_confusion_matrix()` function by passing the confusion matrix to generate the confusion matrix plot.

There's more...

We can also use `GridSearchCV()` from `sklearn.model_selection` to grid search the best parameters and use them in the `BaggingClassifier`:

1. First, we import the required library:

```
from sklearn.model_selection import GridSearchCV
```

2. We then set our parameter values:

```
param_values = {'n_estimators': [10, 20, 25, 30],
'base_estimator__max_leaf_nodes':[5, 10, 15, 20],
'base_estimator__max_depth':[3, 4, 5]}
```

3. We instantiate our `DecisionTreeClassifier` class and pass it to the `BaggingClassifier()` function. Note that we set the `oob_score` to `True` to evaluate the models built on the OOB samples:

```
dt_model = DecisionTreeClassifier()
bag_dt_model_grid = BaggingClassifier(base_estimator=dt_model,
oob_score=True, random_state=1)
```

4. We use `GridSearchCV()` to determine the best parameters:

```
bc_grid = GridSearchCV(estimator=bag_dt_model_grid,
param_grid=param_values, cv=20, n_jobs=-1)
bc_grid.fit(X_train, Y_train)
best_params = bc_grid.best_params_
print(best_params)
```

The preceding code returns the optimum parameters:

```
{'base_estimator__max_depth': 3, 'base_estimator__max_leaf_nodes': 10, 'n_estimators': 20}
```

5. We now take the values returned by `bc_grid.bestparams` and rebuild our decision tree models using the `BaggingClassfier()` function. We pass 10 for the `max_leaf_nodes`, 3 for the `max_depth`, and 20 for the `n_estimators`:

```
best_dt_model = DecisionTreeClassifier(criterion='entropy',
max_leaf_nodes=10, max_depth=3)
final_bag_dt_model =
BaggingClassifier(base_estimator=best_dt_model, n_estimators=150,
bootstrap=True, random_state=1, oob_score=True)
```

We set our `n_estimators` to `150` in the preceding code block. The `n_estimators` parameter indicates the number of trees we want to build. We fit our final model to our training data and make a prediction using our test feature set.

6. We can then look at the accuracy of our OOB samples in the following code block:

```
final_bag_dt_model.fit(X_train, Y_train)
bag_predictedvalues = final_bag_dt_model.predict(X_test)

# See the OOB accuracy
acc_oob = final_bag_dt_model.oob_score_
print(acc_oob)
```

If we plot our confusion matrix, we can see that we have made an improvement with regard to the number of misclassifications that are made. In the earlier example, two instances of class 2 were wrongly predicted as class 3, but we can now see that the number of misclassifications has reduced to one:

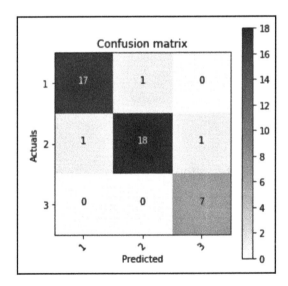

See also

- The scikit-learn guide to bagging classifiers: `https://bit.ly/2zaq81S`

Bagging regressors

Bagging regressors are similar to bagging classifiers. They train each regressor model on a random subset of the original training set and aggregate the predictions. Then, the aggregation averages over the iterations because the target variable is numeric. In the following recipe, we are going to showcase the implementation of a bagging regressor with bootstrap samples.

Getting ready

We will import the required libraries, BaggingRegressor and DecisionTreeRegressor, from sklearn.ensemble and sklearn.tree respectively:

```
from sklearn.ensemble import BaggingRegressor
from sklearn.tree import DecisionTreeRegressor
```

We read our dataset, which is bostonhousing.csv, and look at the dimensions of the DataFrame:

```
df_housingdata = pd.read_csv('bostonhousing.csv')
df_housingdata.shape
```

We now move on to creating our feature set and our target variable set.

How to do it...

1. We first separate our feature and response set. We will also split our data into training and testing subsets in the following code block:

   ```
   X = df_housingdata.iloc[:,1:14]
   Y = df_housingdata.iloc[:,-1]

   X_train, X_test, Y_train, Y_test = train_test_split(X, Y,
   random_state=1)
   ```

2. We will then create an instance of the DecisionTreeClassifier class and pass it to the BaggingClassifier() function:

   ```
   dt_model = DecisionTreeRegressor()
   bag_dt_model = BaggingRegressor(dt_model, max_features=1.0,
   n_estimators=5, bootstrap=True, random_state=1, )
   ```

3. We will fit our model to the training dataset as follows:

```
bag_dt_model.fit(X_train, Y_train)
```

4. We can see the model score in the following code block:

```
bag_dt_model.score(X_test, Y_test)
```

5. We use the `predict()` function and pass the test dataset to predict our target variable as follows:

```
predictedvalues = bag_dt_model.predict(X_test)
```

6. We plot the scatter plot of our actual values and the predicted values of our target variable with the following code:

```
#We can plot the actuals and the predicted values
plt.figure(figsize=(4, 4))
plt.scatter(Y_test, predictedvalues)
plt.xlabel('Actual')
plt.ylabel('Predicted')
plt.tight_layout()
```

Executing the preceding code gives us the following scatter plot:

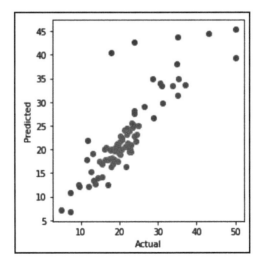

 The `matplotlib.pyplot.tight_layout()` automatically adjusts the subplot parameters to create specified padding.

7. We now change the `n_estimators` parameter to 30 in the following code and re-execute the steps from *Step 3* to *Step 6*:

```
bag_dt_model = BaggingRegressor(dt_model, max_features=1.0,
n_estimators=30, bootstrap=True, random_state=1, )
```

This gives us the following score:

```
0.82224534363352664
```

8. The plot of the actual values against the predicted values looks as follows. This shows us that the values are predicted more accurately than in our previous case when we changed the value of the `n_estimator` parameter from 5 to 30:

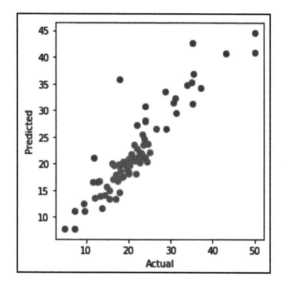

How it works...

In *Step 1*, we separated the features and the target variable set. We also split our data into training and testing subsets. In *Step 2*, we created a decision tree regressor model and passed it to the `BaggingRegressor()` function. Note that we also passed the `n_estimator=5` parameter to the `BaggingRegressor()` function. As mentioned earlier, `n_estimator` is the number of trees in the forest we would like the algorithm to build. In *Step 3*, we trained our model.

In *Step 4*, we looked at the model score, which was 0.71. In *Step 5*, we used the `predict()` function to predict our target variable for the test subset. After that, in *Step 6*, we plotted a scatterplot to explore the relationship between the actual target values and the predicted target values.

In *Step 7*, we changed the `n_estimator` parameter's value from 5 to 30 and re-built our model. This time, we noticed that the model score improved to 0.82. In *Step 8*, we plotted the actual and predicted values and saw that the correlation between the actual and predicted values was much better than our previous model, where we used `n_estimators=5`.

See also

- The scikit-learn guide to bagging regressors: `https://bit.ly/2pZFmUh`
- Single estimator versus bagging: `https://bit.ly/2q08db6`

6
When in Doubt, Use Random Forests

In this chapter, we will cover the following recipes:

- Introduction to random forests
- Implementing a random forest for predicting credit card defaults using scikit-learn
- Implementing a random forest for predicting credit card defaults using H2O

Introduction to random forests

A random forest is a supervised machine learning algorithm based on ensemble learning. It is used for both regression and classification problems. The general idea behind random forests is to build multiple decision trees and aggregate them to get an accurate result. A decision tree is a deterministic algorithm, which means if the same data is given to it, the same tree will be produced each time. They have a tendency to overfit, because they build the best tree possible with the given data, but may fail to generalize when unseen data is provided. All the decision trees that make up a random forest are different because we build each tree on a different random subset of our data. A random forest tends to be more accurate than a single decision tree because it minimizes overfitting.

The following diagram demonstrates bootstrap sampling being done from the source sample. Models are built on each of the samples and then the predictions are combined to arrive at a final result:

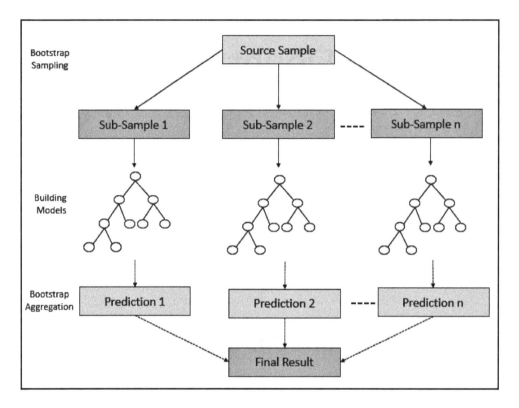

Each tree in a random forest is built using the following steps where A represents the entire forest, a represents a single tree, for *a = 1* to *A*:

1. Create a bootstrap sample with replacement, *D* training from *x, y* label these X_a, Y_a
2. Train the tree f_a on X_a, Y_a
3. Average the predictions or take the majority vote to arrive at a final prediction

In a regression problem, predictions for the test instances are made by taking the mean of the predictions made by all trees. This can be represented as follows:

$$\hat{p} = \frac{1}{N} \sum_{a=1}^{A} f_a(x)$$

Here, N is the total number of trees in the random forest. $a=1$ represents the first tree in a forest, while the last tree in the forest is A. $f_a(x)$ represents the prediction from a single tree.

If we have a classification problem, majority voting or the most common answer is used.

Implementing a random forest for predicting credit card defaults using scikit-learn

The scikit-learn library implements random forests by providing two estimators: RandomForestClassifier and RandomForestRegressor. They take various parameters, some of which are explained as follows:

- n_estimators: This parameter is the number of trees the algorithm builds before taking a maximum vote or the average prediction. In general, the higher the number of trees the better the performance and the accuracy of the predictions, but it also costs more in terms of computation.
- max_features: This parameter is the maximum number of features that the random forest is allowed to try in an individual tree.
- min_sample_leaf: This parameter determines the minimum number of leaves that are required to split an internal node.
- n_jobs: This hyperparameter tells the engine how many jobs to run in parallel for both fitting the model and predicting new instances. If it has a value of None or 1, it runs only one job. A value of -1 means it will use all the processors.
- random_state: This parameter will always produce the same results when it has a definite value of random_state and if it has been given the same hyperparameters and the same training data.
- oob_score: This parameter is also known as **out-of-the-bag sampling**, and is a random forest cross-validation method. In this sampling method, about one-third of the data is not used to train the model and can be used to evaluate its performance. These samples are called the **out-of-the-bag samples**.

Getting ready

In this example, we use a dataset from the UCI ML repository on credit card defaults. This dataset contains the following information:

- Default payments
- Demographic factors
- Credit data
- History of payments
- Bill statements of credit card clients

The data and the data descriptions are provided in the GitHub folder:

We will start by loading the required libraries and reading our dataset:

```
import os
import numpy as np
import pandas as pd
import matplotlib.pyplot as plt
%matplotlib inline
import seaborn as sns
```

We set our working folder as follows:

```
# Set your working directory according to your requirement
os.chdir(".../Chapter 6/Random Forest")
os.getcwd()
```

Let's now read our data. We will prefix the DataFrame name with `df_` so that we can understand it easily:

```
df_creditcarddata = pd.read_csv("UCI_Credit_Card.csv")
```

We check the shape of the dataset:

```
df_creditcarddata.shape
```

We check the datatypes:

```
df_creditcarddata.dtypes
```

We drop the `ID` column, as this is not required:

```
df_creditcarddata = df_creditcarddata.drop("ID", axis= 1)
```

We can explore our data in various ways. Let's take a look at a couple of different methods:

```
selected_columns =
df_creditcarddata[['AGE','BILL_AMT1','BILL_AMT2','BILL_AMT3','BILL_AMT4','B
ILL_AMT5','BILL_AMT6', 'LIMIT_BAL']]

selected_columns.hist(figsize=(16, 20), bins=50, xlabelsize=8,
ylabelsize=8);
```

Note that we have used a semicolon in the last line in the preceding code block. The semicolon helps to hide the verbose information produced by Matplotlib. `xlabelsize` and `ylabelsize` are used to adjust the font size in the x-axis and the y-axis.

The following plot shows the distribution of the numeric variables:

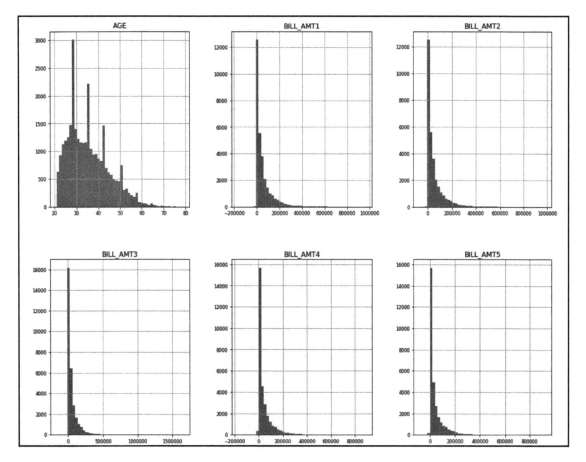

We will now explore the payment defaults by age group. We bucket the age variable and store the binned values in a new variable, age_group, in df_creditcarddata:

```
df_creditcarddata['agegroup'] = pd.cut(df_creditcarddata['AGE'], range(0, 100, 10), right=False)
df_creditcarddata.head()
```

We then use our new age_group variable to plot the number of defaults per age group:

```
# Default vs Age
pd.crosstab(df_creditcarddata.age_group, \
df_creditcarddata["default.payment.next.month"]).plot(kind='bar',stacked=Fa
lse, grid=True)

plt.title('Count of Defaults by AGE')
plt.xlabel('AGE')
plt.ylabel('# of Default')
plt.legend(loc='upper left')
```

The following screenshot shows the amount of defaults per age:

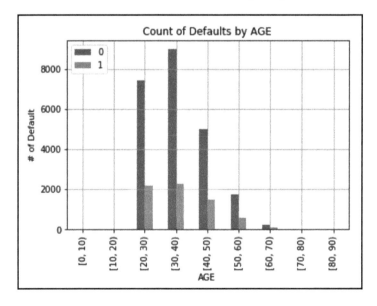

We can drop the age_group variable from df_creditcarddata since we do not need it anymore:

```
df_creditcarddata = df_creditcarddata.drop(columns = ['age_group'])
df_creditcarddata.head()
```

We will now look at the payment defaults according to the credit limits of the account holders:

```
fig_facetgrid = sns.FacetGrid(df_creditcarddata,
hue='default.payment.next.month', aspect=4)
fig_facetgrid.map(sns.kdeplot, 'LIMIT_BAL', shade=True)
max_limit_bal = df_creditcarddata['LIMIT_BAL'].max()
fig_facetgrid.set(xlim=(0,max_limit_bal));
fig_facetgrid.set(ylim=(0.0,0.000007));
fig_facetgrid.set(title='Distribution of limit balance by default.payment')
fig_facetgrid.add_legend()
```

The preceding code gives us the following plot:

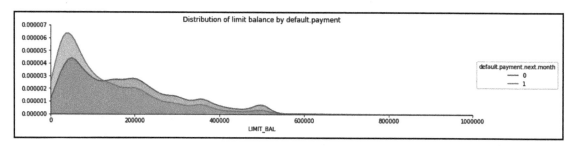

We can also assign labels to some of our variables to make the interpretations better. We assign labels for the Gender, Marriage, and Education variables.

We also change the datatype of the pay variables to the string:

```
GenderMap = {2:'female', 1:'male'}
MarriageMap = {1:'married', 2:'single', 3:'other', 0: 'other'}
EducationMap = {1:'graduate school', 2:'university', 3:'high school',
4:'others', 5:'unknown', 6:'unknown', 0:'unknown'}

df_creditcarddata['SEX'] = df_creditcarddata.SEX.map(GenderMap)
df_creditcarddata['MARRIAGE'] = df_creditcarddata.MARRIAGE.map(MarriageMap)
df_creditcarddata['EDUCATION'] =
df_creditcarddata.EDUCATION.map(EducationMap)
df_creditcarddata['PAY_0'] = df_creditcarddata['PAY_0'].astype(str)
df_creditcarddata['PAY_2'] = df_creditcarddata['PAY_2'].astype(str)
df_creditcarddata['PAY_3'] = df_creditcarddata['PAY_3'].astype(str)
df_creditcarddata['PAY_4'] = df_creditcarddata['PAY_4'].astype(str)
df_creditcarddata['PAY_5'] = df_creditcarddata['PAY_5'].astype(str)
df_creditcarddata['PAY_6'] = df_creditcarddata['PAY_6'].astype(str)
```

There are more explorations available in the code bundle provided with this book. We now move on to training our random forest model.

How to do it...

We will now look at how to use a random forest to train our model:

1. We start by splitting our target and feature variables:

```
predictor= df_creditcarddata.iloc[:, df_creditcarddata.columns !=
'default.payment.next.month']
target= df_creditcarddata.iloc[:, df_creditcarddata.columns ==
'default.payment.next.month']
```

2. We separate the numerical and non-numerical variables in our feature set:

```
# save all categorical columns in list
categorical_columns = [col for col in predictor.columns.values if
predictor[col].dtype == 'object']

# dataframe with categorical features
df_categorical = predictor[categorical_columns]

# dataframe with numerical features
df_numeric = predictor.drop(categorical_columns, axis=1)
```

3. We dummy code the categorical variables:

```
dummy_code_cat_vars =
pd.get_dummies(df_categorical,drop_first=True)
```

4. We concatenate the dummy code variables to our DataFrame:

```
df_predictor = pd.concat([df_numeric, dummy_code_cat_vars], axis=1)
df_predictor.head()
```

5. We split our dataset into training and testing subsets:

```
from sklearn.model_selection import train_test_split
X_train,X_test, y_train, y_test = train_test_split(df_predictor,
target, test_size = 0.30, random_state=0)
print("x_train ",X_train.shape)
print("x_test ",X_test.shape)
print("y_train ",y_train.shape)
print("y_test ",y_test.shape)
```

6. We scale the features with `StandardScaler()`:

```
from sklearn.preprocessing import StandardScaler
scaler = StandardScaler()
```

7. We might notice that the column names have been changed to numbers. We assign the columns names and index values back to the scaled DataFrame:

```
X_train_scaled.columns = X_train.columns.values
X_test_scaled.columns = X_test.columns.values
X_train_scaled.index = X_train.index.values
X_test_scaled.index = X_test.index.values

X_train = X_train_scaled
X_test = X_test_scaled
```

8. We import `RandomForestClassifier()` from `sklearn.ensemble`. We will then build our random forest classifier model:

```
from sklearn.ensemble import RandomForestClassifier

classifier = RandomForestClassifier(random_state = 0, n_estimators
= 100,\
 criterion = 'entropy', max_leaf_nodes= 20,oob_score = True, n_jobs
= -1 )

# fit the model
model_RF = classifier.fit(X_train, y_train)
```

9. After that, we calculate the accuracy of our training model:

```
acc_random_forest = round(classifier.score(X_train, y_train) * 100,
2)
print(round(acc_random_forest,2,), "%")
```

10. We get the **false positive rate (FPR)** and **true positive rate (TPR)** by passing y_test and y_pred_proba to roc_curve(). We also get the auc value using roc_auc_score(). Using the FPR, TPR, and the AUC value, we plot the ROC curve with the AUC value annotated on the plot:

```
from sklearn import metrics

y_pred_proba = model_RF.predict_proba(X_test)[::,1]
fpr, tpr, _ = metrics.roc_curve(y_test, y_pred_proba)
auc = metrics.roc_auc_score(y_test, y_pred_proba)
plt.plot(fpr,tpr,label="AUC="+str(auc))
plt.legend(loc=4)
plt.show()
```

The following graph shows the ROC curve with the AUC value annotated on it:

```
Accuracy Score                          0.811889
Kappa Score                             0.278229
Model                    Random Forest Classifier
Precision Score                         0.673212
ROC Score                               0.60721
Recall Score                            0.247423
dtype: object
```

11. We can also evaluate other scores, as shown here:

```
# predict the model
y_pred_RF = model_RF.predict(X_test)

# evaluate other scores
evaluation_scores = pd.Series({'Model': " Random Forest Classifier
",
'ROC Score' : metrics.roc_auc_score(y_test, y_pred_RF),
'Precision Score': metrics.precision_score(y_test, y_pred_RF),
'Recall Score': metrics.recall_score(y_test, y_pred_RF),
'Accuracy Score': metrics.accuracy_score(y_test, y_pred_RF),
'Kappa Score':metrics.cohen_kappa_score(y_test, y_pred_RF)})

print(evaluation_scores)
```

The preceding code produces the following evaluation scores:

```
Accuracy Score                          0.811889
Kappa Score                             0.278229
Model                    Random Forest Classifier
Precision Score                         0.673212
ROC Score                               0.60721
Recall Score                            0.247423
dtype: object
```

12. We can also evaluate a few statistics based on the class of the target variable, which in this case is 0 or 1:

```
from sklearn.metrics import classification_report
print(classification_report(y_test, y_pred_RF))
```

classification_report from sklearn.metrics gives us the following scores based on each class of the target variable:

	precision	recall	f1-score	support
0	0.82	0.97	0.89	7060
1	0.67	0.25	0.36	1940
avg / total	0.79	0.81	0.78	9000

13. We can plot the top 10 variables by feature importance to see which variables are important for the model:

```
feature_importances = pd.Series(classifier.feature_importances_,
index=X_train.columns)
feature_importances.nlargest(10).plot(kind='barh') #top 10 features
```

The following screenshot shows the top 10 variables with their relative importance:

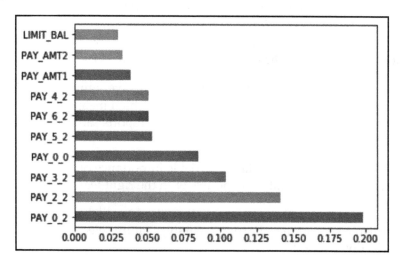

We can change the hyperparameters to see how the model can perform better. We can also perform a grid search over combinations of hyperparameter values to fine-tune our model.

How it works...

In *Step 1*, we split our target and feature variables. In *Step 2*, in our feature set, we separated the numeric and non-numeric variables. In *Step 3* and *Step 4*, we converted the non-numeric variables to dummy coded variables and added them back to the DataFrame. In *Step 5*, we split our dataset into training and testing subsets, and in *Step 6*, we imported `StandardScaler()` from `sklearn.preprocessing` and applied the same scale to our features.

After executing the commands in *Step 6*, we noticed that the column names had changed to sequential numbers. For this reason, in *Step 7*, we assigned the column names and the index values back to the scaled DataFrame. In *Step 8*, we imported `RandomForestClassifier()` from `sklearn.ensemble` and built our first random forest classifier model. After that, in *Step 9* and *Step 10*, we used our model to calculate the accuracy of our training model and plotted the ROC curve respectively. We also annotated the ROC Curve with the AUC value.

In *Step 11*, we evaluated other scores, including the kappa value, the precision, the recall, and the accuracy.

In *Step 12*, we also evaluated these scores based on each class of the target variable, which in this case is 0 or 1, using `classification_report` from `sklearn.metrics`. There, `classification_report()` provides us with metrics such as precision, recall, and f1-score by each class, as well as the average of each of the metrics.

`classification_report()` reports averages, including averaging the total true positives, false negatives and false positives, averaging the unweighted mean per label, and averaging the support-weighted mean per label. It also reports sample averages for multi-label classification.

Finally, in *Step 13*, we looked at the relative variable importance of the top 10 features. This can help in feature selection to build the models with the right features.

There are various feature selection methods available, such as averaged variable, importance, Boruta, recursive feature selection, and variable selection using RF.

There's more...

Isolation forest is another algorithm that is built on the basis of decision trees, and it's used for anomaly and outlier detection. This algorithm is based on the assumption that the outlier data points are rare.

The algorithm works a bit differently to the random forest. It creates a bunch of decision trees, then it calculates the path length necessary to isolate an observation in the tree. The idea is that isolated observations, or anomalies, are easier to separate because there are fewer conditions necessary to distinguish them from normal cases. Thus, the anomalies will have shorter paths than normal observations and will, therefore, reside closer to the root of the tree. When several decision trees are created, the scores are averaged, which gives us a good idea about which observations are truly anomalies. As a result, isolation forests are used for outliers and anomaly detection.

Also, an isolation forest does not utilize any distance or density measures to detect an anomaly. This reduces the computational cost significantly compared to the distance-based and density-based methods.

In scikit-learn, `sklearn.ensemble.IsolationForest` provides an implementation of the isolation forest algorithm.

See also

- The scikit-learn implementation of the isolation forest algorithm can be found here: `https://bit.ly/2DCjGGF`

Implementing random forest for predicting credit card defaults using H2O

H2O is an open source and distributed machine learning platform that allows you to build machine learning models on large datasets. H2O supports both supervised and unsupervised algorithms and is extremely fast, scalable, and easy to implement. H2O's REST API allows us to access all its functionalities from external programs such as R and Python. H2O in Python is designed to be very similar to scikit-learn. At the time of writing this book, the latest version of H2O is H2O v3.

The reason why H2O brought lightning-fast machine learning to enterprises is given by the following explanation:

> *"H2O's core code is written in Java. Inside H2O, a distributed key/value store is used to access and reference data, models, objects, and so on, across all nodes and machines. The algorithms are implemented on top of H2O's distributed Map/Reduce framework and utilize the Java fork/join framework for multi-threading. The data is read in parallel and is distributed across the cluster and stored in memory in a columnar format in a compressed way. H2O's data parser has built-in intelligence to guess the schema of the incoming dataset and supports data ingest from multiple sources in various formats"*

- from h2o.ai

H2O provides us with distributed random forests, which are a powerful tool used for classification and regression tasks. This generates multiple trees, rather than single trees. In a distributed random forest, we use the average predictions of both the classification and regression models to reach a final result.

Getting ready

Java is an absolute must for H2O to run. Make sure you have Java installed with the following command in Jupyter:

```
! apt-get install default-jre
! java -version
```

You will now need to install H2O. To install this from Jupyter, use the following command:

```
! pip install h2o
```

Import the required libraries:

```
import h2o
import seaborn as sns
import numpy as np
import pandas as pd
import seaborn
import matplotlib.pyplot as plt
%matplotlib inline

from h2o.estimators.random_forest import H2ORandomForestEstimator
from sklearn import metrics
```

To use H2O, we need to initialize an instance and connect to it. We can do that as follows:

```
h2o.init()
```

By default, the preceding command tries to connect to an instance. If it fails to do so, it will attempt to start an instance and then connect to it. Once connected to an instance, we will see the details of that instance, as follows:

```
Connecting to H2O server at http://127.0.0.1:54321... successful.
H2O cluster uptime:              02 secs
H2O cluster timezone:            Etc/UTC
H2O data parsing timezone:       UTC
H2O cluster version:             3.22.1.2
H2O cluster version age:         4 hours and 18 minutes
H2O cluster name:                H2O_from_python_unknownUser_zhwtlv
H2O cluster total nodes:         1
H2O cluster free memory:         2.938 Gb
H2O cluster total cores:         2
H2O cluster allowed cores:       2
H2O cluster status:              accepting new members, healthy
H2O connection url:              http://127.0.0.1:54321
H2O connection proxy:            None
H2O internal security:           False
H2O API Extensions:              XGBoost, Algos, AutoML, Core V3, Core V4
Python version:                  3.6.7 final
```

We read our data into a `pandas` DataFrame:

```
df_creditcarddata = pd.read_csv("UCI_Credit_Card.csv")
```

We change our `pandas` DataFrame to an H2O DataFrame using `h2o.H2OFrame()`. We name the `df_creditcarddata` H2O DataFrame:

```
hf_creditcarddata = h2o.H2OFrame(df_creditcarddata)
```

Check whether the data in the H2O DataFrame is properly loaded as follows:

```
hf_creditcarddata.head()
```

We can see the summary statistics with the `describe()` method:

```
hf_creditcarddata.describe()
```

We drop the ID column, as this will not be required for our model building exercise:

```
hf_creditcarddata = hf_creditcarddata.drop(["ID"], axis = 1)
```

We will now move on to explore our data and build our model.

How to do it...

We have performed various explorations on our data in the previous section. There is no limit to the ways in which we can explore our data. In this section, we are going to look at a few more techniques:

1. We check the correlation of each of our feature variables with the target variable:

```
df_creditcarddata.drop(['default.payment.next.month'], \
    axis =
1).corrwith(df_creditcarddata['default.payment.next.month']).\
    plot.bar(figsize=(20,10), \
    title = 'Correlation with Response variable', \
    fontsize = 15, rot = 45, grid = True)
```

The following plot shows how each of the features is correlated with the target variable:

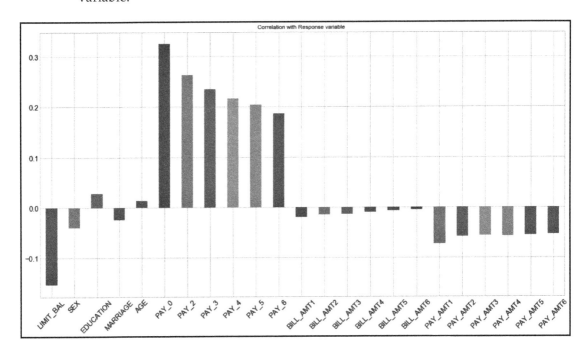

2. We check the datatypes in the H2O DataFrame. Note that for the `pandas` DataFrame, we used `dtypes`. For the H2O DataFrame, we use types:

```
hf_creditcarddata.types
```

3. We notice that they are all of the integer datatype. We will convert them to factor type, which is categorical in nature:

```
hf_creditcarddata['SEX'] = hf_creditcarddata['SEX'].asfactor()
hf_creditcarddata['EDUCATION'] =
hf_creditcarddata['EDUCATION'].asfactor()
hf_creditcarddata['MARRIAGE'] =
hf_creditcarddata['MARRIAGE'].asfactor()
hf_creditcarddata['PAY_0'] = hf_creditcarddata['PAY_0'].asfactor()
hf_creditcarddata['PAY_2'] = hf_creditcarddata['PAY_2'].asfactor()
hf_creditcarddata['PAY_3'] = hf_creditcarddata['PAY_3'].asfactor()
hf_creditcarddata['PAY_4'] = hf_creditcarddata['PAY_4'].asfactor()
hf_creditcarddata['PAY_5'] = hf_creditcarddata['PAY_5'].asfactor()
hf_creditcarddata['PAY_6'] = hf_creditcarddata['PAY_6'].asfactor()
```

We can check the datatypes with `hf_creditcarddata.types` to see that the datatype conversion has taken place.

4. We will encode the binary target variable as a factor type variable:

```
hf_creditcarddata['default.payment.next.month'] = \
hf_creditcarddata['default.payment.next.month'].asfactor()
hf_creditcarddata['default.payment.next.month'].levels()
```

5. We select the features and the `target` variable:

```
predictors =
['LIMIT_BAL','SEX','EDUCATION','MARRIAGE','AGE','PAY_0','PAY_2','PA
Y_3','PAY_4','PAY_5','PAY_6','BILL_AMT1','BILL_AMT2','BILL_AMT3','B
ILL_AMT4','BILL_AMT5','BILL_AMT6','PAY_AMT1','PAY_AMT2','PAY_AMT3',
'PAY_AMT4','PAY_AMT5','PAY_AMT6']

target = 'default.payment.next.month'
```

6. We now split the H2O DataFrame into training and testing subsets. We use 70% of our data for training the model and the remaining 30% for validation:

```
splits = hf_creditcarddata.split_frame(ratios=[0.7], seed=123)
train = splits[0]
test = splits[1]
```

7. We build our random forest model with the default settings. You can check the model performance on the test data with the following commands:

```
from h2o.estimators.random_forest import H2ORandomForestEstimator

RF_D = H2ORandomForestEstimator(model_id = 'RF_D',seed = 123)
RF_D.train(x = predictors, y = target, training_frame = train)

print(RF_D.model_performance(test))
```

This gives us the following performance metrics:

```
ModelMetricsBinomial: drf
** Reported on test data. **

MSE: 0.13916702510839007
RMSE: 0.3730509685128697
LogLoss: 0.4404003566729752
Mean Per-Class Error: 0.3021721562099693
AUC: 0.7689912083007103
pr_auc: 0.5367690443947648
Gini: 0.5379824166014207
Confusion Matrix (Act/Pred) for max f1 @ threshold = 0.31553293049335485:
```

	0	1	Error	Rate
0	6035.0	902.0	0.13	(902.0/6937.0)
1	969.0	1034.0	0.4838	(969.0/2003.0)
Total	7004.0	1936.0	0.2093	(1871.0/8940.0)

How it works...

In the *Getting ready* section, we installed JRE and H2O. We initialized and connected to an H2O instance with h2o.init(). We then read our data using pandas and converted it to an H2O DataFrame. We used the head() and describe() methods on the H2O DataFrame, just like we used them on a pandas DataFrame. We then dropped the ID column from the H2O DataFrame.

After we did these data explorations in the *Getting ready* section, we moved on to the next steps. In *Step 1*, we checked the correlation of each of the features with the target variable. In *Step 2*, we used the h2o DataFrame and checked the datatypes.

Note that for the `pandas` DataFrame we used `dtypes`, whereas we used `types` with the `h2o` DataFrame.

In *Step 3*, we used `asfactor()` to convert the numeric variables to the categorical type. We performed this on variables that were supposed to be of a categorical type but were appearing as numeric.

 In previous examples, we used the `astype()` method on a `pandas` DataFrame. With an H2O DataFrame, we used the `asfactor()` method.

In *Step 4*, we used `asfactor()` on our `target` variable to convert it to a categorical variable.

In *Step 5*, we separated our features and the `target` variable. In *Step 6*, we split the H2O DataFrame into training and testing subsets using `split_frame()` on our H2O DataFrame. We used the `ratios` parameter and set it to `ratios=[0.7]` for `split_frame()` to allocate 70% of the data to the training set and 30% of the data to the testing set.

In *Step 7*, we imported `H2ORandomForestEstimator` from `h2o.estimators.random_forest`. We passed `model_id` and then referred to it to call the `train()` function and pass the predictor and the `target` variables. We then looked at the performance metrics by passing the test subset to `model_performance()`.

There's more...

In our preceding example, we have an AUC of `0.76` and a log loss of `0.44`:

1. We can apply cross-validation by passing `nfolds` as a parameter to `H2ORandomForestEstimator()`:

```
RF_cv = H2ORandomForestEstimator(model_id = 'RF_cv',
                                 seed = 12345,
                                 ntrees = 500,
                                 sample_rate = 0.9,
                                 col_sample_rate_per_tree = 0.9,
                                 nfolds = 10)
RF_cv.train(x = predictors, y = target, training_frame = train)
print(RF_cv.model_performance(test))
```

We notice that the AUC has slightly improved to 0.77 and that the log loss has dropped to 0.43:

```
ModelMetricsBinomial: drf
** Reported on test data. **

MSE: 0.1377514905065363
RMSE: 0.3711488791664826
LogLoss: 0.4364918401503112
Mean Per-Class Error: 0.29563198088840503
AUC: 0.7738851575598977
pr_auc: 0.5456525571043274
Gini: 0.5477703151197955
Confusion Matrix (Act/Pred) for max f1 @ threshold = 0.300957882463187:
```

	0	1	Error	Rate
0	6027.0	910.0	0.1312	(910.0/6937.0)
1	945.0	1058.0	0.4718	(945.0/2003.0)
Total	6972.0	1968.0	0.2075	(1855.0/8940.0)

2. We can also apply a grid search to extract the best model from the given options. We set our options as follows:

```
search_criteria = {'strategy': "RandomDiscrete"}

hyper_params = {'sample_rate': [0.5, 0.6, 0.7],\
                'col_sample_rate_per_tree': [0.7, 0.8, 0.9],\
                'max_depth': [3, 5, 7]}
```

3. We build the model with the preceding search parameters:

```
from h2o.grid.grid_search import H2OGridSearch

RF_Grid = H2OGridSearch(
                H2ORandomForestEstimator(
                    model_id = 'RF_Grid',
                    ntrees = 200,
                    nfolds = 10,
                    stopping_metric = 'AUC',
                    stopping_rounds = 25),
                search_criteria = search_criteria, # full grid
search
                hyper_params = hyper_params)
RF_Grid.train(x = predictors, y = target, training_frame = train)
```

4. We now sort all models by AUC in a descending manner and then pick the first model, which has the highest AUC:

```
RF_Grid_sorted = RF_Grid.get_grid(sort_by='auc',decreasing=True)
print(RF_Grid_sorted)

best_RF_model = RF_Grid_sorted.model_ids[0]
best_RF_from_RF_Grid = h2o.get_model(best_RF_model)
```

5. We apply the best model for our test data:

```
best_RF_from_RF_Grid.model_performance(test)
```

6. We can plot the variable importance from the best model that we have achieved so far:

```
best_RF_from_RF_G
rid.varimp_plot()
```

This gives us the following plot:

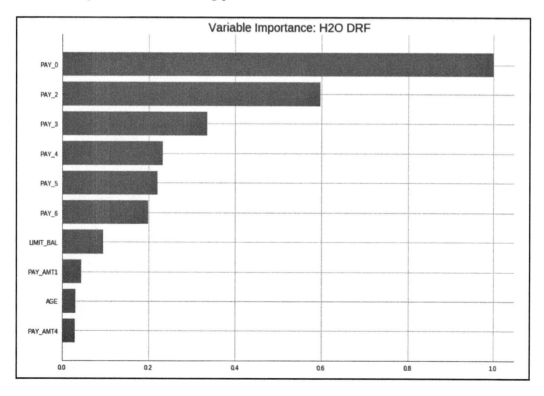

See also

You may want to look into extremely randomized trees, which have a slightly different implementation but can sometimes perform better than random forests.

In ensemble methods, each model learns differently in terms of the subset of the dataset and the subset of the feature vector used for training. These subsets are taken randomly. Extremely randomized trees possess a high randomness factor in the way they compute the splits and the subset of the features selected. Unlike random forests, in which the splitting threshold is chosen randomly, in extremely randomized trees, a discriminative threshold is used as the splitting rule. Due to this, the overall variance of the ensemble decreases and the overall performance may be better.

The scikit-learn implementation of extremely randomized trees can be found at the following link: `https://bit.ly/2zWsNNS`. H2O also supports extremely randomized trees.

Boosting Model Performance with Boosting

7

In this chapter, we will cover the following recipes:

- Introduction to boosting
- Implementing AdaBoost for disease risk prediction using scikit-learn
- Implementing gradient boosting for disease risk prediction using scikit-learn
- Implementing extreme gradient boosting for glass identification using XGBoost with scikit-learn

Introduction to boosting

A boosting algorithm is an ensemble technique that helps to improve model performance and accuracy by taking a group of weak learners and combining them to form a strong learner. The idea behind boosting is that predictors should learn from mistakes that have been made by previous predictors.

Boosting algorithms have two key characteristics:

- First, they undergo multiple iterations
- Second, each iteration focuses on the instances that were wrongly classified by previous iterations

When an input is misclassified by a hypothesis, its weight is altered in the next iteration so that the next hypothesis can classify it correctly. More weight will be given to those that provide better performance on the training data. This process, through multiple iterations, converts weak learners into a collection of strong learners, thereby improving the model's performance.

In bagging, no bootstrap sample depends on any other bootstrap, so they all run in parallel. Boosting works in a sequential manner and does not involve bootstrap sampling. Both bagging and boosting reduce the variance of a single estimate by combining several estimates from different models into a single estimate. However, it is important to note that boosting does not help significantly if the single model is overfitting. Bagging would be a better option if the model overfits. On the other hand, boosting tries to reduce bias, while bagging rarely improves bias.

In this chapter, we will introduce different boosting algorithms such as **Adaptive Boosting** (**AdaBoost**), gradient boosting, and **extreme gradient boosting** (**XGBoost**).

Implementing AdaBoost for disease risk prediction using scikit-learn

AdaBoost is one of the earliest boosting algorithms that was used for binary classification. It was proposed by Freund and Schapire in 1996. Many other boosting-based algorithms have since been developed on top of AdaBoost.

 Another variation of adaptive boosting is known as **AdaBoost-abstain**. AdaBoost-abstain allows each baseline classifier to abstain from voting if its dependent feature is missing.

AdaBoost focuses on combining a set of weak learners into a strong learner. The process of an AdaBoost classifier is as follows:

1. Initially, a short decision tree classifier is fitted onto the data. The decision tree can just have a single split, which is known as a **decision stump**. The overall errors are evaluated. This is the first iteration.
2. In the second iteration, whatever data is correctly classified will be given lowerweights, while higher weights will be given to the misclassified classes.
3. In the third iteration, another decision stump will be fitted to the data and the weights will be changed again in the next iteration.
4. Once these iterations are over, the weights are automatically calculated for each classifier at each iteration based on the error rates to come up with a strong classifier.

The following screenshot shows how AdaBoost works:

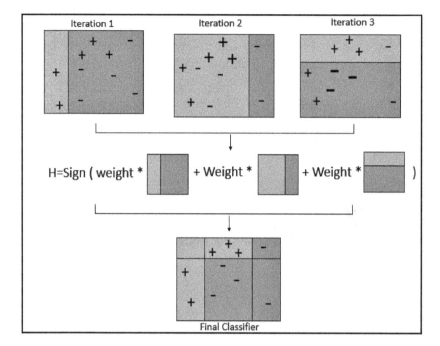

The concept behind this algorithm is to distribute the weights to the training example and select the classifier with the lowest weighted error. Finally, it constructs a strong classifier as a linear combination of these weak learners.

The general equation for an AdaBoost as follows:

$$F(x) = \alpha_1 f_1(x) + \alpha_2 f_2(x) + \ldots + \alpha_n f_n(x)$$

Here, **F(x)** represents a strong classifier, α represent the weights, and **f(x)** represents a weak classifier.

The AdaBoost classifier takes various parameters. The important ones are explained as follows:

- `base_estimator`: The learning algorithm that is used to train the models. If a value is not provided for this parameter, the base estimator is `DecisionTreeClassifier (max_depth=1)`.
- `n_estimators`: The number of models to iteratively train.
- `learning_rate`: The contribution of each model to the weights. By default, `learning_rate` has a value of `1`. A lower value for the learning rate forces the model to train slower but might result in better performance scores.

Getting ready

To start with, import the `os` and the `pandas` packages and set your working directory according to your requirements:

```
# import required packages
import os
import pandas as pd
import numpy as np

from sklearn.ensemble import AdaBoostClassifier
from sklearn.model_selection import GridSearchCV
from sklearn.model_selection import train_test_split
from sklearn.tree import DecisionTreeClassifier

from sklearn.metrics import roc_auc_score, roc_curve, auc
from sklearn.model_selection import train_test_split

# Set working directory as per your need
os.chdir(".../.../Chapter 8")
os.getcwd()
```

Download the `breastcancer.csv` dataset from GitHub and copy it to your working directory. Read the dataset:

```
df_breastcancer = pd.read_csv("breastcancer.csv")
```

Take a look at the first few rows with the `head()` function:

```
df_breastcancer.head(5)
```

Notice that the `diagnosis` variable has values such as M and B, representing Malign and Benign, respectively. We will perform label encoding on the `diagnosis` variable so that we can convert the M and B values into numeric values.

We use `head()` to see the changes:

```
# import LabelEncoder from sklearn.preprocessing
from sklearn.preprocessing import LabelEncoder

lb = LabelEncoder()
df_breastcancer['diagnosis']
=lb.fit_transform(df_breastcancer['diagnosis'])
df_breastcancer.head(5)
```

We then check whether the dataset has any null values:

```
df_breastcancer.isnull().sum()
```

We check the shape of the dataset with `shape()`:

```
df_breastcancer.shape
```

We now separate our target and feature set. We also split our dataset into training and testing subsets:

```
# Create feature & response variables
# Drop the response var and id column as it'll not make any sense to the
analysis
X = df_breastcancer.iloc[:,2:31]

# Target
Y = df_breastcancer.iloc[:,0]

# Create train & test sets
X_train, X_test, Y_train, Y_test = train_test_split(X, Y, test_size=0.30,
random_state=0, stratify= Y)
```

Now, we will move on to building our model using the `AdaBoost` algorithm.

 It is important to note that the accuracy and AUC scores may differ because of random splits and other randomness factors.

How to do it...

We will now look at how to use an AdaBoost to train our model:

1. Before we build our first `AdaBoost` model, let's train our model using the `DecisionTreeClassifier`:

```
dtree = DecisionTreeClassifier(max_depth=3, random_state=0)
dtree.fit(X_train, Y_train)
```

2. We can see our accuracy and **Area Under the Curve** (**AUC**) with the following code:

```
# Mean accuracy
print('The mean accuracy is:
',(dtree.score(X_test,Y_test))*100,'%')

#AUC score
y_pred_dtree = dtree.predict_proba(X_test)
fpr_dtree, tpr_dtree, thresholds = roc_curve(Y_test,
y_pred_dtree[:,1])
auc_dtree = auc(fpr_dtree, tpr_dtree)
print ('AUC Value: ', auc_dtree)
```

We get an accuracy score and an AUC value of 91.81% and 0.91, respectively. Note that these values might be different for different users due to randomness.

3. Now, we will build our AdaBoost model using the scikit-learn library. We will use the `AdaBoostClassifier` to build our `AdaBoost` model. `AdaBoost` uses `dtree` as the base classifier by default:

```
AdaBoost = AdaBoostClassifier(n_estimators=100,
base_estimator=dtree, learning_rate=0.1, random_state=0)
AdaBoost.fit(X_train, Y_train)
```

4. We check the accuracy and AUC value of the model on our test data:

```
# Mean accuracy
print('The mean accuracy is:
',(AdaBoost.score(X_test,Y_test))*100,'%')

#AUC score
y_pred_adaboost = AdaBoost.predict_proba(X_test)
fpr_ab, tpr_ab, thresholds = roc_curve(Y_test,
y_pred_adaboost[:,1])
auc_adaboost = auc(fpr_ab, tpr_ab)
print ('AUC Value: ', auc_adaboost)
```

We notice that we get an accuracy score of 92.82% and an AUC value of 0.97. Both of these metrics are higher than the decision tree model we built in *Step 1*.

5. Then, we must fine-tune our hyperparameters. We set n_estimators to 100 and learning_rate to 0.4:

```
# Tuning the hyperparams
AdaBoost_with_tuning = AdaBoostClassifier(n_estimators=100,
base_estimator=dtree, learning_rate=0.4, random_state=0)
AdaBoost_with_tuning.fit(X_train, Y_train)
```

6. Now, we will check the accuracy and AUC values of our new model on our test data:

```
# Mean accuracy
print('The mean accuracy is:
', (AdaBoost_with_tuning.score(X_test,Y_test))*100,'%')

#AUC score
y_pred_adaboost_tune = AdaBoost.predict_proba(X_test)
fpr_ab_tune, tpr_ab_tune, thresholds = roc_curve(Y_test,
y_pred_adaboost_tune[:,1])
auc_adaboost_tune = auc(fpr_ab_tune, tpr_ab_tune)
print ('AUC Value: ', auc_adaboost_tune)
```

We notice the accuracy drops to 92.39%, but that we get an improved AUC value of 0.98.

How it works...

In *Step 1*, we used the DecisionTreeClassifier to build our model. In *Step 2*, we noticed that our mean accuracy and the AUC score were 91.81% and 0.91, respectively. We aimed to improve this using the AdaBoost algorithm.

Note that the AdaBoost algorithm uses a decision tree as the base classifier by default. In *Step 3*, we trained our model using AdaBoost with the default base learner. We set n_estimators to 100 and the learning_rate to 0.1. We checked our mean accuracy and AUC value in *Step 4*. We noticed that we got a decent improvement in the mean accuracy and the AUC as they jumped to 93.57% and 0.977, respectively.

In *Step 5*, we fine-tuned some of the hyperparameters for our AdaBoost algorithm, which used a decision tree as the base classifier. We set the n_estimators to 100 and the learning_rate to 0.4. *Step 6* gave us the accuracy and AUC values for the model we built in *Step 5*. We saw that the accuracy dropped to 93.56% and that the AUC stayed similar at 0.981.

There's more...

Here, we will showcase training a model using AdaBoost with a **support vector machine** (**SVM**) as the base learner.

By default, AdaBoost uses a decision tree as the base learner. We can use different base learners as well. In the following example, we have used an SVM as our base learner with the `AdaBoost` algorithm. We use `SVC` with `rbf` as the kernel:

```
from sklearn.svm import SVC

Adaboost_with_svc_rbf = AdaBoostClassifier(n_estimators=100,
base_estimator=SVC(probability=True, kernel='rbf'), learning_rate=1,
random_state=0)
Adaboost_with_svc_rbf.fit(X_train, Y_train)
```

We can check the accuracy and the AUC values of our AdaBoost model with **support vector classifier** (**SVC**) as the base learner:

```
# Mean accuracy
print('The mean accuracy is:
',(Adaboost_with_svc_rbf.score(X_test,Y_test))*100,'%')

#AUC score
y_pred_svc_rbf = Adaboost_with_svc_rbf.predict_proba(X_test)
fpr_svc_rbf, tpr_svc_rbf, thresholds = roc_curve(Y_test,
y_pred_svc_rbf[:,1])
auc_svc_rbf = auc(fpr_svc_rbf, tpr_svc_rbf)
print ('AUC Value: ', auc_svc_rbf)
```

We noticed that the accuracy and AUC values fall to 62.57 and 0.92, respectively.

Now, we will rebuild our AdaBoost model with SVC. This time, we will use a linear kernel:

```
Adaboost_with_svc_linear =AdaBoostClassifier(n_estimators=100,
base_estimator=SVC(probability=True, kernel='linear'), learning_rate=1,
random_state=0)
Adaboost_with_svc_linear.fit(X_train, Y_train)
```

We now get a mean accuracy of 90.64% and a decent AUC value of 0.96.

We will now plot a graph to compare the AUC value of each model using the following code:

```
import matplotlib.pyplot as plt
% matplotlib inline
plt.figure(figsize=(8,8))
```

```
plt.plot(fpr_dtree, tpr_dtree,label="Model1: Dtree, auc="+str(auc_dtree))
plt.plot(fpr_ab, tpr_ab,label="Model2: Adaboost, auc="+str(auc_adaboost))
plt.plot(fpr_ab_tune,tpr_ab_tune,label="Model3: Adaboost with Tuning,
auc="+str(auc_adaboost_tune))
plt.plot(fpr_svc_rbf, tpr_svc_rbf, label="Model4: Adaboost with SVC (RBF
Kernel), auc="+str(auc_svc_rbf))
plt.plot(fpr_svc_lin, tpr_svc_lin, label="Model5: Adaboost with SVC (Linear
Kernel), auc="+str(auc_svc_linear))

plt.legend(loc=5)
plt.show()
```

This gives us the following plot:

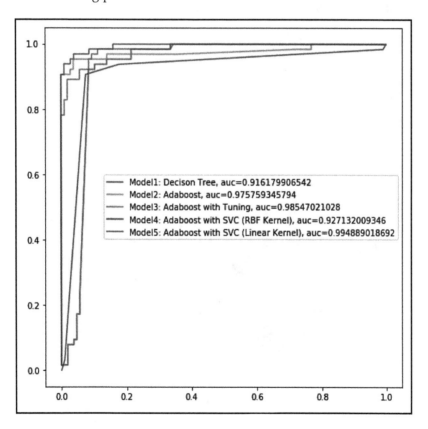

We can also plot the accuracy of all the models with the following code:

```
import matplotlib.pyplot as plt
% matplotlib inline
plt.figure(figsize=(8,8))
```

```
label = ['Decison Tree', 'Adaboost', 'Adaboost with Tuning', 'Adaboost with
SVC (RBF)', 'Adaboost with SVC (Linear)']

values = [dtree.score(X_test,Y_test),
        AdaBoost.score(X_test,Y_test),
        AdaBoost_with_tuning.score(X_test,Y_test),
        Adaboost_with_svc_rbf.score(X_test,Y_test),
        Adaboost_with_svc_linear.score(X_test,Y_test)]

def plot_bar_accuracy():
    # this is for plotting purpose
    index = np.arange(len(label))
    plt.bar(index, values)
    plt.xlabel('Algorithms', fontsize=10)
    plt.ylabel('Accuracy', fontsize=10)
    plt.xticks(index, label, fontsize=10, rotation=90)
    plt.title('Model Accuracies')
    plt.show()

plot_bar_accuracy()
```

This gives us the following output:

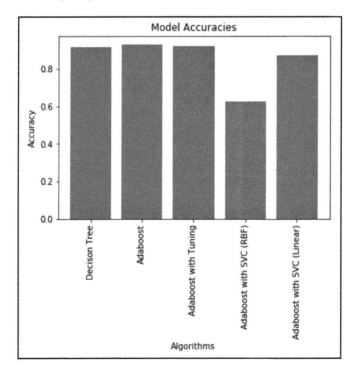

See also

We can also use grid search with AdaBoost:

```
#grid search using svm
Adaboost_with_svc = AdaBoostClassifier(n_estimators=100,
base_estimator=SVC(probability=True, kernel='linear'), learning_rate=1,
algorithm= 'SAMME')

Ada_Grid = {'n_estimators': [10,30,40,100],
            'learning_rate': [0.1, 0.2, 0.3]}

estimator = Adaboost_with_svc
Adaboost_with_grid_search = GridSearchCV(estimator,Ada_Grid).fit(X_train,
Y_train)
print(Adaboost_with_grid_search.best_params_)
print(Adaboost_with_grid_search.best_score_)
```

In the preceding code, we performed a grid search with the `n_estimators` set to `10`, `30`, `40`, and `100`, and `learning_rate` set to `0.1`, `0.2`, and `0.3`.

Implementing a gradient boosting machine for disease risk prediction using scikit-learn

Gradient boosting is a machine learning technique that works on the principle of boosting, where weak learners iteratively shift their focus toward error observations that were difficult to predict in previous iterations and create an ensemble of weak learners, typically decision trees.

Gradient boosting trains models in a sequential manner, and involves the following steps:

1. Fitting a model to the data
2. Fitting a model to the residuals
3. Creating a new model

While the AdaBoost model identifies errors by using weights that have been assigned to the data points, gradient boosting does the same by calculating the gradients in the loss function. The loss function is a measure of how a model is able to fit the data on which it is trained and generally depends on the type of problem being solved. If we are talking about regression problems, mean squared error may be used, while in classification problems, the logarithmic loss can be used. The gradient descent procedure is used to minimize loss when adding trees one at a time. Existing trees in the model remain the same.

There are a handful of hyperparameters that may be tuned for this:

- N_estimators: This represents the number of trees in the model. Usually, the higher it is, the better the model learns the data.
- max_depth: This signifies how deep our tree is. It is used to control overfitting.
- min_samples_split: This is the minimum number of samples required to split an internal node. Values that are too high can prevent the model from learning relations.
- learning_rate: This controls the magnitude of change in the estimates. Lower values with a higher number of trees are generally preferred.
- loss: This refers to the loss function that is minimized in each split. deviance is used in the algorithm as the default parameter, while the other is exponential.
- max_features: This represents the number of features we have to consider when looking for the best split.
- criterion: This function measures the quality of the split and supports friedman_mse and mae to evaluate the performance of the model.
- subsample: This represents the fraction of samples to be used for fitting the individual base learners. Choosing a subsample that is less than 1.0 leads to a reduction of variance and an increase in bias.
- min_impurity_split: This is represented as a threshold to stop tree growth early.

Getting ready

We will take the same dataset that we used for training our AdaBoost model. In this example, we will see how we can train our model using gradient boosting machines. We will also look at a handful of hyperparameters that can be tuned to improve the model's performance.

First, we must import all the required libraries:

```
import os
import pandas as pd
import numpy as np

from sklearn.model_selection import train_test_split

from sklearn.ensemble import GradientBoostingClassifier
from sklearn.metrics import classification_report, confusion_matrix,
accuracy_score, roc_auc_score
from sklearn.preprocessing import MinMaxScaler

import matplotlib.pyplot as plt
import itertools
```

Then, we read our data and label encode our target variables to 1 and 0:

```
# Read the Dataset
df_breastcancer = pd.read_csv("breastcancer.csv")

from sklearn.preprocessing import LabelEncoder
lb = LabelEncoder()
df_breastcancer['diagnosis'] =
lb.fit_transform(df_breastcancer['diagnosis'])
df_breastcancer.head(5)
```

Then, separate our target and feature variables. We split our data into train and test subsets:

```
# create feature & response variables
# drop the response var and id column as it'll not make any sense to the
analysis
X = df_breastcancer.iloc[:,2:31]

# Target variable
Y = df_breastcancer.iloc[:,0]

# Create train & test sets
X_train, X_test, Y_train, Y_test = train_test_split(X, Y, test_size=0.20,
random_state=0, stratify= Y)
```

 This is the same code that we used in the *Getting ready* section of the AdaBoost **example**.

How to do it...

We will now look at how to use a Gradient Boosting Machines to train our model:

1. We imported `GradientBoostingClassifier` from `sklearn.ensemble` in the last section, *Getting ready*. We trained our model using `GradieBoostingClassfier`:

```
GBM_model = GradientBoostingClassifier()
GBM_model.fit(X_train, Y_train)
```

2. Here, we must pass our test data to the `predict()` function to make the predictions using the model we built in *Step 1*:

```
Y_pred_gbm = GBM_model.predict(X_test)
```

3. Now, we use `classification_report` to see the following metrics:

```
print(classification_report(Y_test, Y_pred_gbm))
```

`classification_report` gives us the following output:

	precision	recall	f1-score	support
0	0.97	0.96	0.97	72
1	0.93	0.95	0.94	42
avg / total	0.96	0.96	0.96	114

4. We will use `confusion_matrix()` to generate the confusion matrix. We then pass the output of the `confusion_matrix` to our predefined function, that is, `plot_confusion_matrix()`, to plot the matrix:

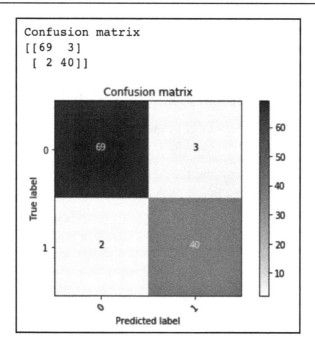

```
Confusion matrix
[[69  3]
 [ 2 40]]
```

5. We can check the test accuracy and the AUC value with `accuracy_score()` and `roc_auc_score()`.

Note that `accuracy_score` and `roc_auc_score` have been imported from `sklearn.metrics`:

```
Accuracy score = 0.96
Area under ROC curve = 0.96
```

How it works...

In *Step 1*, we trained a gradient boosting classifier model. In *Step 2*, we used the `predict()` method to make predictions on our test data.

In *Step 3*, we used `classification_report()` to see various metrics such as `precision`, `recall`, and `f1-score` for each class, as well as the average of each of the metrics. The `classification_report()` reports the averages for the total true positives, false negatives, false positives, unweighted mean per label, and support-weighted mean per label. It also reports a sample average for multi-label classification.

Precision refers to the classifier's ability not to label an instance that is negative as positive, while recall refers to the ability of the classifier to find all positive instances. The f_1 score is a weighted harmonic mean of precision and recall. The best f_1 score is 1.0 and the worst is 0.0. The support is the number of observations of each class.

In *Step 4*, we used `confusion_matrix()` to generate the confusion matrix to see the true positives, true negatives, false positives, and false negatives.

In *Step 5*, we looked at the accuracy and the AUC values of our test data using the `accuracy_score()` and `roc_auc_score()` functions.

In the next section, we will tune our hyperparameters using a grid search to find the optimal model.

There's more...

We will now look at how to fine-tune the hyperparameters for gradient boosting machines:

1. First, we import `GridSearchCV` from `sklearn.model_selection`:

```
from sklearn.model_selection import GridSearchCV
```

2. We set the grid parameters to a variable:

```
parameters = {
    "n_estimators":[100,150,200],
    "loss":["deviance"],
    "learning_rate": [0.01, 0.05, 0.1, 0.2, 0.3, 0.4, 0.5, 0.6,
0.7, 0.8, 0.9, 1],
    "min_samples_split":np.linspace(0.1, 0.5, 4),
    "min_samples_leaf": np.linspace(0.1, 0.5, 4),
    "max_depth":[3, 5, 8],
    "max_features":["log2","sqrt"],
    "criterion": ["friedman_mse", "mae"],
    "subsample":[0.3, 0.6, 1.0]
    }
```

3. We use `GridSeacrhCV`, which lets us combine an estimator with a grid search to tune the hyperparameters. The `GridSeacrhCV` method selects the optimal parameter from the grid values and uses it with the estimator:

```
grid = GridSearchCV(GradientBoostingClassifier(), parameters, cv=3,
n_jobs=-1)
grid.fit(X_train, Y_train)
```

4. Then, we can view the optimal parameters:

```
grid.best_estimator_
```

Take a look at the following screenshot:

```
GradientBoostingClassifier(criterion='friedman_mse', init=None,
          learning_rate=0.6, loss='deviance', max_depth=3,
          max_features='sqrt', max_leaf_nodes=None,
          min_impurity_decrease=0.0, min_impurity_split=None,
          min_samples_leaf=0.10000000000000001,
          min_samples_split=0.10000000000000001,
          min_weight_fraction_leaf=0.0, n_estimators=100,
          presort='auto', random_state=None, subsample=0.6, verbose=0,
          warm_start=False)
```

5. We pass our test data to the `predict` method to get the predictions:

```
grid_predictions = grid.predict(X_test)
```

6. Again, we can see the metrics that are provided by `classification_report`:

```
print(classification_report(Y_test, grid_predictions))
```

This gives us the following output. We notice that the average `precision` and `f1-score` improved from the previous case:

	precision	recall	f1-score	support
0	0.99	0.96	0.97	72
1	0.93	0.98	0.95	42
avg / total	0.97	0.96	0.97	114

7. Now, we will take a look at the confusion matrix and plot it, like we did earlier:

```
cnf_matrix = confusion_matrix(Y_test, grid_predictions)
plot_confusion_matrix(cnf_matrix,classes=[0,1])
```

We get the following plot from the preceding code:

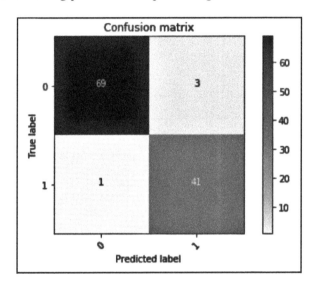

8. Now, we will look at the accuracy and AUC values again:

```
print("Accuracy score = {:0.2f}".format(accuracy_score(Y_test,
grid_predictions)))
print("Area under ROC curve = {:0.2f}".format(roc_auc_score(Y_test,
grid_predictions)))
```

We notice that the accuracy remains the same but that the AUC improves from 0.96 to 0.97:

```
Accuracy score = 0.96
Area under ROC curve = 0.97
```

Implementing the extreme gradient boosting method for glass identification using XGBoost with scikit-learn

XGBoost stands for extreme gradient boosting. It is a variant of the gradient boosting machine that aims to improve performance and speed. The XGBoost library in Python implements the gradient boosting decision tree algorithm. The name gradient boosting comes from its us of the gradient descent algorithm to minimize loss when adding new models. XGBoost can handle both regression and classification tasks.

XGBoost is the algorithm of choice among those participating in Kaggle competitions because of its performance and speed of execution in difficult machine learning problems.

Some of the important parameters that are used in XGBoost are as follows:

- `n_estimators`/`ntrees`: This specifies the number of trees to build. The default value is 50.
- `max_depth`: This specifies the maximum tree depth. The default value is 6. Higher values will make the model more complex and may lead to overfitting. Setting this value to 0 specifies no limit.
- `min_rows`: This specifies the minimum number of observations for a leaf. The default value is 1.
- `learn_rate`: This specifies the learning rate by which to shrink the feature weights. Shrinking feature weights after each boosting step makes the boosting process more conservative and prevents overfitting. The range is 0.0 to 1.0. The default value is 0.3.
- `sample_rate`: This specifies the row sampling ratio of the training instance (the *x axis*). For example, setting this value to 0.5 tells XGBoost to randomly collect half of the data instances to grow trees. The default value is 1 and the range is 0.0 to 1.0. Higher values may improve training accuracy.
- `col_sample_rate`: This specifies the column sampling rate (the *y axis*) for each split in each level. The default value is 1.0 and the range is from 0 to 1.0. Higher values may improve training accuracy.

Getting ready...

You will need the XGBoost library installed to continue with this recipe. You can use the pip command to install the XGBoost library as follows:

```
!pip install xgboost
```

Import the required libraries:

```
# Import required libraries
import os
import pandas as pd
import numpy as np

from numpy import sort

from xgboost import XGBClassifier
from xgboost import plot_tree
from xgboost import plot_importance

from sklearn.feature_selection import SelectFromModel
from sklearn.model_selection import train_test_split, KFold,
cross_val_score, StratifiedKFold

import matplotlib.pyplot as plt
from sklearn.metrics import accuracy_score, confusion_matrix

import itertools
```

Set your working folder and read your data:

```
os.chdir("/.../Chapter 7")
os.getcwd()

df_glassdata = pd.read_csv('glassdata.csv')
df_glassdata.shape
```

This data has been taken from the UCI ML repository. The column names have been changed according to the data description that's provided at the following link: https:// bit.ly/2EZX6IC.

We take a look at the data:

```
df_glassdata.head()
```

We split our data into a target and feature set, and verify it. Note that we ignore the ID column:

```
# split data into X and Y
X = df_glassdata.iloc[:,1:10]
Y = df_glassdata.iloc[:,10]

print(X.shape)
print(Y.shape)
```

We confirm that there are no missing values:

```
df_glassdata.isnull().sum()
```

We split our dataset into train and test subsets:

```
# Create train & test sets
X_train, X_test, Y_train, Y_test = train_test_split(X, Y, test_size=0.30,
random_state=0)
```

How to do it...

Now, we will proceed to build our first XGBoost model:

1. First, we fit our train data into the XGBoost classifier:

```
xg_model = XGBClassifier()
xg_model.fit(X_train, Y_train)
```

2. We can visualize a single XGBoost decision tree from our trained model. Visualizing decision trees can provide insight into the gradient boosting process:

```
plot_tree(xg_model, num_trees=0, rankdir='LR')
fig = pyplot.gcf()
fig.set_size_inches(30, 30)
```

This gives us the following output:

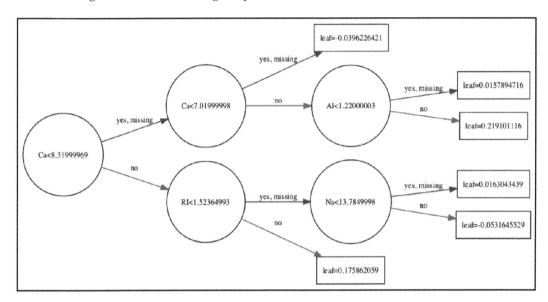

With `num_trees=0`, we get the first boosted tree. We can view the other boosted trees by setting the index value to the `num_trees` parameter.

3. We set `num_trees=5` in the following example:

```
plot_tree(xg_model, num_trees=5, rankdir='LR')
fig = pyplot.gcf()
fig.set_size_inches(30, 30)
```

The following screenshot shows us the 6th boosted tree:

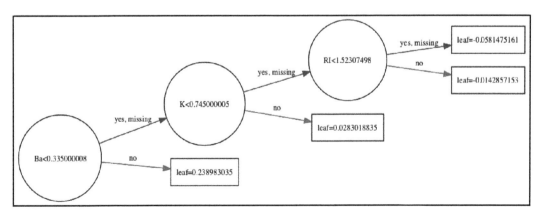

You will need the `graphviz` library installed on your system to plot the boosted trees.

4. We will now use `predict()` on our test data to get the predicted values. We can see our test accuracy with `accuracy_score()`:

```
test_predictions = xg_model.predict(X_test)
test_accuracy = accuracy_score(Y_test, test_predictions)

print("Test Accuracy: %.2f%%" % (test_accuracy * 100.0))
```

By executing this code, we can see the test accuracy is 69.23%.

5. We can see our confusion matrix by using the following code:

```
confusion_matrix(Y_test, predictions)
```

6. We can then use a predefined function, `plot_confusion_matrix()`, which we have sourced from `https://scikit-learn.org`:

```
def plot_confusion_matrix(cm, classes,
                          normalize=False,
                          title='Confusion matrix',
                          cmap=plt.cm.Blues):
    plt.imshow(cm, interpolation='nearest', cmap=cmap)
    plt.title(title)
    plt.colorbar()
    tick_marks = np.arange(len(classes))
    plt.xticks(tick_marks, classes, rotation=45)
    plt.yticks(tick_marks, classes)

    fmt = '.2f' if normalize else 'd'
    thresh = cm.max() / 2.
    for i, j in itertools.product(range(cm.shape[0]),
range(cm.shape[1])):
        plt.text(j, i, format(cm[i, j], fmt),
                 horizontalalignment="center",
                 color="white" if cm[i, j] > thresh else "black")

    plt.ylabel('True label')
    plt.xlabel('Predicted label')
    plt.tight_layout()
```

7. We then look at the `unique` values of our target variable to set the names of each level of our target variable:

```
Y.unique()
```

In the following code block, we can see the `target_names` values as 1, 2, 3, 5, 6, and 7. We set the names to each level of our target variable accordingly:

```
# Set names to each level of our target variable
target_names = [ '1', '2', '3', '5', '6', '7']

# Pass Actual & Predicted values to confusion_matrix()
cm = confusion_matrix(Y_test, predictions)

plt.figure()
plot_confusion_matrix(cm, classes=target_names)
plt.show()
```

We can now visualize the confusion matrix, as shown in the following screenshot:

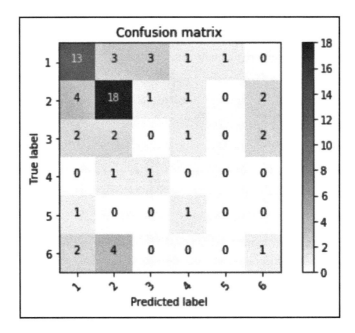

How it works...

In *Step 1*, we fit the XGBoostClassfier to our train data. In *Step 2* and *Step 3*, we visualized the individual boosted trees. To do this, we used the plot_tree() function. We passed our XGBoost model to the plot_tree() and set the index of the tree by setting the num_trees parameter. The rankdir='LR' parameter plotted the tree from left to right. Setting rankdir to UT would plot a vertical tree.

In *Step 4*, we passed our test subset to predict() to get the test accuracy. *Step 5* gave us the confusion matrix. In *Step 6*, we sourced a predefined function, plot_confusion_matrix(), from scikit-learn.org. We used this function to plot our confusion matrix. In *Step 7*, we looked at the unique values of our target variable so that we could set the names for each class of our confusion matrix plot. We then plotted our confusion matrix to evaluate our model.

There's more...

In this section, we will look at how we can check feature importance and perform feature selection based on that. We will also look at how we can evaluate the performance of our XGBoost model using cross-validation.

We can check feature importance with model.feature_importances_:

```
print(xg_model.feature_importances_)
```

We can also visualize feature importance using plot_importance():

 Note that we have imported plot_importance from the xgboost library.

```
plot_importance(xg_model)
```

After executing the preceding code, we get to see the following chart, which shows feature importance in descending order of importance:

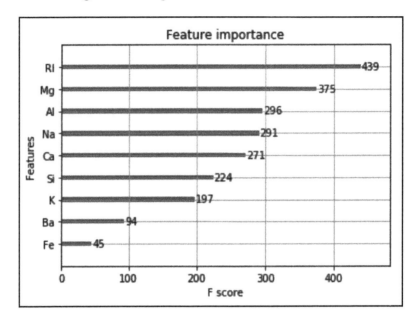

Feature importance can be used for feature selection using `SelectFromModel`.

The `SelectFromModel` class is imported from `sklearn.feature_selection`.

In the following example, the `SelectFromModel` takes the pretrained `XGBoost` model and provides a subset from our dataset with the selected features. It decides on the selected features based on a threshold value.

Features that have an importance that is greater than or equal to the threshold value are kept, while any others are discarded:

```
# The threshold value to use for feature selection.
feature_importance = sort(xg_model.feature_importances_)

# select features using threshold
for each_threshold in feature_importance:
    selection = SelectFromModel(xg_model, threshold=each_threshold,
prefit=True)
    # Reduce X_train only to the selected feature
```

```
    selected_feature_X_train = selection.transform(X_train)
    # Train the model
    selection_model = XGBClassifier()
    selection_model.fit(selected_feature_X_train, Y_train)
    # Reduce X_test only to the selected feature
    selected_feature_X_test = selection.transform(X_test)
    # Predict using the test value of the selected feature
    predictions = selection_model.predict(selected_feature_X_test)
    accuracy = accuracy_score(Y_test, predictions)
    print("Threshold=%.5f, Number of Features=%d, Model Accuracy: %.2f%%" %
(each_threshold, selected_feature_X_train.shape[1],accuracy*100))
```

From the preceding code, we get to see the following output:

```
Threshold=0.02016, Number of Features=9, Model Accuracy: 0.69%
Threshold=0.04211, Number of Features=8, Model Accuracy: 0.71%
Threshold=0.08826, Number of Features=7, Model Accuracy: 0.69%
Threshold=0.10036, Number of Features=6, Model Accuracy: 0.68%
Threshold=0.12142, Number of Features=5, Model Accuracy: 0.72%
Threshold=0.13038, Number of Features=4, Model Accuracy: 0.71%
Threshold=0.13262, Number of Features=3, Model Accuracy: 0.66%
Threshold=0.16801, Number of Features=2, Model Accuracy: 0.69%
Threshold=0.19668, Number of Features=1, Model Accuracy: 0.49%
```

We notice that the performance of the model fluctuates with the number of selected features. Based on the preceding output, we decide to opt for five features that give us an accuracy value of 72%. Also, if we use the Occam's razor principle, we can probably opt for a simpler model with four features that gives us a slightly lower accuracy of 71%.

We can also evaluate our models using cross-validation. To perform k-fold cross-validation, we must import the KFold class from sklearn.model_selection.

First, we create the KFold object and mention the number of splits that we would like to have:

```
kfold = KFold(n_splits=40, random_state=0)
xg_model_with_kfold = XGBClassifier()

cv_results = cross_val_score(xg_model_with_kfold, X_train, Y_train,
cv=kfold, verbose=True)
print("Mean Accuracy: %.2f%% Standard Deviation %.2f%%" %
(cv_results.mean()*100, cv_results.std()*100))
```

With `cross_val_score()`, we evaluate our model, which gives us the mean and standard deviation classification accuracy. We notice that we get a mean accuracy of 77.92% and a standard deviation of 22.33%.

In our case, we have a target variable with six classes.

If you have many classes for a multi-class classification task, you may use stratified folds when performing cross-validation:

```
Stratfold = StratifiedKFold(n_splits=40, random_state=0)
xg_model_with_stratfold = XGBClassifier()

sf_results = cross_val_score(xg_model_with_stratfold, X_train, Y_train,
cv=Stratfold, verbose=True)
print("Mean Accuracy: %.2f%% Standard Deviation %.2f%%" %
(sf_results.mean()*100, sf_results.std()*100))
```

With `StratifiedKFold()`, we get an improved mean accuracy of 81.18% and a reduced standard deviation of 21.37%.

Note that `n_splits` cannot be greater than the number of members in each class.

See also

- LightGBM is an open source software for the gradient boosting framework that was developed by Microsoft. It uses the tree-based algorithm differently to other **Gradient Boosting Machines** (**GBMs**): `https://bit.ly/2QW53jH`

8
Blend It with Stacking

In this chapter, we will cover the following recipes:

- Understanding stacked generalization
- Implementing stacked generalization by combining the predictions
- Implementing stacked generalization for marketing campaign outcome prediction using H2O

Technical requirements

The technical requirements for this chapter remain the same as those we detailed in earlier chapters.

Visit the GitHub repository to find the dataset and the code. The datasets and code files are arranged according to chapter numbers, and by the name of the topic.

Understanding stacked generalization

Stacked generalization is an ensemble of a diverse group of models that introduces the concept of a meta-learner. A meta-learner is a second-level machine learning algorithm that learns from an optimal combination of base learners:

> *"Stacked generalization is a means of non-linearly combining generalizers to make a new generalizer, to try to optimally integrate what each of the original generalizers has to say about the learning set. The more each generalizer has to say (which isn't duplicated in what the other generalizers have to say), the better the resultant stacked generalization."*

> *- Wolpert (1992), Stacked Generalization*

The steps for stacking are as follows:

1. Split your dataset into a training set and a testing set.
2. Train several base learners on the training set.
3. Apply the base learners on the testing set to make predictions.
4. Use the predictions as inputs and the actual responses as outputs to train a higher-level learner.

Because the predictions from the base learners are blended together, stacking is also referred to as blending.

The following diagram gives us a conceptual representation of stacking:

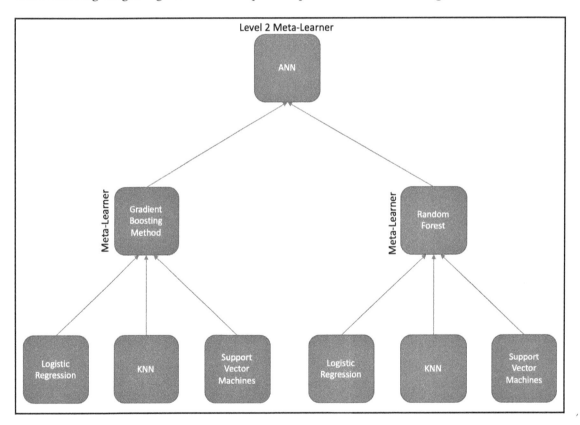

It's of significance for stack generalization that the predictions from the base learners are not correlated with each other. In order to get uncorrelated predictions from the base learners, algorithms that use different approaches internally may be used to train the base learners. Stacked generalization is used mainly for minimizing the generalization error of the base learners, and can be seen as a refined version of cross-validation. It uses a strategy that's more sophisticated than cross-validation's **winner-takes-all** approach for combining the predictions from the base learners.

Implementing stacked generalization by combining predictions

In this section, we'll look at how to implement stacked generalization from scratch.

We will carry out the following steps to get started:

1. Build three base learners for stacking.
2. Combine the predictions from each of the base learners.
3. Build the meta-learner using another algorithm.

Getting ready...

In this example, we use a dataset from the UCI ML Repository on credit card defaults. This dataset contains information on default payments, demographic factors, credit data, history of payments, and bill statements of credit card clients. The data and the data descriptions are provided in the GitHub.

We will start by loading the required libraries and reading our dataset:

```
import os
import numpy as np
import pandas as pd
from sklearn.metrics import accuracy_score
```

We set our working folder as follows:

```
# Set your working directory according to your requirement
os.chdir(".../Chapter 8/")
os.getcwd()
```

Let's now read our data. We will prefix the DataFrame name with `df_` so that we can understand it easily:

```
df_creditcarddata = pd.read_csv("UCI_Credit_Card.csv")
```

We drop the `ID` column, as this isn't required:

```
df_creditcarddata = df_creditcarddata.drop("ID", axis= 1)
```

We check the shape of the dataset:

```
df_creditcarddata.shape
```

We notice that the dataset now has 30,000 observations and 24 columns. Let's now move on to training our models.

How to do it...

1. We split our target and feature variables:

   ```
   from sklearn.model_selection import train_test_split

   X = df_creditdata.iloc[:,0:23]
   Y = df_creditdata['default.payment.next.month']
   ```

2. Split the data into training, validation, and testing subsets:

   ```
   # We first split the dataset into train and test subset
   X_train, X_test, Y_train, Y_test = train_test_split(X, Y,
   test_size=0.1, random_state=1)

   # Then we take the train subset and carve out a validation set from
   the same
   X_train, X_val, Y_train, Y_val = train_test_split(X_train, Y_train,
   test_size=0.2, random_state=1)
   ```

3. Check the dimensions of each subset to ensure that our splits are correct:

   ```
   # Dimensions for train subsets
   print(X_train.shape)
   print(Y_train.shape)

   # Dimensions for validation subsets
   print(X_val.shape)
   print(Y_val.shape)
   ```

```
# Dimensions for test subsets
print(X_test.shape)
print(Y_test.shape)
```

4. Import the required libraries for the base learners and the meta-learner:

```
# for the base learners
from sklearn.naive_bayes import GaussianNB
from sklearn.neighbors import KNeighborsClassifier
from sklearn.tree import DecisionTreeClassifier



# for the meta learner
from sklearn.linear_model import LogisticRegression
```

5. Create instances of the base learners and fit the model on our training data:

```
# The base learners
model_1 = GaussianNB()
model_2 = KNeighborsClassifier(n_neighbors=1)
model_3 = DecisionTreeClassifier()

# Now we train a list of models
base_learner_1 = model_1.fit(X_train, Y_train)
base_learner_2 = model_2.fit(X_train, Y_train)
base_learner_3 = model_3.fit(X_train, Y_train)
```

6. Use the base learners on our validation subset to make predictions:

```
# We then use the models to make predictions on validation data
val_prediction_base_learner_1 = base_learner_1.predict(X_val)
val_prediction_base_learner_2 = base_learner_2.predict(X_val)
val_prediction_base_learner_3 = base_learner_3.predict(X_val)
```

7. We have three sets of prediction results from three base learners. We use them to create a stacked array:

```
# And then use the predictions to create a new stacked dataset
import numpy as np
prediction_test_stack = np.dstack([val_prediction_base_learner_1,
val_prediction_base_learner_2, val_prediction_base_learner_3])

# Now we stack the actual outcomes i.e. Y_Test with the
prediction_stack
final_train_stack = np.dstack([prediction_test_stack, Y_val])
```

8. We convert the `final_train_stack` stacked array to a DataFrame and add column names to each of the columns. Verify the dimensions and take a look at the first few rows:

```
stacked_train_dataframe = pd.DataFrame(final_train_stack[0,0:5400],
columns='NB_VAL KNN_VAL DT_VAL Y_VAL'.split())

print(stacked_train_dataframe.shape)
print(stacked_train_dataframe.head(5))
```

In the following image, we see that the stacked array now has 5,400 observations and 4 columns:

```
(5400, 4)
    NB_VAL   KNN_VAL   DT_VAL   Y_VAL
0      1         0        0        0
1      1         0        0        1
2      1         0        0        0
3      1         0        1        1
4      1         0        0        0
```

9. Train the meta-learner using the stacked array that we created in *Step 8*:

```
# Build the Mata-learner
meta_learner = LogisticRegression()
meta_learner_model =
meta_learner.fit(stacked_train_dataframe.iloc[:,0:3],
stacked_train_dataframe['Y_VAL'])
```

10. Create the stacked test set with the testing subset:

```
# Take the test data (new data)
# Apply the base learners on this new data to make predictions

# We now use the models to make predictions on the test data and
create a new stacked dataset
test_prediction_base_learner_1 = base_learner_1.predict(X_test)
test_prediction_base_learner_2 = base_learner_2.predict(X_test)
test_prediction_base_learner_3 = base_learner_3.predict(X_test)

# Create the stacked data
final_test_stack = np.dstack([test_prediction_base_learner_1,
test_prediction_base_learner_2, test_prediction_base_learner_3])
```

11. Convert the `final_test_stack` stacked array to a DataFrame and add column names to each of the columns. Verify the dimensions and take a look at the first few rows:

```
stacked_test_dataframe = pd.DataFrame(final_test_stack[0,0:3000],
columns='NB_TEST KNN_TEST DT_TEST'.split())
print(stacked_test_dataframe.shape)
print(stacked_test_dataframe.head(5))
```

We see that the stacked array now has 3,000 observations and 3 columns in `stacked_test_dataframe`:

```
(3000, 3)
  NB_TEST   KNN_TEST   DT_TEST
0       1          0         0
1       1          1         0
2       0          1         1
3       1          1         1
4       1          0         1
```

12. Check the accuracy of `base_learner` on our original test data:

```
test_prediction_base_learner_1 = base_learner_1.predict(X_test)
test_prediction_base_learner_2 = base_learner_2.predict(X_test)
test_prediction_base_learner_3 = base_learner_3.predict(X_test)

print("Accuracy from GaussianNB:", accuracy_score(Y_test,
test_prediction_base_learner_1))
print("Accuracy from KNN:", accuracy_score(Y_test,
test_prediction_base_learner_2))
print("Accuracy from Decision Tree:", accuracy_score(Y_test,
test_prediction_base_learner_3))
```

We notice that the accuracy is as follows. Note that based on the sampling strategy and hyperparameters, the results may vary:

```
Accuracy from GaussianNB: 0.391333333333
Accuracy from KNN: 0.697
Accuracy from Decision Tree: 0.732666666667
```

13. Use the meta-learner on the stacked test data and check the accuracy:

```
test_predictions_meta_learner =
meta_learner_model.predict(stacked_test_dataframe)
print("Accuracy from Meta Learner:", accuracy_score(Y_test,
test_predictions_meta_learner))
```

We see the following output returned by the meta-learner applied on the stacked test data. This accuracy is higher than the individual base learners:

```
Accuracy from Meta Learner: 0.774666666667
```

How it works...

In *Step 1*, we split our dataset into target and feature sets. In *Step 2*, we created our training, validation, and testing subsets. We took a look at the dimensions of each of the subset in *Step 3* to verify that the splits were done correctly.

We then moved on to building our base learners and the meta-learner. In *Step 4*, we imported the required libraries for the base learners and the meta-learner. For the base learners, we used Gaussian Naive Bayes, KNN, and a decision tree, while for the meta-learner we used logistic regression.

In *Step 5*, we fitted the base learners to our train dataset. Single models, including Gaussian Naive Bayes, KNN, and a decision tree, are established in the level 0 space. We then had three base models.

In *Step 6*, we used these three base models on our validation subset to predict the target variable. We then had three sets of predictions given by the respective base learners.

Now the base learners will be integrated by logistic regression in the level 1 space via stacked generalization. In *Step 7*, we stacked the three sets of predicted values to create an array. We also stacked the actual target variable of our training dataset to the array. We then had four columns in our array: three columns from the three sets of predicted values of the base learners and a fourth column from the target variable of our training dataset. We called it `final_train_stack` known as `stacked_train_dataframe`, and we named the columns according to the algorithm used for the base learners. In our case, we used the names `NB_VAL`, `KNN_VAL`, and `DT_VAL` since we used Gaussian Naive Bayes, KNN, and a decision tree classifier, respectively. Because the base learners are fitted to our validation subset, we suffixed the column names with `_VAL` to make them easier to understand.

In *Step 9*, we built the meta-learner with logistic regression and fitted it to our stacked dataset, `stacked_train_dataframe`. Notice that we moved away from our original dataset to a stacked dataset, which contains the predicted values from our base learners.

In *Step 10*, we used the base models on our test subset to get the predicted results. We called it `final_test_stack`. In *Step 11*, we converted the `final_test_stack` array to a DataFrame called `stacked_test_dataframe`. Note that in our `stacked_test_dataframe`, we only had three columns, which held the predicted values returned by the base learners applied on our test subset. The three columns were named after the algorithm used, suffixed with `_TEST`, so we have `NB_TEST`, `KNN_TEST`, and `DT_TEST` as the three columns in `stacked_test_dataframe`.

In *Step 12*, we checked the accuracy of the base models on our original test subset. The Gaussian Naive Bayes, KNN, and decision tree classifier models gave us accuracy ratings of 0.39, 0.69, and 0.73, respectively.

In *Step 13*, we checked the accuracy that we get by applying the meta-learner model on our stacked test data. This gave us an accuracy of 0.77, which we can see is higher than the individual base learners. However, bear in mind that simply adding more base learners to your stacking algorithm doesn't guarantee that you'll get better accuracy.

There's more...

Creating a stacking model can be tedious. The `mlxtend` library provides tools that simplify building the stacking model. It provides StackingClassifier, which is the ensemble-learning meta-classifier for stacking, and it also provides StackingCVClassifier, which uses cross-validation to prepare the input for the second level meta-learner to prevent overfitting.

You can download the library from `https://pypi.org/project/mlxtend/` or use the `pip install mlxtend` command to install it. You can find some great examples of simple stacked classification and stacked classification with grid search at `http://rasbt.github.io/mlxtend/user_guide/classifier/StackingClassifier/`.

See also

You can also take a look at the ML-Ensemble library. To find out more about ML-Ensemble, visit `http://ml-ensemble.com/`. A guide to using ML-Ensemble is available at `https://bit.ly/2GFsxJN`.

Implementing stacked generalization for campaign outcome prediction using H2O

H2O is an open source platform for building machine learning and predictive analytics models. The algorithms are written on H2O's distributed map-reduce framework. With H2O, the data is distributed across nodes, read in parallel, and stored in the memory in a compressed manner. This makes H2O extremely fast.

H2O's stacked ensemble method is an ensemble machine learning algorithm for supervised problems that finds the optimal combination of a collection of predictive algorithms using stacking. H2O's stacked ensemble supports regression, binary classification, and multiclass classification.

In this example, we'll take a look at how to use H2O's stacked ensemble to build a stacking model. We'll use the bank marketing dataset which is available in the Github.

Getting ready...

First, import the h2o library and other modules from H2O:

```
import h2o
from h2o.estimators.random_forest import H2ORandomForestEstimator
from h2o.estimators.gbm import H2OGradientBoostingEstimator
from h2o.estimators.glm import H2OGeneralizedLinearEstimator
from h2o.estimators.stackedensemble import
H2OStackedEnsembleEstimator
from h2o.grid.grid_search import H2OGridSearch
```

Initialize the h2o instance using the init() function:

```
h2o.init()
```

Once we run the preceding code, the h2o instance gets initialized and we will see the following output:

```
Connecting to H2O server at http://127.0.0.1:54321... successful.
```

H2O cluster uptime:	02 secs
H2O cluster timezone:	Asia/Kolkata
H2O data parsing timezone:	UTC
H2O cluster version:	3.20.0.8
H2O cluster version age:	3 months and 2 days
H2O cluster name:	H2O_from_python_Dippies_s1thwh
H2O cluster total nodes:	1
H2O cluster free memory:	3.556 Gb
H2O cluster total cores:	8
H2O cluster allowed cores:	8
H2O cluster status:	accepting new members, healthy
H2O connection url:	http://127.0.0.1:54321
H2O connection proxy:	None
H2O internal security:	False
H2O API Extensions:	XGBoost, Algos, AutoML, Core V3, Core V4
Python version:	3.6.5 final

Now that we have instantiated an H2O instance, we move onto reading our dataset and building stacking models.

How to do it...

1. We read our data using the h2o.import_file() function. We pass the filename to the function as the parameter:

```
df_bankdata = h2o.import_file("bank-full.csv")
```

2. We split our data into training and testing subsets:

```
# split into train and validation sets
train, test = df_bankdata.split_frame(ratios = [.8], seed = 1234)
```

3. We check the dimensions of the training and testing subsets to verify that the splits are OK:

```
train.shape, test.shape
```

4. We take a look at the first few rows to ensure that data is loaded correctly:

```
df_bankdata.head()
```

5. We separate the target and predictor column names, which are the `response` and `predictors`, respectively:

```
# Set the predictor names
predictors = train.columns

# Set the response column name
response = "y"

# Remove the 'y' variable from the predictors
predictors.remove(response)

print(predictors)
```

6. We convert the `response` variable to a categorical type with the `asfactor()` function:

```
train[response] = train[response].asfactor()
test[response] = test[response].asfactor()
```

7. We will train our base learners using cross-validation. We set the `nfolds` value to 5.We also set a variable 'encoding' to 'OneHotExplicit'. We will use this variable to encode our categorical variables.

```
# Number of CV folds
nfolds = 5

# Using the `categorical_encoding` parameter
encoding = "OneHotExplicit"
```

8. We start training our base learners. We choose the Gradient Boosting Machine algorithm to build our first base learner:

```
# Train and cross-validate a GBM
base_learner_gbm =
H2OGradientBoostingEstimator(distribution="bernoulli",\
                                                   ntrees=100,\
                                                   max_depth=5,\
```

```
                                                          min_rows=2, \
                                                          learn_rate=0.01, \
                                                          nfolds=nfolds, \
fold_assignment="Modulo", \
categorical_encoding = encoding, \
keep_cross_validation_predictions=True)

base_learner_gbm.train(x=predictors, y=response,
training_frame=train)
```

9. For our second base learner, we use a Random Forest:

```
# Train and cross-validate a RF
base_learner_rf = H2ORandomForestEstimator(ntrees=250, \
                                            nfolds=nfolds, \
fold_assignment="Modulo", \
                                          categorical_encoding =
encoding, \
keep_cross_validation_predictions=True)
base_learner_rf.train(x=predictors, y=response,
training_frame=train)
```

10. For our third base learner, we implement a **Generalized Linear Model (GLM)**:

```
# Train and cross-validate a GLM
base_learner_glm =
H2OGeneralizedLinearEstimator(family="binomial", \
                                            model_id="GLM", \
lambda_search=True, \
                                            nfolds = nfolds, \
                                            fold_assignment =
"Modulo", \
keep_cross_validation_predictions = True)

base_learner_glm.train(x = predictors, y = response, training_frame
= train)
```

11. Get the best-performing base learner on the test set in terms of the `test` AUC. Compare this with the `test` AUC of the stacked ensemble model:

```
# Compare to base learner performance on the test set
gbm_test_performance = base_learner_gbm.model_performance(test)
rf_test_performance = base_learner_rf.model_performance(test)
glm_test_performance = base_learner_glm.model_performance(test)

print("Best AUC from the GBM", gbm_test_performance.auc())
print("Best AUC from the Random Forest", rf_test_performance.auc())
print("Best AUC from the GLM", glm_test_performance.auc())
```

```
baselearner_best_auc_test = max(gbm_test_performance.auc(),
rf_test_performance.auc(), glm_test_performance.auc())
print("Best AUC from the base learners", baselearner_best_auc_test)


stack_auc_test = perf_stack_test.auc()
print("Best Base-learner Test AUC: ", baselearner_best_auc_test)
print("Ensemble Test AUC: ", stack_auc_test)
```

12. We train a stacked ensemble using the base learners we built in the preceding steps:

```
all_models = [base_learner_glm, base_learner_gbm, base_learner_rf]

# Set up Stacked Ensemble. Using Deep Learning as the meta learner
ensemble_deep = H2OStackedEnsembleEstimator(model_id
="stack_model_d", base_models = all_models, metalearner_algorithm =
'deeplearning')

ensemble_deep.train(y = response, training_frame = train)

# Eval ensemble performance on the test data
perf_stack_test = ensemble_deep.model_performance(test)
stack_auc_test = perf_stack_test.auc()
print("Ensemble_deep Test AUC: {0}".format(stack_auc_test))
```

How it works...

In *Step 1*, we used the h2o.import_file() function to read our dataset.

> The h2o.import_file() function returns an H2OFrame instance.

In *Step 2*, we split our H2OFrame into training and testing subsets. In *Step 3*, we checked the dimensions of these subsets to verify that our split is adequate for our requirements.

In *Step 4*, we took a look at the first few rows to check if the data is correctly loaded. In *Step 5*, we separated out the column names of our response and predictor variables, and in *Step 6*, we converted the response variables into a categorical type with the asfactor() function.

We defined a variable called `nfolds` in *Step 7*, which we used for cross-validation. We have also defined a variable `encoding` which we used in the next steps to instruct H2O to use one-hot encoding for categorical variables. In *Step 8* to *Step 10*, we built our base learners.

In *Step 11*, we trained a Gradient Boosting Machine model. We passed some values to a few hyperparameters as follows:

- `nfolds`: Number of folds for K-fold cross-validation.
- `fold_assignment`: This option specifies the scheme to use for cross-validation fold assignment. This option is only applicable if a value for `nfolds` is specified and a `fold_column` isn't specified.
- `distribution`: Specifies the distribution. In our case, since the response variable has two classes, we set `distribution` to `"bernoulli"`.
- `ntrees`: Number of trees.
- `max_depth`: Denotes the maximum tree depth.
- `min_rows`: Fewest allowed observations in a leaf.
- `learn_rate`: Learning rate takes value from `0.0` to `1.0`.

 Note that for all base learners, cross-validation folds must be the same and `keep_cross_validation_predictions` must be set to `True`.

In *Step 9*, we trained a random forest base learner using the following hyperparameters: `ntrees, nfolds, fold_assignment`.

In *Step 10*, we trained our algorithm with a GLM. Note that we have not encoded the categorical variables in GLM.

 H2O recommends users to allow GLM handle categorical columns, as it can take advantage of the categorical column for better performance and efficient memory utilization.
From H2o.ai: "We strongly recommend avoiding one-hot encoding categorical columns with any levels into many binary columns, as this is very inefficient. This is especially true for Python users who are used to expanding their categorical variables manually for other frameworks".

In *Step 11*, we generated the test AUC values for each of the base learners and printed the best AUC.

In *Step 12*, we trained a stacked ensemble model by combining the output of the base learners using `H2OStackedEnsembleEstimator`. We used the trained ensemble model on our test subset. Note that by default GLM is used as the meta-learner for `H2OStackedEnsembleEstimator`. However, we have used deep learning as the meta-learner in our example.

 Note that we have used default hyperparameters values for our meta-learner. We can specify the hyperparameter values with `metalearner_params`. The `metalearner_params` option allows you to pass in a dictionary/list of hyperparameters to use for the algorithm that is used as meta-learner.

Fine-tuning the hyperparameters can deliver better results.

There's more...

You may also assemble a list of models to stack together in different ways. In the preceding example, we trained individual models and put them in a list to ensemble them. We can also train a grid of models:

1. We specify the random forest hyperparameters for the grid:

```
hyper_params = {"max_depth": [3, 4, 5, 8, 10],
                "min_rows": [3,4,5,6,7,8,9,10],
                "mtries": [10,15, 20],
                "ntrees": [100,250,500, 750],
                "sample_rate": [0.7, 0.8, 0.9, 1.0],
                "col_sample_rate_per_tree": [0.5, 0.6, 0.7, 0.8,
0.9, 1.0]}

search_criteria = {"strategy": "RandomDiscrete", "max_models": 3,
"seed": 1}
```

2. We train the grid using the hyperparameters defined in the preceding code:

```
# Train the grid
grid = H2OGridSearch(model=H2ORandomForestEstimator(nfolds=nfolds,\
fold_assignment="Modulo",\
keep_cross_validation_predictions=True),\
                    hyper_params=hyper_params,\
                    search_criteria=search_criteria,\
                    grid_id="rf_grid_binomial")

grid.train(x=predictors, y=response, training_frame=train)
```

3. We train the ensemble using the random forest grid:

```
# Train a stacked ensemble using the RF grid
ensemble =
H2OStackedEnsembleEstimator(model_id="ensemble_rf_grid_binomial_9",
base_models=grid.model_ids)

ensemble.train(x=predictors, y=response, training_frame=train)

# Evaluate ensemble performance on the test data
perf_stack_test = ensemble.model_performance(test)

# Compare to base learner performance on the test set
baselearner_best_auc_test =
max([h2o.get_model(model).model_performance(test_data=test).auc()
for model in grid.model_ids])

stack_auc_test = perf_stack_test.auc()

print("Best Base-learner Test AUC: ", baselearner_best_auc_test)
print("Ensemble Test AUC: ", stack_auc_test)
```

The preceding code will give the best base-learner test AUC and test the AUC from the ensemble model. If the response variable is highly imbalanced, consider fine-tuning the following hyperparameters to control oversampling and under-sampling:

- `balance_classes`: This option can be used to balance the class distribution. When enabled, H2O will either under-sample the majority classes or oversample the minority classes. If this option is enabled, you can also specify a value for the `class_sampling_factors` and `max_after_balance_size` options.
- `class_sampling_factors`: By default, sampling factors will be automatically computed to obtain class balance during training. This behavior may be changed using the `class_sampling_factors` parameter. This option sets an over- or under-sampling ratio for each class and requires `balance_classes=true`.
- `max_after_balance_size`: In most cases, setting `balance_classes` to true will increase the size of the DataFrame. To reduce the DataFrame size, you can use the `max_after_balance_size` parameter. This specifies the maximum relative size of the training data after balancing the class counts and defaults to 5.0.

See also

Take a look at `StackNet`, which was developed by Marios Michailidis as part of his PhD. `StackNet` is available under the MIT licence. It's a scalable and analytical framework that resembles a feed-forward neural network, and uses Wolpert's stacked-generalization concept to improve accuracy in machine learning predictive tasks. It uses the notion of meta-learners, in that it uses the predictions of some algorithms as features for other algorithms. StackNet can also generalize stacking on multiple levels. It is, however, computationally intensive. It was originally developed in Java, but a lighter Python version of `StackNet`, named `pystacknet`, is now available as well.

Let's think about how StackNet works. In the case of a neural network, the output of one layer is inserted as an input to the next layer and an activation function, such as sigmoid, tanh, or relu, is applied. Similarly, in the case of StackNet, the activation functions can be replaced with any supervised machine learning algorithm.

The stacking element can be run on two modes: a normal stacking mode and a re-stacking mode. In the case of a normal stacking mode, each layer uses the predictions of the previous one. In the case of re-stacking mode, each layer uses the neurons and activations of the previous layers.

Sample code that uses StackNet would consist of the following steps:

1. Import the required libraries (note that we have imported `StackNetClassifier` and `StackNetRegressor` from the `pystacknet` library):

```
import numpy as np

# import required libraries from sklearn
from sklearn.tree import DecisionTreeClassifier
from sklearn.ensemble import RandomForestClassifier,
GradientBoostingClassifier
from sklearn.linear_model import LogisticRegression

from sklearn.metrics import roc_auc_score, log_loss
from sklearn.model_selection import StratifiedKFold

# import StackNetClassifier and StackNetRegressor from pystacknet
from pystacknet.pystacknet import
StackNetClassifier,StackNetRegressor
from pystacknet.metrics import rmse,mae
```

2. We read the data, drop the `ID` column, and check the dimensions of the dataset:

```
df_creditcarddata = pd.read_csv("UCI_Credit_Card.csv")

#dropping the ID column, as it would not be required
df_creditcarddata.drop(["ID"],axis=1,inplace=True)

# Check the shape of the data
df_creditcarddata.shape
```

3. We separate our target and predictor variables. We also split the data into training and testing subsets:

```
#create the predictor & target set
X = df_creditcarddata.iloc[:,0:23]
Y = df_creditcarddata['default.payment.next.month']

# Create train & test sets
X_train, X_test, Y_train, Y_test = \
train_test_split(X, Y, test_size=0.20, random_state=1)
```

4. We define the models for the base learners and the meta-learner:

```
models=[[DecisionTreeClassifier(criterion="entropy", max_depth=5,
max_features=0.5, random_state=1),
GradientBoostingClassifier(n_estimators=100, learning_rate=0.1,
max_depth=5, max_features=0.5, random_state=1),
LogisticRegression(random_state=1)],
[RandomForestClassifier (n_estimators=500, criterion="entropy",
max_depth=5, max_features=0.5, random_state=1)]]
```

5. We now use `StackNetClassifier` to build the stacking ensemble. However, note that we use `restacking=False`, which means that it uses the normal stacking mode:

```
model=StackNetClassifier(models, metric="accuracy", folds=4,
restacking=False, use_retraining=True, use_proba=True,
random_state=12345, n_jobs=1, verbose=1)

model.fit(X_train,Y_train )

# Uses the meta-learner model to predict the outcome
preds=model.predict_proba(X_test)[:,1]
print ("TEST ACCURACY without RESTACKING, auc %f " %
(roc_auc_score(Y_test,preds)))
```

With `restacking=True`, `StackNetClassifier` would use the re-stacking mode to build the models.

There are various case studies of StackNet being used in winning competitions in Kaggle. An example of how `StackNet` can be used is available at `https://bit.ly/2T7339y`.

9
Homogeneous Ensembles Using Keras

In this chapter, we will cover the following topics:

- An ensemble of homogeneous models for energy prediction
- An ensemble of homogeneous models for handwritten digit classification

Introduction

In the case of ensemble models, each base classifier must have some degree of diversity within itself. This diversity can be obtained in one of the following manners:

- By using different subsets of training data through various resampling methods or randomization of the training data
- By using different learning hyperparameters for different base learners
- By using different learning algorithms

In the case of ensemble models, where different algorithms are used for the base learners, the ensemble is called a **heterogeneous ensemble method**. If the same algorithm is used for all the base learners on different distributions of the training set, the ensemble is called a **homogeneous ensemble**.

An ensemble of homogeneous models for energy prediction

In the following example, we will use the Keras API. Keras is an open source high-level framework for building deep neural networks. It's written on top of TensorFlow or Theano and uses them for its calculations behind the scenes. Keras can run on both CPU and GPU. The default settings of Keras are designed to deliver good results in most cases.

The focus of Keras is the idea of a model. Keras supports two types of models. The main type of model is a sequence of layers, called **sequential**. The other type of model in Keras is the non-sequential model, called **model**.

To build a sequential model, carry out the following steps:

1. Instantiate a sequential model using `Sequential()`
2. Add layers to it one by one using the `Dense` class
3. Compile the model with the following:
     - A mandatory loss function
     - A mandatory optimizer
     - Optional evaluation parameters
4. Use data to fit the model
5. Evaluate the model

Here's a diagrammatic flow of the preceding steps:

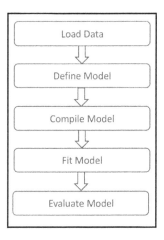

In the following code block, we can see a short code example:

```
# Instantiate a sequential model
seqmodel = Sequential()

# Add layers using the Dense class
seqmodel.add(Dense8, activation='relu')

# Compile the model
seqmodel.compile(loss='binary_crossentropy, optimizer='adam',
metric=['accuracy'])

# Fit the model
seqmodel.fit(X_train, Y_train, batch_size=10)
```

Getting ready

We'll start by installing Keras. In order to install Keras, you will need to have Theano or TensorFlow installed in your system. In this example, we'll go with TensorFlow as the backend for Keras.

There are two variants of TensorFlow: a CPU version and a GPU version.

To install the current CPU-only version, use the following command:

```
pip install tensorflow
```

If you have to install the GPU package, use the following command:

```
pip install tensorflow-gpu
```

Once you've installed TensorFlow, you'll need to install Keras using the following command:

```
sudo pip install keras
```

In order to upgrade your already-installed Keras library, use the following command:

```
sudo pip install --upgrade keras
```

Once we're done with installing the libraries, let's import the required libraries:

```
import os
import pandas as pd
import numpy as np
from sklearn.model_selection import train_test_split
```

```
from sklearn.metrics import mean_squared_error

from keras.models import Sequential
from keras.layers import Dense
```

We set our working directory according to our requirements:

```
os.chdir("..../Chapter 9")
os.getcwd()
```

We read our `energydata.csv` dataset:

```
df_energydata = pd.read_csv("energydata.csv")
```

We check whether there are any null values in our dataset:

```
df_energydata.isnull().sum()
```

How to do it...

We'll now build our `test` subset and train our neural network models:

1. Separate the `test` subset to apply the models in order to make predictions:

   ```
   df_traindata, df_testdata = train_test_split(df_energydata,
   test_size=0.3)
   ```

2. Check the shape of the `train` and `test` subsets:

   ```
   print(df_traindata.shape)
   print(df_testdata.shape)
   ```

3. Take the `test` subset and split it into target and feature variables:

   ```
   X_test = df_testdata.iloc[:,3:27]
   Y_test = df_testdata.iloc[:,28]
   ```

4. Validate the preceding split by checking the shape of `X_test` and `Y_test`:

   ```
   print(X_test.shape)
   print(Y_test.shape)
   ```

5. Let's create multiple neural network models using Keras. We use `For...Loop` to build multiple models:

   ```
   ensemble = 20
   frac = 0.7
   ```

```python
predictions_total = np.zeros(5921, dtype=float)

for i in range(ensemble):
    print("number of iteration:", i)
    print("predictions_total", predictions_total)

    # Sample randomly the train data
    Traindata = df_traindata.sample(frac=frac)
    X_train = Traindata.iloc[:,3:27]
    Y_train = Traindata.iloc[:,28]

    ################################################################
    model = Sequential()
    # Adding the input layer and the first hidden layer
    model.add(Dense(units=16, kernel_initializer = 'normal',
activation = 'relu', input_dim = 24))

    # Adding the second hidden layer
    model.add(Dense(units = 24, kernel_initializer = 'normal',
activation = 'relu'))
    # Adding the third hidden layer
    model.add(Dense(units = 32, kernel_initializer = 'normal',
activation = 'relu'))

    # Adding the output layer
    model.add(Dense(units = 1, kernel_initializer = 'normal',
activation = 'relu'))

    # Compiling the ANN
    adam = optimizers.Adam(lr=0.001, beta_1=0.9, beta_2=0.9,
epsilon=None, decay=0.0)
    model.compile(loss='mse', optimizer=adam,
metrics=['mean_squared_error'])
    # Fitting the ANN to the Training set

    model.fit(X_train, Y_train, batch_size = 16, epochs = 25)

    ################################################################
    # We use predict() to predict our values
    model_predictions = model.predict(X_test)
    model_predictions = model_predictions.flatten()
    print("TEST MSE for individual model: ",
mean_squared_error(Y_test, model_predictions))
    print("")
    print(model_predictions)
    print("")

predictions_total = np.add(predictions_total, model_predictions)
```

6. Take the summation of the predicted values and divide them by the number of iterations to get the average predicted values. We use the average predicted values to calculate the **mean-squared error** (**MSE**) for our ensemble:

```
predictions_total = predictions_total/ensemble
print("MSE after ensemble: ", mean_squared_error(np.array(Y_test),
predictions_total))
```

How it works...

Here's a diagrammatic representation of the ensemble homogeneous model workflow:

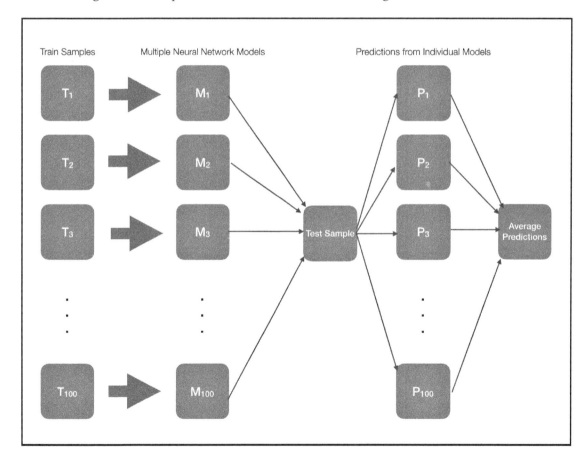

In the preceding diagram, we assume that we have 100 train samples. We train 100 models on our 100 train samples and apply them to our test sample. We get 100 sets of predictions, which we ensemble by averaging whether the target variable is a numeric variable or whether we are calculating probabilities for a classification problem. In the case of class predictions, we would opt for max voting.

In *Step 1*, we separated our train and test samples. This is the same test sample that we used for our predictions with all the models we built in this recipe. In *Step 2*, we checked the shape of the `train` and `test` subsets. In *Step 3*, we split our test subset into target and predictor variables, and then checked the shape again in *Step 4* to ensure we got the right split.

In *Step 5*, we used the Keras library to build our neural network models. We initialized two variables, `ensemble` and `frac`. We used the `ensemble` variable to run a `for` loop for a certain number of iterations (in our case, we set it to `200`). We then used the `frac` variable to assign the proportion of data we took for our bootstrap samples from the training subset. In our example, we set `frac` to `0.8`.

In *Step 5*, within the `for...loop` iteration, we built multiple neural network models and applied the models to our test subset to get the predictions. We created sequential models by passing a list of layers using the `add()` method. In the first layer, we specified the input dimensions using the `input_dim` argument. Because we have 24 input dimensions, we set `input_dim` to `24`. We also mentioned the `Activation` function to use in each layer by setting the `Activation` argument.

You can also set the `Activation` function through an `Activation` layer, as follows:

```
# Example code to set activation function through the activation layer

from keras.layers import Activation, Dense

model.add(Dense(64))
model.add(Activation('tanh'))
```

In this step, before we build our model, we configure the learning process using the `compile` method. The `compile` method takes the mandatory `loss function`, the mandatory `optimizer`, and the optional `metrics` as an argument.

The `optimizer` argument can take values such as **Stochastic Gradient Descent (SGD)**, `RMSprop`, `Adagrad`, `Adadelta`, `Adam`, `Adamax`, or `Nadam`.

`loss function` can take values such as `mean_squared_error`, `mean_absolute_error`, `mean_absolute_percentage_error`, `mean_squared_logarithmic_error`, `squared_hinge`, `categorical_hinge`, or `binary_crossentropy`. More details are available at `https://keras.io/losses/`.

We also keep adding the predictions array to an array variable, called `predictions_total`, using the `np.add()` method.

Once we finished all the iterations in the `for` loop in *Step 5*, we divided the summation of predictions by the number of iterations, which is held in the `ensemble` variable and set to `200`, to get the average predictions. We used the average predictions to calculate the MSE of the ensemble result.

There's more...

If you have high computational requirements, you can use Google Colaboratory. Colaboratory is a free Jupyter notebook environment that requires no setup and runs entirely in the cloud. It's a free cloud service that supports free GPU. You can use Google Colab to build your deep learning applications using TensorFlow, Keras, PyTorch, and OpenCV.

Once you create your account with `https://colab.research.google.com/`, you can log in using your credentials.

Once you're logged in, you can move straight to the `File` menu to create your Python notebook:

Once you click on the **File** tab, you'll see **New Python 3 notebook**; a new notebook is created that supports Python 3.

You can click on **Untitled0.ipynb** in the top-left corner to rename the file:

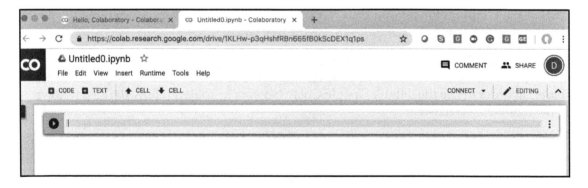

Go to **Edit** and then **Notebook settings.** A window pops up to indicate the different settings that you can have:

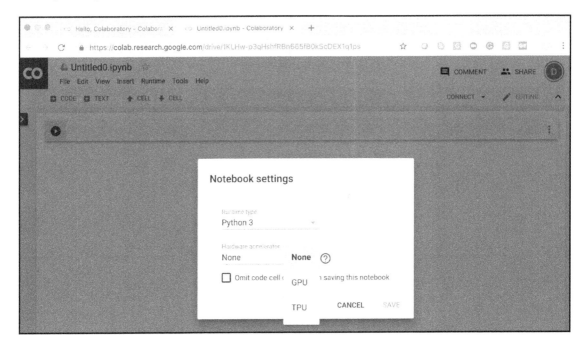

Choose the **Graphics Processing Unit** (**GPU**) option as the **Hardware accelerator**, as shown in the preceding screenshot, in order to use the free GPU.

One neat thing about Google Colab is it can work on your own Google Drive. You can choose to create your own folder in your Google Drive or use the default Colab Notebooks folder. In order to use the default Google Colab Notebooks folder, follow the steps shown in the following screenshot:

To start reading your datasets, you can store them in folders in Google Drive.

After you have logged in to Google Colab and created a new notebook, you will have to mount the drive by executing the following code in your notebook:

```
from google.colab import drive

# This can be your folder path as per your drive
drive.mount('/content/drive')
```

When the preceding code is run, it will ask for the authorization code to be entered, as shown here:

```
...  Go to this URL in a browser: https://accounts.google.com/o/oauth2/auth?client_id=947318989803-6bn6qk8qdgf4n4g3pfee6491hc0brc4i.apps.googleuser
Enter your authorization code:
```

Click on the preceding URL to get an authorization code:

Paste the authorization code into the text box. You'll get a different authorization code each time. Upon authorization, the drive is mounted.

Once the drive is mounted, you can read `.csv` file using `pandas`, as we showed earlier in the chapter. The rest of the code, as shown in the *How to do it* section, runs as it is. If you use the GPU, you'll notice that there is a substantial increase in the speed of your computational performance.

In order to install additional libraries in Google Colab, you'll need to run the `pip install` command with a ! sign before it. For example, you can run `!pip install utils` to install utils in the Google Colab instance.

See also

There are various activation functions available for use with the Keras library:

- Softmax activation function
- Exponential linear unit
- Scaled exponential linear unit
- Softplus activation function
- Rectified linear unit
- Hyperbolic tangent activation function
- Sigmoid activation function
- Linear activation function
- Exponential activation function

For more information about the preceding activation functions, visit `https://keras.io/activations/`.

An ensemble of homogeneous models for handwritten digit classification

In this example, we will use a dataset called The **Street View House Numbers** (**SVHN**) dataset from `http://ufldl.stanford.edu/housenumbers/`. The dataset is also provided in the GitHub in `.hd5f` format.

This dataset is a real-world dataset and is obtained from house numbers in Google Street View images.

We use Google Colab to train our models. In the first phase, we build a single model using Keras. In the second phase, we ensemble multiple homogeneous models and ensemble the results.

Getting ready

The dataset has 60,000 house number images. Each image is labeled between 1 and 10. Digit 1 is labelled as 1, digit 9 is labelled as 9, and digit 0 is labelled as 10. The images are 32 x 32 images centered around a single character. In some cases, we can see the images are visually indistinct.

We import the required libraries:

```
import os
import matplotlib.pyplot as plt
import numpy as np
from numpy import array

from sklearn.metrics import accuracy_score

from keras.models import Sequential, load_model
from keras.layers.core import Dense, Dropout, Activation
```

We mount the Google Drive:

```
from google.colab import drive
drive.mount('/content/drive')
```

Now, we import a library called h5py to read the HDF5 format file and our data file, which is called SVHN_single_grey.h5:

```
import h5py

# Open the file as readonly
h5f = h5py.File('/content/drive/My Drive/DLCP/SVHN_single_grey.h5', 'r')
```

We load the training and test subsets and close the file:

```
# Load the training and test set
x_train = h5f['X_train'][:]
y_train = h5f['y_train'][:]
x_test = h5f['X_test'][:]
y_test = h5f['y_test'][:]

# Close this file
h5f.close()
```

We reshape our train and test subsets. We also change the datatype to float:

```
x_train = x_train.reshape(x_train.shape[0], 1024)
x_test = x_test.reshape(x_test.shape[0], 1024)
```

We now normalize our data by dividing it by 255.0. This also converts the data type of the values to float:

```
# normalize inputs from 0-255 to 0-1
x_train = x_train / 255.0
x_test = x_test / 255.0
```

We check the shape of the train and test subsets:

```
print("X_train shape", x_train.shape)
print("y_train shape", y_train.shape)
print("X_test shape", x_test.shape)
print("y_test shape", y_test.shape)
```

We see that the shape of the `train` and `test` features and our target subsets are as follows:

```
X_train shape (42000, 1024)
y_train shape (42000, 10)
X_test shape (18000, 1024)
y_test shape (18000, 10)
Train data matrix shape (42000, 1024)
Test data matrix shape (18000, 1024)
```

We visualize some of the images. We also print labels on top of the images:

```python
# Visualizing the 1st 10 images in our dataset
# along with the labels
%matplotlib inline
import matplotlib.pyplot as plt
plt.figure(figsize=(10, 1))
for i in range(10):
  plt.subplot(1, 10, i+1)
  plt.imshow(x_train[i].reshape(32,32), cmap="gray")
  plt.title(y_train[i], color='r')
  plt.axis("off")
plt.show()
```

The first 10 images are shown as follows:

We now perform one-hot encoding on our target variable. We also store our `y_test` labels in another variable, called `y_test_actuals`, for later use:

```python
# Let us store the original y_test to another variable y_test_actuals
y_test_actuals = y_test

# one-hot encoding using keras' numpy-related utilities
n_classes = 10

print("Before one-hot encoding:")
print("Shape of Y_TRAIN before one-hot encoding: ", y_train.shape)
print("Shape of Y_TEST before one-hot encoding: ", y_test.shape)

y_train = np_utils.to_categorical(y_train, n_classes)
y_test = np_utils.to_categorical(y_test, n_classes)
```

```
print("After one-hot encoding:")
print("Shape of Y_TRAIN after one-hot encoding: ", y_train.shape)
print("Shape of Y_TRAIN after one-hot encoding: ", y_test.shape)
```

The shapes before and after one-hot encoding are as follows:

```
Before one-hot encoding:
Shape of Y_TRAIN before one-hot encoding:  (42000, 10)
Shape of Y_TEST before one-hot encoding:  (18000, 10)
After one-hot encoding:
Shape of Y_TRAIN after one-hot encoding:  (42000, 10, 10)
Shape of Y_TRAIN after one-hot encoding:  (18000, 10, 10)
```

How to do it...

We'll now build a single model with the Keras library:

1. Build a linear stack of layers with the sequential model:

```
# building a linear stack of layers with the sequential model
model = Sequential()
model.add(Dense(512, input_shape=(1024,)))
model.add(Activation('relu'))

model.add(Dense(512))
model.add(Activation('relu'))

model.add(Dense(10))
model.add(Activation('softmax'))
```

2. Compile the model:

```
# compiling the sequential model
model.compile(loss='categorical_crossentropy',
metrics=['accuracy'], optimizer='adam')
```

3. Fit the model to the `train` data and validate it with the `test` data:

```
# training the model and saving metrics in history
svhn_model = model.fit(x_train, y_train,
            batch_size=128, epochs=100,
            verbose=2,
            validation_data=(x_test, y_test))
```

4. Plot the model's accuracy at every epoch:

```
# plotting the metrics
fig = plt.figure(figsize=(12,4))

#plt.subplot(2,1,1)
plt.plot(svhn_model.history['acc'])
plt.plot(svhn_model.history['val_acc'])
plt.title('Model Accuracy')
plt.ylabel('Accuracy')
plt.xlabel('Epochs')
plt.legend(['Train', 'Test'], loc='uppper left')

plt.tight_layout()
```

We see the following model accuracy plot:

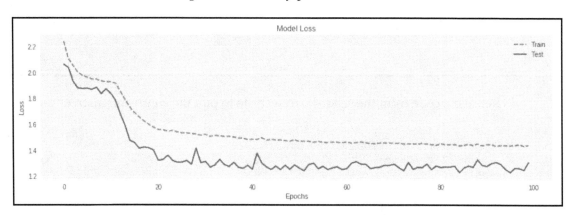

5. Plot the loss at every epoch:

```
# plotting the metrics
fig = plt.figure(figsize=(12,4))

plt.plot(svhn_model.history['loss'])
plt.plot(svhn_model.history['val_loss'])
plt.title('Model Loss')
plt.ylabel('Loss')
plt.xlabel('Epochs')
plt.legend(['Train', 'Test'], loc='upper right')

plt.tight_layout()
```

We see the following model loss plot:

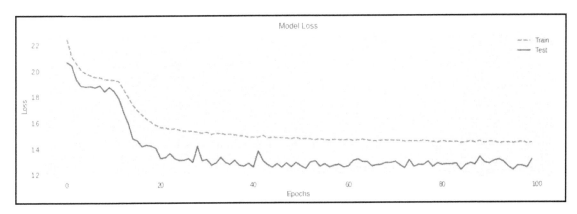

6. Reuse the code from the scikit-learn website to plot the confusion matrix:

```
# code from http://scikit-learn.org
def plot_confusion_matrix(cm, classes,
normalize=False,
title='Confusion matrix',
cmap=plt.cm.Blues):
    """
    This function prints and plots the confusion matrix.
    """
    plt.imshow(cm, cmap=cmap)
    plt.title(title)
    plt.colorbar()
    tick_marks = np.arange(len(classes))
    plt.xticks(tick_marks, classes, rotation=45)
    plt.yticks(tick_marks, classes)
```

```
thresh = cm.max() / 2.
for i, j in itertools.product(range(cm.shape[0]),
range(cm.shape[1])):
plt.text(j, i, cm[i, j],
horizontalalignment="center",
color="white" if cm[i, j] > thresh else "black")

plt.ylabel('Actuals')
plt.xlabel('Predicted')
```

7. Plot the confusion matrix both numerically and graphically:

```
target_names = [ '0', '1', '2', '3', '4', '5', '6', '7', '8', '9']

# Formulating the Confusion Matrix
import itertools
from sklearn.metrics import confusion_matrix

cm = confusion_matrix(y_test_actuals, predicted_classes)
print(cm)

plt.figure(figsize=(10,10))
plot_confusion_matrix(cm, classes=target_names, normalize=False)
plt.show()
```

The confusion matrix appears as follows:

```
[[1019   107   141    28    52    30   107    46    69   215]
 [  98  1093    78    70   108    34    16   252    36    43]
 [  49   143   761   127    53    34    11   527    34    64]
 [  40   186   130   865    36   160    17   196    54    35]
 [  63   190    78    25  1298    16    65    31    22    24]
 [  78   136   109   366    80   604    62    41   158   134]
 [ 209    90    55    19   200    56   984    37   162    20]
 [  50   168   361    51    33    22    20  1059    18    26]
 [ 166   128    77   121   119   280   220    31   533   137]
 [ 337   117   185   150    57    86    34    65    88   685]]
```

Confusion matrix

8. We'll now look at how to ensemble the results of multiple homogeneous models. Define a function to fit the model to the training data:

```
# fit model on dataset
def train_models(x_train, y_train):
    # building a linear stack of layers with the sequential model
    model = Sequential()
    model.add(Dense(512, input_shape=(1024,)))
    model.add(Activation('relu'))
    model.add(Dropout(0.2))

    model.add(Dense(512))
    model.add(Activation('relu'))
    model.add(Dropout(0.2))

    model.add(Dense(10))
    model.add(Activation('softmax'))
    # compiling the sequential model
    model.compile(loss='categorical_crossentropy', optimizer='adam',
metrics=['accuracy'])
    # training the model and saving metrics in history
    svhn_model = model.fit(x_train, y_train, batch_size=32,
epochs=25)
    return model
```

9. Write a function to ensemble the predictions of all the models:

```
# make an ensemble prediction for multi-class classification
def ensemble_predictions(models, x_test):
    # make predictions
    y_predicted = [model.predict(x_test) for model in models]
    y_predicted = np.array(y_predicted)
    # sum predictions from all ensemble models
    predicted_total = np.sum(y_predicted, axis=0)
    # argmax across classes
    result = np.argmax(predicted_total, axis=1)
    return result
```

numpy.argmax returns indices of the max element of the array in a particular axis.

10. Write a function to evaluate the models and get the accuracy score of each model:

```
# evaluate a specific number of members in an ensemble
def evaluate_models(models, no_of_models, x_test, y_test):
 # select a subset of members
 subset = models[:no_of_models]

 # make prediction
 y_predicted_ensemble = ensemble_predictions(subset, x_test)

 # calculate accuracy
 return accuracy_score(y_test_actuals, y_predicted_ensemble)
```

11. Fit all the models:

```
# fit all models
no_of_models = 50

models = [train_models(x_train, y_train) for _ in
range(no_of_models)]

# evaluate different numbers of ensembles
all_scores = list()
for i in range(1, no_of_models+1):
  score = evaluate_models(models, i, x_test, y_test)
  print("Accuracy Score of model ", i, " ", score)
  all_scores.append(score)
```

12. Plot the accuracy score against each epoch:

```
# plot score vs number of ensemble members
x_axis = [i for i in range(1, no_of_models+1)]
plt.plot(x_axis, all_scores)
plt.show()
```

How it works...

In *Step 1* to *Step 7*, we built a single neural network model to see how to use a labelled image dataset to train our model and predict the actual label for an unseen image.

In *Step 1*, we built a linear stack of layers with the sequential model using Keras. We defined the three layers: one input layer, one hidden layer, and one output layer. We provided input_shape=1024 to the input layer since we have 32 x 32 images. We used the relu activation function in the first and second layers. Because ours is a multi-class classification problem, we used softmax as the activation function for our output layer.

In *Step 2*, we compiled the model with `loss='categorical_crossentropy'` and `optimizer='adam'`. In *Step 3*, we fitted our model to our train data and validated it on our test data.

In *Step 4* and *Step 5*, we plotted the model accuracy and the loss metric for every epoch.

In *Step 6* and *Step 7*, we reused a `plot_confusion_matrix()` function from the scikit-learn website to plot our confusion matrix both numerically and visually.

From *Step 8* onward, we ensembled multiple models. We wrote three custom functions:

- `train_models()`: To train and compile our model using sequential layers.
- `ensemble_predictions()`: To ensemble the predictions and find the maximum value across classes for all observations.
- `evaluate_models()`: To calculate the accuracy score for every model.

In *Step 11*, we fitted all the models. We set the `no_of_models` variable to 50. We trained our models in a loop by calling the `train_models()` function. We then passed `x_train` and `y_train` to the `train_models()` function for every model built at every iteration. We also called `evaluate_models()`, which returned the accuracy scores of each model built. We then appended all the accuracy scores.

In *Step 12*, we plotted the accuracy scores for all the models.

10
Heterogeneous Ensemble Classifiers Using H2O

In this chapter, we will cover the following recipe:

- Predicting credit card defaulters using heterogeneous ensemble classifiers

Introduction

In this chapter, we'll showcase how to build heterogeneous ensemble classifier using H2O, which is an open source, distributed, in-memory, machine learning platform. There are a host of supervised and unsupervised algorithms available in H2O.

Among the supervised algorithms, H2O provides us with neural networks, random forest (RF), generalized linear models, a Gradient-Boosting Machine, a naive Bayes classifier, and XGBoost.

H2O also provides us with a stacked ensemble method that aims to find the optimal combination of a collection of predictive algorithms using the stacking process. H2O's stacked ensemble supports both regression and classification.

Predicting credit card defaulters using heterogeneous ensemble classifiers

We will use Taiwan's credit card payment defaulters data as an example. This is the same dataset we used earlier, in Chapter 3, *Resampling Methods*, to build a logistic regression model. In this recipe, we'll build multiple models using different algorithms, and finally, build a stacked ensemble model.

This dataset contains information about credit card clients in Taiwan. This includes information to do with payment defaulters, customers' demographic factors, their credit data, and their payment history. The dataset is provided in GitHub. It is also available from its main source, the UCI ML Repository: `https://bit.ly/2EZX6IC`.

In our example, we'll use the following supervised algorithms from H2O to build our models:

- Generalized linear model
- Distributed random forest
- Gradient-boosting machine
- Stacked ensemble

We'll see how to use these algorithms in Python and learn how to set some of the hyperparameters for each of the algorithms.

Getting ready

We'll use Google Colab to build our model. In `Chapter 10`, *Heterogeneous Ensemble Classifiers Using H2O*, we explained how to use Google Colaboratory in the *There's more* section.

We'll start by installing H2O in Google Colab as follows:

```
! pip install h2o
```

Executing the preceding command will show you a few instructions, with the final line showing the following message (the version number of H2O will be different depending on the latest version available):

```
Successfully installed colorama-0.4.1 h2o-3.22.1.2
```

We import all the required libraries, as follows:

```
import pandas as pd
import numpy as np

from sklearn.model_selection import train_test_split
from sklearn.metrics import confusion_matrix, roc_curve, auc
from sklearn import tree

import h2o
from h2o.estimators.glm import H2OGeneralizedLinearEstimator
from h2o.estimators.random_forest import H2ORandomForestEstimator
```

```
from h2o.estimators.gbm import H2OGradientBoostingEstimator
from h2o.grid.grid_search import H2OGridSearch
from h2o.estimators.stackedensemble import H2OStackedEnsembleEstimator


import seaborn as sns
import matplotlib.pyplot as plt
%matplotlib inline
```

We'll then initialize H2O:

```
# Initialize H2o
h2o.init()
```

Upon successful initialization, we'll see the information shown in the following screenshot. This information might be different, depending on the environment:

```
Connecting to H2O server at http://127.0.0.1:54321... successful.
H2O cluster uptime:          02 secs
H2O cluster timezone:        Etc/UTC
H2O data parsing timezone:   UTC
H2O cluster version:         3.22.1.2
H2O cluster version age:     4 hours and 18 minutes
H2O cluster name:            H2O_from_python_unknownUser_zhwtlv
H2O cluster total nodes:     1
H2O cluster free memory:     2.938 Gb
H2O cluster total cores:     2
H2O cluster allowed cores:   2
H2O cluster status:          accepting new members, healthy
H2O connection url:          http://127.0.0.1:54321
H2O connection proxy:        None
H2O internal security:       False
H2O API Extensions:          XGBoost, Algos, AutoML, Core V3, Core V4
Python version:              3.6.7 final
```

We'll read our dataset from Google Drive. In order to do this, we first need to mount the drive:

```
from google.colab import drive
drive.mount('/content/drive')
```

It will instruct you to go to a URL to get the authorization code. You'll need to click on the URL, copy the authorization code, and paste it. Upon successful mounting, you can read your file from the respective folder in Google Drive:

```
# Reading dataset from Google drive
df_creditcarddata = h2o.import_file("/content/drive/My Drive/Colab
Notebooks/UCI_Credit_Card.csv")
```

Note that with `h2o.import_file`, we create `h2o.frame.H2OFrame`. This is similar to a `pandas` DataFrame. However, in the case of a `pandas` DataFrame, the data is held in the memory, while in this case, the data is located on an H2O cluster.

You can run similar methods on an H2O DataFrame as you can on pandas. For example, in order to see the first 10 observations in the DataFrame, you can use the following command:

```
df_creditcarddata.head()
```

To check the dimensions of the DataFrame, we use the following command:

```
df_creditcarddata.shape
```

In order to see all the column names, we run the following syntax:

```
df_creditcarddata.columns
```

In the `pandas` DataFrame, we used `dtypes` to see the datatypes of each column. In the H2o DataFrame, we would use the following:

```
df_creditcarddata.types
```

This gives us the following output. Note that the categorical variables appear as `'enum'`:

```
{'AGE': 'int',
 'BILL_AMT1': 'int',
 'BILL_AMT2': 'int',
 'BILL_AMT3': 'int',
 'BILL_AMT4': 'int',
 'BILL_AMT5': 'int',
 'BILL_AMT6': 'int',
 'EDUCATION': 'enum',
 'LIMIT_BAL': 'int',
 'MARRIAGE': 'enum',
 'PAY_0': 'enum',
 'PAY_2': 'enum',
 'PAY_3': 'enum',
 'PAY_4': 'enum',
 'PAY_5': 'enum',
 'PAY_6': 'enum',
 'PAY_AMT1': 'int',
 'PAY_AMT2': 'int',
 'PAY_AMT3': 'int',
 'PAY_AMT4': 'int',
 'PAY_AMT5': 'int',
 'PAY_AMT6': 'int',
 'SEX': 'enum',
 'default.payment.next.month': 'enum'}
```

We have our target variable, `default.payment.next.month`, in the dataset. This tells us which customers have and have not defaulted on their payments. We want to see the distribution of the defaulters and non-defaulters:

```
df_creditcarddata['default.payment.next.month'].table()
```

This gives us the count of each class in the `default.payment.next.month` variable:

default.payment.next.month	Count
0	23364
1	6636

We don't need the `ID` column for predictive modeling, so we remove it from our DataFrame:

```
df_creditcarddata = df_creditcarddata.drop(["ID"], axis = 1)
```

We can see the distribution of the numeric variables using the `hist()` method:

```
import pylab as pl
df_creditcarddata[['AGE','BILL_AMT1','BILL_AMT2','BILL_AMT3','BILL_AMT4','B
ILL_AMT5','BILL_AMT6', 'LIMIT_BAL']].as_data_frame().hist(figsize=(20,20))
pl.show()
```

The following screenshot shows us the plotted variables . This can help us in our analysis of each of the variables:

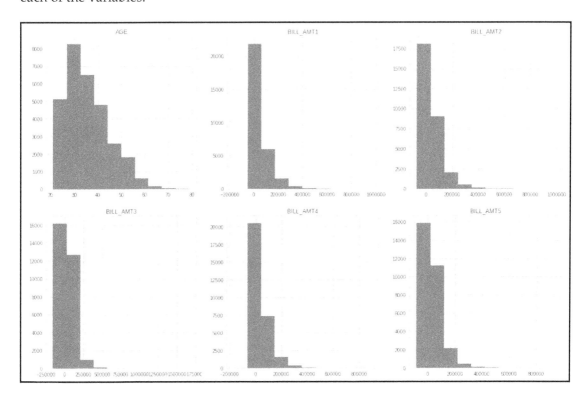

To extend our analysis, we can see the distribution of defaulters and non-defaulters by gender, education, and marital status:

```
# Defaulters by Gender
columns = ["default.payment.next.month","SEX"]
default_by_gender = df_creditcarddata.group_by(by=columns).count(na ="all")
print(default_by_gender.get_frame())

# Defaulters by education
columns = ["default.payment.next.month","EDUCATION"]
default_by_education = df_creditcarddata.group_by(by=columns).count(na
```

```
="all")
print(default_by_education.get_frame())

# Defaulters by MARRIAGE
columns = ["default.payment.next.month","MARRIAGE"]
default_by_marriage = df_creditcarddata.group_by(by=columns).count(na
="all")
print(default_by_marriage.get_frame())
```

In the following screenshot, we get to see the distribution of defaulters by different categories:

default.payment.next.month	SEX	nrow
0	1	9015
0	2	14349
1	1	2873
1	2	3763

default.payment.next.month	EDUCATION	nrow
0	0	14
0	1	8549
0	2	10700
0	3	3680
0	4	116
0	5	262
0	6	43
1	1	2036
1	2	3330
1	3	1237

default.payment.next.month	MARRIAGE	nrow
0	0	49
0	1	10453
0	2	12623
0	3	239
1	0	5
1	1	3206
1	2	3341
1	3	84

We'll now convert the categorical variables into factors:

```
# Convert the categorical variables into factors

df_creditcarddata['SEX'] = df_creditcarddata['SEX'].asfactor()
df_creditcarddata['EDUCATION'] = df_creditcarddata['EDUCATION'].asfactor()
df_creditcarddata['MARRIAGE'] = df_creditcarddata['MARRIAGE'].asfactor()
df_creditcarddata['PAY_0'] = df_creditcarddata['PAY_0'].asfactor()
df_creditcarddata['PAY_2'] = df_creditcarddata['PAY_2'].asfactor()
df_creditcarddata['PAY_3'] = df_creditcarddata['PAY_3'].asfactor()
df_creditcarddata['PAY_4'] = df_creditcarddata['PAY_4'].asfactor()
df_creditcarddata['PAY_5'] = df_creditcarddata['PAY_5'].asfactor()
df_creditcarddata['PAY_6'] = df_creditcarddata['PAY_6'].asfactor()
```

We also encode the dichotomous target variable, `default.payment.next.month`, as a factor variable. After the conversion, we check the classes of the target variable with the `levels()` method:

```
# Also, encode the binary response variable as a factor
df_creditcarddata['default.payment.next.month'] =
df_creditcarddata['default.payment.next.month'].asfactor()
df_creditcarddata['default.payment.next.month'].levels()
```

We'll then define our predictor and target variables:

```
# Define predictors manually
predictors =
['LIMIT_BAL','SEX','EDUCATION','MARRIAGE','AGE','PAY_0','PAY_2','PAY_3',\
 'PAY_4','PAY_5','PAY_6','BILL_AMT1','BILL_AMT2','BILL_AMT3','BILL_AMT4',\
 'BILL_AMT5','BILL_AMT6','PAY_AMT1','PAY_AMT2','PAY_AMT3','PAY_AMT4','PAY_AM
T5','PAY_AMT6']

target = 'default.payment.next.month'
```

We then split our DataFrame using the `split_frame()` method:

```
splits = df_creditcarddata.split_frame(ratios=[0.7], seed=1)
```

The following code gives us two split output:

```
splits
```

In the following screenshot, we get to see the following two splits:

LIMIT_BAL	SEX	EDUCATION	MARRIAGE	AGE	PAY_0	PAY_2	PAY_3	PAY_4	PAY_5	PAY_6	BILL_AMT1	BILL_AMT2	BILL_AMT3	BILL_AMT4	BILL_AMT5	BILL_AMT6
20000	2	2	1	24	2	2	-1	-1	-2	-2	3913	3102	689	0	0	0
120000	2	2	2	26	-1	2	0	0	0	2	2682	1725	2682	3272	3455	3261
50000	2	2	1	37	0	0	0	0	0	0	46990	48233	49291	28314	28959	29547
50000	1	1	2	37	0	0	0	0	0	0	64400	57069	57808	19394	19619	20024
100000	2	2	2	23	0	-1	-1	0	0	-1	11876	380	601	221	-159	567
140000	2	3	1	28	0	0	2	0	0	0	11285	14096	12108	12211	11793	3719
260000	2	1	2	51	-1	-1	-1	-1	-1	2	12261	21670	9966	8517	22287	13668
70000	1	2	2	30	1	2	2	0	0	2	65802	67369	65701	66782	36137	36894
250000	1	1	2	29	0	0	0	0	0	0	70887	67060	63561	59696	56875	55512
50000	2	3	3	23	1	2	0	0	0	0	50614	29173	28116	28771	29531	30211
LIMIT_BAL	SEX	EDUCATION	MARRIAGE	AGE	PAY_0	PAY_2	PAY_3	PAY_4	PAY_5	PAY_6	BILL_AMT1	BILL_AMT2	BILL_AMT3	BILL_AMT4	BILL_AMT5	BILL_AMT6
90000	2	2	2	34	0	0	0	0	0	0	29239	14027	13559	14331	14948	15549
50000	1	2	1	57	-1	0	-1	0	0	0	8617	5670	35835	20940	19146	19131
500000	1	1	2	29	0	0	0	0	0	0	367965	412023	445007	542653	483003	473944
20000	1	3	2	35	-2	-2	-2	-2	-1	-1	0	0	0	0	13007	13912
200000	2	3	2	34	0	0	2	0	0	-1	11073	9787	5535	2513	1828	3731
630000	2	2	2	41	-1	0	-1	-1	-1	-1	12137	6500	6500	6500	6500	2870
130000	2	3	2	39	0	0	0	0	0	-1	38358	27688	24489	20616	11802	930
60000	2	2	2	22	0	0	0	0	0	-1	15054	9806	11068	6026	-28335	18660
280000	1	1	2	31	-1	-1	2	-1	0	-1	498	9075	4641	9976	17976	9477
100000	2	3	3	43	0	0	0	0	0	0	61559	51163	43824	39619	35762	33258

We separate the splits into train and test subsets:

```
train = splits[0]
test = splits[1]
```

How to do it...

Let's move on to training our models using the algorithms we mentioned earlier in this chapter. We'll start by training our **generalized linear model** (**GLM**) models. We'll build three GLM models:

- A GLM model with default values for the parameters
- A GLM model with Lambda search (regularization)
- A GLM model with grid search

Now we will start with training our models in the following section.

1. Let's train our first model:

```
GLM_default_settings =
H2OGeneralizedLinearEstimator(family='binomial', \
model_id='GLM_default',nfolds = 10, \
                                    fold_assignment =
"Modulo", \
keep_cross_validation_predictions = True)
```

H2OGeneralizedLinearEstimator fits a generalized linear model. It takes in a response variable and a set of predictor variables.

H2OGeneralizedLinearEstimator can handle both regression and classification tasks. In the case of a regression problem, it returns an H2ORegressionModel subclass, while for classification, it returns an H2OBinomialModel subclass.

2. We created predictor and target variables in the *Getting ready* section. Pass the predictor and target variables to the model:

```
GLM_default_settings.train(x = predictors, y = target,
training_frame = train)
```

3. Train the GLM model using the `lambda_search` parameter:

```
GLM_regularized = H2OGeneralizedLinearEstimator(family='binomial',
model_id='GLM', \
                                              lambda_search=True,
nfolds = 10, \
                                              fold_assignment =
"Modulo", \
keep_cross_validation_predictions = True)

GLM_regularized.train(x = predictors, y = target, training_frame =
train)
```

`lambda_search` helps the GLM to find an optimal regularization parameter, λ. The `lambda_search` parameter takes in a Boolean value. When set to `True`, the GLM will first fit a model with the highest lambda value, which is known as **maximum regularization**. It then decreases this at each step until it reaches the minimum lambda. The resulting optimum model is based on the best lambda value.

4. Train the model using the GLM with a grid search:

```
hyper_parameters = { 'alpha': [0.001, 0.01, 0.05, 0.1, 1.0],
                     'lambda': [0.001, 0.01, 0.1, 1] }
search_criteria = { 'strategy': "RandomDiscrete", 'seed': 1,
                    'stopping_metric': "AUTO",
                    'stopping_rounds': 5 }

GLM_grid_search =
H2OGridSearch(H2OGeneralizedLinearEstimator(family='binomial', \
                nfolds = 10, fold_assignment = "Modulo", \
                keep_cross_validation_predictions = True),\
                hyper_parameters, grid_id="GLM_grid",
search_criteria=search_criteria)

GLM_grid_search.train(x= predictors,y= target,
training_frame=train)
```

5. We get the grid result sorted by the `auc` value with the `get_grid()` method:

```
# Get the grid results, sorted by validation AUC
GLM_grid_sorted = GLM_grid_search.get_grid(sort_by='auc',
decreasing=True)
GLM_grid_sorted
```

In the following screenshot, we can see the `auc` score for each model, which consists of different combinations of the `alpha` and `lambda` parameters:

	alpha	lambda	model_ids	auc
0	[0.1]	[0.001]	GLM_grid_model_42	0.7713781111059813
1	[0.001]	[0.001]	GLM_grid_model_36	0.7709312585464846
2	[0.001]	[0.001]	GLM_grid_model_36	0.7709312585464846
3	[0.001]	[0.001]	GLM_grid_model_29	0.7709312585464846
4	[0.01]	[0.001]	GLM_grid_model_33	0.7708762163954489
5	[0.01]	[0.001]	GLM_grid_model_12	0.7708762163954489
6	[0.05]	[0.001]	GLM_grid_model_23	0.7708584425688997
7	[0.05]	[0.001]	GLM_grid_model_4	0.7708584425688997
8	[0.1]	[0.001]	GLM_grid_model_37	0.7707119599447292
9	[0.1]	[0.001]	GLM_grid_model_21	0.7707119599447292
10	[0.1]	[0.001]	GLM_grid_model_15	0.7707119599447292
11	[0.001]	[0.01]	GLM_grid_model_39	0.7701545977486606
12	[0.001]	[0.01]	GLM_grid_model_40	0.7701448601663852
13	[1.0E-4]	[0.01]	GLM_grid_model_43	0.7701052782799948
14	[0.01]	[0.01]	GLM_grid_model_41	0.7699872479561195
15	[1.0]	[0.001]	GLM_grid_model_20	0.7696323643156521
16	[1.0]	[0.001]	GLM_grid_model_5	0.7696323643156521
17	[0.001]	[0.01]	GLM_grid_model_31	0.7694406029005699
18	[0.001]	[0.01]	GLM_grid_model_38	0.7694406029005699
19	[0.01]	[0.01]	GLM_grid_model_16	0.7693231848005969
20	[0.01]	[0.01]	GLM_grid_model_25	0.7693231848005969
21	[0.05]	[0.01]	GLM_grid_model_2	0.7689357888486935
22	[0.1]	[0.01]	GLM_grid_model_34	0.7685357488620949
23	[0.1]	[0.01]	GLM_grid_model_14	0.7685357488620949
24	[0.001]	[0.1]	GLM_grid_model_17	0.7618706605730926
25	[0.01]	[0.1]	GLM_grid_model_3	0.7614101006426495
26	[0.01]	[0.1]	GLM_grid_model_32	0.7614101006426495
27	[0.05]	[0.1]	GLM_grid_model_22	0.7561812316279662

6. We can see the model metrics on our train data and our cross-validation data:

```
# Extract the best model from random grid search
Best_GLM_model_from_Grid = GLM_grid_sorted.model_ids[0]

# model performance
Best_GLM_model_from_Grid = h2o.get_model(Best_GLM_model_from_Grid)
print(Best_GLM_model_from_Grid)
```

From the preceding code block, you can evaluate the model metrics, which include MSE, RMSE, Null and Residual Deviance, AUC, and Gini, along with the Confusion Matrix. At a later stage, we will use the best model from the grid search for our stacked ensemble.

Let us look at the following image and evaluate the model metrics:

```
ModelMetricsBinomialGLM: glm
** Reported on cross-validation data. **

MSE: 0.13760225425088768
RMSE: 0.37094777833394244
LogLoss: 0.4394365568279339
Null degrees of freedom: 21100
Residual degrees of freedom: 21039
Null deviance: 22491.611606980696
Residual deviance: 18545.101571252468
AIC: 18669.101571252468
AUC: 0.7713781111059813
pr_auc: 0.5420207583434027
Gini: 0.5427562222119626
Confusion Matrix (Act/Pred) for max f1 @ threshold = 0.2298965437009241:
```

	0	1	Error	Rate
0	13661.0	2697.0	0.1649	(2697.0/16358.0)
1	1995.0	2748.0	0.4206	(1995.0/4743.0)
Total	15656.0	5445.0	0.2224	(4692.0/21101.0)

7. Train the model using random forest. The code for random forest using default settings looks as follows:

```
# Build a RF model with default settings
RF_default_settings = H2ORandomForestEstimator(model_id = 'RF_D',\
                            nfolds = 10, fold_assignment =
"Modulo", \
                            keep_cross_validation_predictions =
True)

# Use train() to build the model
RF_default_settings.train(x = predictors, y = target,
training_frame = train)
```

8. To get the summary output of the model, use the following code:

```
RF_default_settings.summary()
```

9. Train the random forest model using a grid search. Set the hyperparameters as shown in the following code block:

```
hyper_params = {'sample_rate':[0.7, 0.9],
                'col_sample_rate_per_tree': [0.8, 0.9],
                'max_depth': [3, 5, 9],
                'ntrees': [200, 300, 400]
                }
```

10. Use the hyperparameters on `H2OGridSearch()` to train the `RF` model using gridsearch:

```
RF_grid_search = H2OGridSearch(H2ORandomForestEstimator(nfolds =
10, \
                                fold_assignment = "Modulo", \
                                keep_cross_validation_predictions =
True, \
                                stopping_metric =
'AUC',stopping_rounds = 5), \
                                hyper_params = hyper_params, \
                                grid_id= 'RF_gridsearch')

# Use train() to start the grid search
RF_grid_search.train(x = predictors, y = target, training_frame =
train)
```

11. Sort the results by AUC score to see which model performs best:

```
# Sort the grid models
RF_grid_sorted = RF_grid_search.get_grid(sort_by='auc',
decreasing=True)
print(RF_grid_sorted)
```

12. Extract the best model from the grid search result:

```
Best_RF_model_from_Grid = RF_grid_sorted.model_ids[0]

# Model performance
Best_RF_model_from_Grid = h2o.get_model(Best_RF_model_from_Grid)
print(Best_RF_model_from_Grid)
```

In the following screenshot, we see the model metrics for the grid model on the train data and the cross-validation data:

```
Model Details
=============
H2ORandomForestEstimator :  Distributed Random Forest
Model Key:  RF_gridsearch_model_29

ModelMetricsBinomial: drf
** Reported on train data. **

MSE: 0.13794252425933623
RMSE: 0.37140614461709737
LogLoss: 0.439212061123055
Mean Per-Class Error: 0.29017439406262435
AUC: 0.7775937549400496
pr_auc: 0.5444830285801324
Gini: 0.5551875098800991
Confusion Matrix (Act/Pred) for max f1 @ threshold = 0.2533025703444073:
```

	0	1	Error	Rate
0	13744.0	2605.0	0.1593	(2605.0/16349.0)
1	2027.0	2714.0	0.4275	(2027.0/4741.0)
Total	15771.0	5319.0	0.2196	(4632.0/21090.0)

13. Train the model using GBM. Here's how to train a GBM with the default settings:

```
GBM_default_settings = H2OGradientBoostingEstimator(model_id =
'GBM_default', \
                        nfolds = 10, \
                        fold_assignment = "Modulo", \
                        keep_cross_validation_predictions = True)

# Use train() to build the model
GBM_default_settings.train(x = predictors, y = target,
training_frame = train)
```

14. Use a grid search on the GBM. To perform a grid search, set the hyperparameters as follows:

```
hyper_params = {'learn_rate': [0.001,0.01, 0.1],
                'sample_rate': [0.8, 0.9],
                'col_sample_rate': [0.2, 0.5, 1],
                'max_depth': [3, 5, 9]}
```

15. Use the hyperparameters on `H2OGridSearch()` to train the GBM model using grid search:

```
GBM_grid_search = H2OGridSearch(H2OGradientBoostingEstimator(nfolds
= 10, \
                              fold_assignment = "Modulo", \
                              keep_cross_validation_predictions = True,\
                              stopping_metric = 'AUC', stopping_rounds =
5),
                              hyper_params = hyper_params, grid_id=
'GBM_Grid')

# Use train() to start the grid search
GBM_grid_search.train(x = predictors, y = target, training_frame =
train)
```

16. As with the earlier models, we can view the results sorted by AUC:

```
# Sort and show the grid search results
GBM_grid_sorted = GBM_grid_search.get_grid(sort_by='auc',
decreasing=True)
print(GBM_grid_sorted)
```

17. Extract the best model from the grid search:

```
Best_GBM_model_from_Grid = GBM_grid_sorted.model_ids[0]

Best_GBM_model_from_Grid = h2o.get_model(Best_GBM_model_from_Grid)
print(Best_GBM_model_from_Grid)
```

We can use `H2OStackedEnsembleEstimator` to build a stacked ensemble ML model that can use the models we have built using H2O algorithms to improve the predictive performance. `H2OStackedEnsembleEstimator` helps us find the optimal combination of a collection of predictive algorithms.

18. Create a list of the best models from the earlier models that we built using grid search:

```
# list the best models from each grid
all_models = [Best_GLM_model_from_Grid, Best_RF_model_from_Grid,
Best_GBM_model_from_Grid]
```

19. Set up a stacked ensemble model using `H2OStackedEnsembleEstimator`:

```
# Set up Stacked Ensemble
ensemble = H2OStackedEnsembleEstimator(model_id = "ensemble",
base_models = all_models, metalearner_algorithm = "deeplearning")

# uses GLM as the default metalearner
ensemble.train(y = target, training_frame = train)
```

20. Evaluate the ensemble performance on the test data:

```
# Eval ensemble performance on the test data
Ens_model = ensemble.model_performance(test)
Ens_AUC = Ens_model.auc()
```

21. Compare the performance of the base learners on the `test` data. The following code tests the model performance of all the GLM models we've built:

```
# Checking the model performance for all GLM models built
model_perf_GLM_default =
GLM_default_settings.model_performance(test)
model_perf_GLM_regularized =
GLM_regularized.model_performance(test)
model_perf_Best_GLM_model_from_Grid =
Best_GLM_model_from_Grid.model_performance(test)
```

The following code tests the model performance of all the random forest models we've built:

```
# Checking the model performance for all RF models built
model_perf_RF_default_settings =
RF_default_settings.model_performance(test)
model_perf_Best_RF_model_from_Grid =
Best_RF_model_from_Grid.model_performance(test)
```

The following code tests the model performance of all the GBM models we've built:

```
# Checking the model performance for all GBM models built
model_perf_GBM_default_settings =
GBM_default_settings.model_performance(test)
model_perf_Best_GBM_model_from_Grid =
Best_GBM_model_from_Grid.model_performance(test)
```

22. To get the best AUC from the base learners, execute the following commands:

```
# Best AUC from the base learner models
best_auc = max(model_perf_GLM_default.auc(),
model_perf_GLM_regularized.auc(), \
 model_perf_Best_GLM_model_from_Grid.auc(), \
 model_perf_RF_default_settings.auc(), \
 model_perf_Best_RF_model_from_Grid.auc(), \
 model_perf_GBM_default_settings.auc(), \
 model_perf_Best_GBM_model_from_Grid.auc())

print("Best AUC out of all the models performed: ",
format(best_auc))
```

23. The following commands show the AUC from the stacked ensemble model:

```
# Eval ensemble performance on the test data
Ensemble_model = ensemble.model_performance(test)
Ensemble_model = Ensemble_model.auc()
```

How it works...

We used Google Colab to train our models. After we installed H2O in Google Colab, we initialized the H2O instance. We also imported the required libraries.

In order to use the H2O libraries, we imported `H2OGeneralizedLinearEstimator`, `H2ORandomForestEstimator`, and `H2OGradientBoostingEstimator` from `h2o.estimators`. We also imported `H2OStackedEnsembleEstimator` to train our model using a stacked ensemble.

We mounted Google Drive and read our dataset using `h2o.import_file()`. This created an H2O DataFrame, which is very similar to a `pandas` DataFrame. Instead of holding it in the memory, however, the data is located in one of the remote H2O clusters.

We then performed basic operations on the H2O DataFrame to analyze our data. We took a look at the dimensions, the top few rows, and the data types of each column. The `shape` attribute returned a tuple with the number of rows and columns. The `head()` method returned the top 10 observations. The `types` attribute returned the data types of each column.

 Note that a categorical variable in an H2O DataFrame is marked as an enum.

Our target variable was `default.payment.next.month`. With the `table()` method, we saw the distribution of both classes of our target variable. The `table()` method returned the count for classes `1` and `0` in this case.

We didn't need the `ID` column, so we removed it using the `drop()` method with `axis=1` as a parameter. With `axis=1`, it dropped the columns. Otherwise, the default value of `axis=0` would have dropped the labels from the index.

We analyzed the distribution of the numeric variables. There's no limit to how far you can explore your data. We also saw the distribution of both of the classes of our target variable by various categories, such as gender, education, and marriage.

We then converted the categorical variables to factor type with the `asfactor()` method. This was done for the target variable as well.

We created a list of predictor variables and target variables. We split our DataFrame into the train and test subsets with the `split_frame()` method.

We passed ratios to the `split_frame()` method. In our case, we split the dataset into 70% and 30%. However, note that this didn't give an exact split of 70%-30%. H2O uses a probabilistic splitting method instead of using the exact ratios to split the dataset. This is to make the split more efficient on big data.

After we split our datasets into train and test subsets, we moved onto training our models. We used GLM, random forest, a **gradient-boosting machine** (**GBM**), and stacked ensembles to train the stacking model.

In the *How to do it...* section, in *Step 1* and *Step 2*, we showcased the code to train a GLM model with the default settings. We used cross-validation to train our model.

In *Step 3*, we trained a GLM model with `lambda_search`, which helps to find the optimal regularization parameter.

In *Step 4*, we used grid-search parameters to train our GLM model. We set our hyper-parameters and provided these to the `H2OGridSearch()` method. This helps us search for the optimum parameters across models. In the `H2OGridSearch()` method, we used the `RandomDiscrete` search-criteria strategy.

The default search-criteria strategy is Cartesian, which covers the entire space of hyperparameter combinations. The random discrete strategy carries out a random search of all the combinations of the hyperparameters provided.

In *Step 5*, with the `get_grid()` method, we looked at the AUC score of each model built with different combinations of the parameters provided. In *Step 6*, we extracted the `best` model from the random grid search. We can also use the `print()` method on the best model to see the model performance metrics on both the train data and the cross-validation data.

In *Step 7*, we trained a random forest model with default settings and looked at the summary of the resulting model in step 8. In *Step 9* and *Step 10*, we showcased the code to train a random forest model using grid-search. We set multiple values for various acceptable hyper-parameters, such as `sample_rate`, `col_sample_rate_per_tree`, `max_depth`, and `ntrees`. `sample_rate` refers to row sampling without replacement. It takes a value between `0` and `1`, indicating the sampling percentage of the data. `col_sample_rate_per_tree` is the column sampling for each tree without replacement. `max_depth` is set to specify the maximum depth to which each tree should be built. Deeper trees may perform better on the training data but will take more computing time and may overfit and fail to generalize on unseen data. The `ntrees` parameter is used for tree-based algorithms to specify the number of trees to build on the model.

In *Step 11* and *Step 12*, we printed the AUC score of each model generated by the grid-search and extracted the best model from it.

We also trained GBM models to fit our data. In *Step 13*, we built the GBM using the default settings. In *Step 14*, we set the hyperparameter space for the grid search. We used this in *Step 15*, where we trained our GBM. In the GBM, we set values for hyperparameters, such as `learn_rate`, `sample_rate`, `col_sample_rate`, `max_depth`, and `ntrees`. The `learn_rate` parameter is used to specify the rate at which the GBM algorithm trains the model. A lower value for the `learn_rate` parameter is better and can help in avoiding overfitting, but can be costly in terms of computing time.

 In H2O, `learn_rate` is available in GBM and XGBoost.

Step 16 showed us the AUC score of each resulting model from the grid search. We extracted the best grid-searched GBM in *Step 17*.

In *Step 18* through to *Step 20,* we trained our stacked ensemble model using `H2OStackedEnsembleEstimator` from H2O. We evaluated the performance of the resulting model on the test data.

In *Step 21*, we evaluated all the GLM models we built on our test data. We did the same with all the models we trained using RF and GBM. *Step 22* gave us the model with the maximum AUC score. In *Step 23*, we evaluated the AUC score of the stacked ensemble model on the test data in order to compare the performance of the stacked ensemble model with the individual base learners.

There's more...

Note that we used cross-validation to train all our models. We used the `nfolds` option to set the number of folds to use for cross-validation. In our example, we used `nfolds=5`, but we can also set it to higher numbers.

The number of folds needs to be the same across every models you build.

With a value for `nfolds` specified, we can also provide a value for the `fold_assignment` parameters. `fold_assignment` takes values such as `auto`, `random`, `modulo`, and `stratified`. If we set it to `Auto`, the algorithm automatically chooses an option; currently, it chooses `Random`. With `fold_assignment` set to `Random`, it will enable a random split of the data into `nfolds` sets. When `fold_assignment` is set to `Modulo`, it uses a deterministic method to evenly split the data into `nfolds` that don't depend on the `seed` parameter.

When we use cross-validation method to build models, ensure that you specify a `seed` value for all models or use `fold_assignment="Modulo"`.

In grid search, we used two parameters: `stopping_metric` and `stopping_rounds`. These parameters are available for GBM and random forest algorithms, but they aren't available for GLM. `stopping_metric` specifies the metric to consider when early stopping is specified, which can be done by setting `stopping_rounds` to a value greater than zero.

In our examples, we set `stopping_metric` to AUC and `stopping_rounds` to five. This means that the algorithm will measure the AUC before it stops training any further if the AUC doesn't improve in the specified number of rounds, which is five in our case.

> If `stopping_metric` is specified, `stopping_rounds` must be set as well. When `stopping_tolerance` is also set, the model will stop training after reaching the number of rounds mentioned in `stopping_rounds` if the model's `stopping_metric` doesn't improve by the `stopping_tolerance` value.

See also

The H2O documentation is available at `http://docs.h2o.ai/`.

11
Heterogeneous Ensemble for Text Classification Using NLP

In this chapter, we will cover the following topics:

- Spam filtering using an ensemble of heterogeneous algorithms
- Sentiment analysis of movie reviews using an ensemble model

Introduction

Text classification is a widely studied area of language processing and text mining. Using text classification mechanisms, we can classify documents into predefined categories based on their content.

In this chapter, we'll take a look at how to classify short text messages that get delivered to our mobile phones. While some messages we receive are important, others might represent a serious threat to our privacy. We want to be able to classify the text messages correctly in order to avoid spam and to avoid missing important messages.

Spam filtering using an ensemble of heterogeneous algorithms

We will use the SMS Spam Collection dataset from the UCI ML repository to create a spam classifier. Using the spam classifier, we can estimate the polarity of these messages. We can use various classifiers to classify the messages either as spam or ham.

In this example, we opt for algorithms such as Naive Bayes, random forest, and support vector machines to train our models.

We prepare our data using various data-cleaning and preparation mechanisms. To preprocess our data, we will perform the following sequence:

1. Convert all text to lowercase
2. Remove punctuation
3. Remove stop words
4. Perform stemming
5. Tokenize the data

We also process our data using **term frequency-inverse data frequency (TF-IDF)**, which tells us how often a word appears in a message or a document. TF is calculated as:

```
TF = No. of times a word appears in a document / Total No. of words in
the document
```

TF-IDF numerically scores the importance of a word based on how often the word appears in a document or a collection of documents. Simply put, the higher the TF-IDF score, the rarer the term. The lower the score, the more common it is. The mathematical representation of TD-IDF would be as follows:

$$\text{tfidf}(w,d,D) = \text{tf}(t,d) \times \text{idf}(t,D)$$

where w represents the word, d represents a document and D represents the collection of documents.

In this example, we'll use the SMS spam collection dataset, which has labelled messages that have been gathered for cellphone spam research. This dataset is available in the UCI ML repository and is also provided in the GitHub repository.

Getting ready

We start by importing the required libraries:

```
import os
import numpy as np
import pandas as pd
import itertools
import warnings
import string
import matplotlib.pyplot as plt
from nltk.corpus import stopwords
from nltk.stem import WordNetLemmatizer
from sklearn.feature_extraction.text import CountVectorizer
```

```
from sklearn.feature_extraction.text import TfidfVectorizer
from sklearn.model_selection import train_test_split
from sklearn.naive_bayes import MultinomialNB
from sklearn.metrics import confusion_matrix
from sklearn.model_selection import GridSearchCV
from sklearn.ensemble import RandomForestClassifier
from sklearn.metrics import classification_report
from sklearn.metrics import roc_auc_score as auc
from sklearn.metrics import roc_curve
from sklearn.metrics import accuracy_score
from scipy.stats import mode
```

Note that for this example we import libraries such as `nltk` to prepare our data. We also import the `CountVectorizer` and `TfidVectorizer` modules from `sklearn.feature_extraction`. These modules are used for feature extraction in ML algorithms.

We reuse `plot_confusion_matrix` from the scikit-learn website to plot our confusion matrix. This is the same function that we've used in earlier chapters as well:

```
def plot_confusion_matrix(cm, classes,
                          normalize=False,
                          title='Confusion matrix',
                          cmap=plt.cm.Blues):

    plt.imshow(cm, interpolation='nearest', cmap=cmap)
    plt.title(title)
    plt.colorbar()
    tick_marks = np.arange(len(classes))
    plt.xticks(tick_marks, classes, rotation=45)
    plt.yticks(tick_marks, classes)

    fmt = '.2f' if normalize else 'd'
    thresh = cm.max() / 2.
    for i, j in itertools.product(range(cm.shape[0]), range(cm.shape[1])):
        plt.text(j, i, format(cm[i, j], fmt),
                horizontalalignment="center",
                color="white" if cm[i, j] > thresh else "black")

    plt.ylabel('True label')
    plt.xlabel('Predicted label')
    plt.tight_layout()
```

We set our working directory and read the dataset:

```
os.chdir("/.../Chapter 11/CS - SMS Classification")
os.getcwd()

df_sms = pd.read_csv("sms_labeled_data.csv", encoding = 'utf8')
```

 Note that we use `encoding='utf8'`. This is to instruct the `read_csv()` method to use UTF encoding to read the file. Python comes with a number of codecs. An exhaustive list is available at `https://docs.python.org/3/library/codecs.html#standard-encodings`.

After reading the data, we check whether it has been loaded properly:

```
df_sms.head()
```

We also check the number of observations and features in the dataset with `dataframe.shape`:

```
df_sms.shape
```

We take a look at the counts of spam and ham messages:

```
# Gives the count for ham messages
print(df_sms["type"].value_counts()[0])
no_of_ham_messages = df_sms["type"].value_counts()[0]

# Gives the count for spam messages
print(df_sms["type"].value_counts()[1])
no_of_spam_messages = df_sms["type"].value_counts()[1]
```

We can also visualize the proportion of spam and ham messages:

```
sms_count = pd.value_counts(df_sms["type"], sort= True)
ax = sms_count.plot(kind='bar', figsize=(10,10), color= ["green",
"orange"], fontsize=13)

ax.set_alpha(0.8)
ax.set_title("Percentage Share of Spam and Ham Messages")
ax.set_ylabel("Count of Spam & Ham messages");
ax.set_yticks([0, 500, 1000, 1500, 2000, 2500, 3000, 3500, 4000, 4500,
5000, 5500])

totals = []
for i in ax.patches:
totals.append(i.get_height())

total = sum(totals)
```

```
# set individual bar lables using above list
for i in ax.patches:
string = str(round((i.get_height()/total)*100, 2))+'%'
# get_x pulls left or right; get_height pushes up or down
ax.text(i.get_x()+0.16, i.get_height(), string, fontsize=13, color='black')
```

With the preceding code, we see the following plot:

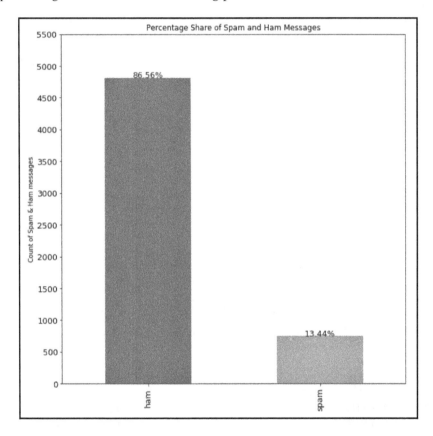

We also define a function to remove punctuation, convert the text to lowercase, and remove stop words:

```
lemmatizer = WordNetLemmatizer()

# Defining a function to remove punctuations, convert text to lowercase and
remove stop words
def process_text(text):
    no_punctuations = [char for char in text if char not in
string.punctuation]
    no_punctuations = ''.join(no_punctuations)
```

```
        clean_words = [word.lower() for word in nopunc.split() if word.lower()
    not in stopwords.words('english')]
        clean_words = [lemmatizer.lemmatize(lem) for lem in clean_words]
        clean_words = " ".join(clean_words)

        return clean_words
```

We apply the defined `process_text()` function to our text variable in the dataset:

```
df_sms['text'] = df_sms['text'].apply(text_processing)
```

We separate our feature and target variables, and split our data into `train` and `test` subsets:

```
X = df_sms.loc[:,'text']
Y = df_sms.loc[:,'type']
Y = Y.astype('int')

X_train, X_test, Y_train, Y_test = train_test_split(X, Y, test_size=.3,
random_state=1)
```

We use the `CountVectorizer` module to convert the text into vectors:

```
count_vectorizer = CountVectorizer(stop_words='english')

count_train = count_vectorizer.fit_transform(X_train)
count_test = count_vectorizer.transform(X_test)
```

We also use the `TfidfVectorizer` module to convert the text into TF-IDF vectors:

```
tfidf = TfidfVectorizer(stop_words='english')

tfidf_train = tfidf.fit_transform(X_train)
tfidf_test = tfidf.transform(X_test)
```

Let's now move on to training our models. We use the following algorithms both on the count data and the TF-IDF data and see how the individual models perform:

- Naive Bayes
- Support vector machine
- Random forest

We also combine the model predictions to see the result from the ensemble.

How to do it...

Let's begin with training our models, and see how they perform in this section:

1. Train the model using the Naive Bayes algorithm. Apply this algorithm to both the count data and the TF-IDF data.

   The following is the code to train the Naive Bayes on the count data:

   ```
   from sklearn.naive_bayes import MultinomialNB
   nb = MultinomialNB()

   nb.fit(count_train, Y_train)
   nb_pred_train = nb.predict(count_train)
   nb_pred_test = nb.predict(count_test)
   nb_pred_train_proba = nb.predict_proba(count_train)
   nb_pred_test_proba = nb.predict_proba(count_test)

   print('The accuracy for the training data is
   {}'.format(nb.score(count_train, Y_train)))
   print('The accuracy for the testing data is
   {}'.format(nb.score(count_test, Y_test)))
   ```

   Take a look at the `train` and `test` accuracy for the preceding model:

   ```
   The accuracy for the training data is 0.9940858832604783
   The accuracy for the testing data is 0.9808038392321535
   ```

2. Print the classification report using the `classification_report()` method. Pass `Y_test` and `nb_pred_test` to the `classification_report()` method:

   ```
   print(classification_report(Y_test, nb_pred_test))
   ```

   This gives us the following output, which shows the `precision`, `recall`, `f1-score`, and `support` for each class in the target variable:

	precision	recall	f1-score	support
0	0.93	0.93	0.93	230
1	0.99	0.99	0.99	1437
micro avg	0.98	0.98	0.98	1667
macro avg	0.96	0.96	0.96	1667
weighted avg	0.98	0.98	0.98	1667

3. Pass `Y_test` and `nb_pred_test` to the `plot_confusion_matrix()` function to plot the confusion matrix, as follows:

```
target_names = ['Spam','Ham']

# Pass actual & predicted values to the confusion matrix()
cm = confusion_matrix(Y_test, nb_pred_test)
plt.figure()
plot_confusion_matrix(cm, classes=target_names)
plt.show()
```

The following plot shows us the true negative, false positive, false negative, and true positive values:

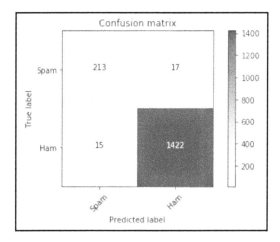

 Note that in the *Getting ready* section earlier, we used the `TfidfVectorizer` module to convert text into TF-IDF vectors.

4. Fit the Naive Bayes model to the TF-IDF train data:

```
nb.fit(tfidf_train, Y_train)
nb_pred_train_tfidf = nb.predict(tfidf_train)
nb_pred_test_tfidf = nb.predict(tfidf_test)

nb_tfidf_pred_train_proba = nb.predict_proba(tfidf_train)
nb_tfidf_pred_test_proba = nb.predict_proba(tfidf_test)

print('The accuracy for the training data is
```

```
{}'.format(nb.score(count_train, Y_train)))
print('The accuracy for the testing data is
{}'.format(nb.score(count_test, Y_test)))
```

5. Check the performance statistics of the TF-IDF test data:

```
print(classification_report(Y_test, nb_pred_test_tfidf))

target_names = ['Spam','Ham']

# Pass actual & predicted values to the confusion matrix()
cm = confusion_matrix(Y_test, nb_pred_test_tfidf)
plt.figure()

plot_confusion_matrix(cm, classes=target_names)
plt.show()
```

In the following screenshot, we can see the output from the preceding code block:

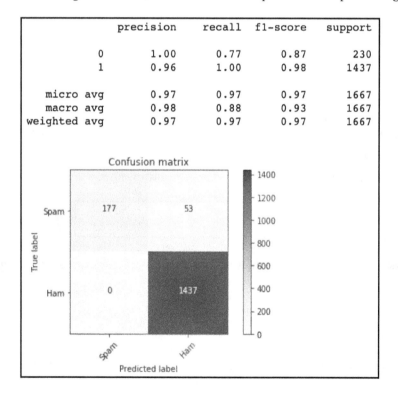

	precision	recall	f1-score	support
0	1.00	0.77	0.87	230
1	0.96	1.00	0.98	1437
micro avg	0.97	0.97	0.97	1667
macro avg	0.98	0.88	0.93	1667
weighted avg	0.97	0.97	0.97	1667

6. Fit the model with the support vector machine classifier with the count data. Use `GridSearchCV` to perform a search over the specified parameter values for the estimator:

```
from sklearn.svm import SVC

svc = SVC(kernel='rbf',probability=True)
svc_params = {'C':[0.001, 0.01, 0.1, 1, 10]}

svc_gcv_rbf_count = GridSearchCV(svc, svc_params, cv=5)
svc_gcv_rbf_count.fit(count_train, Y_train)

# We use the grid model to predict the class
svc_rbf_train_predicted_values =
svc_gcv_rbf_count.predict(count_train)
svc_rbf_test_predicted_values =
svc_gcv_rbf_count.predict(count_test)

# We use the grid model to predict the class probabilities
svc_gcv_train_proba_rbf =
svc_gcv_rbf_count.predict_proba(count_train)
svc_gcv_test_proba_rbf =
svc_gcv_rbf_count.predict_proba(count_test)

print('The best parameters
{}'.format(svc_gcv_rbf_count.best_params_))
print('The best score {}'.format(svc_gcv_rbf_count.best_score_))
```

The grid-search provides us with the optimum model. We get to see the parameter values and the score of the optimum model:

```
The best parameters {'C': 10}
The best score 0.8794034456158395
```

7. Take a look at the `test` accuracy of the count data with the following code:

```
print(classification_report(Y_test, svc_rbf_test_predicted_values))

target_names = ['Spam','Ham']

# Pass actual & predicted values to the confusion matrix()
cm = confusion_matrix(Y_test, svc_rbf_test_predicted_values)
plt.figure()
plot_confusion_matrix(cm,classes=target_names)
plt.show()
```

Here's the output from `classification_report()` and the confusion matrix:

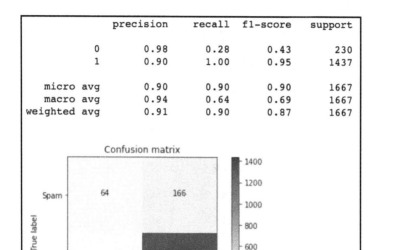

	precision	recall	f1-score	support
0	0.98	0.28	0.43	230
1	0.90	1.00	0.95	1437
micro avg	0.90	0.90	0.90	1667
macro avg	0.94	0.64	0.69	1667
weighted avg	0.91	0.90	0.87	1667

8. Use SVM with the TF-IDF data:

```
svc = SVC(kernel='rbf',probability=True)
svc_params = {'C':[0.001, 0.01, 0.1, 1, 10]}

svc_gcv = GridSearchCV(svc,svc_params,cv=5)
svc_gcv.fit(tfidf_train, Y_train)

# We use the grid model to predict the class
svc_tfidf_rbf_train_predicted_values = svc_gcv.predict(tfidf_train)
svc_tfidf_rbd_test_predicted_values = svc_gcv.predict(tfidf_test)

# We use the grid model to predict the class probabilities
svc_gcv_tfidf_train_proba_rbf = svc_gcv.predict_proba(tfidf_train)
svc_gcv_tfidf_test_proba_rbf = svc_gcv.predict_proba(tfidf_test)

print('The best parameters {}'.format(svc_gcv.best_params_))
print('The best score {}'.format(svc_gcv.best_score_))
```

The following output shows the best score of the model trained with the SVM and RBF kernel on the TF-IDF data:

```
The best parameters {'C': 0.001}
The best score 0.8670609411159681
```

9. Print the classification report and the confusion matrix for the preceding model:

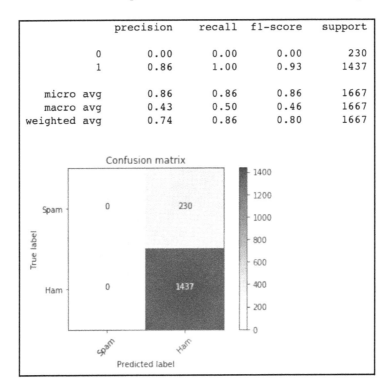

```
              precision    recall  f1-score   support

           0       0.00      0.00      0.00       230
           1       0.86      1.00      0.93      1437

   micro avg       0.86      0.86      0.86      1667
   macro avg       0.43      0.50      0.46      1667
weighted avg       0.74      0.86      0.80      1667
```

10. Fit the random forest model on the count data with grid search cross-validation, as we did for SVM:

```
# Set the parameters for grid search
rf_params =
{"criterion":["gini","entropy"],"min_samples_split":[2,3],"max_dept
h":[None,2,3],"min_samples_leaf":[1,5],"max_leaf_nodes":[None],"oob
_score":[True]}

# Create an instance of the Random Forest Classifier()
rf = RandomForestClassifier()
```

```
# Use gridsearchCV(), pass the values you have set for grid search
rf_gcv = GridSearchCV(rf, rf_params, cv=5)

# Fit the model onto the train data
rf_gcv.fit(count_train, Y_train)

# We use the grid model to predict the class
rf_train_predicted_values = rf_gcv.predict(count_train)
rf_test_predicted_values = rf_gcv.predict(count_test)

# We use the grid model to predict the class probabilities
rf_gcv_pred_train_proba = rf_gcv.predict_proba(count_train)
rf_gcv_pred_test_proba = rf_gcv.predict_proba(count_test)

print('The best parameters {}'.format(rf_gcv.best_params_))
print('The best score {}'.format(rf_gcv.best_score_))
```

A grid search of the random forest with the grid parameters returns the best
parameters and the best score, as seen in the following screenshot:

```
The best parameters {'criterion': 'gini', 'max_depth': None, 'max_leaf_nodes': None, 'min_samples_leaf': 1, 'min_samp
les_split': 3, 'oob_score': True}
The best score 0.9748007199794292
```

11. Using a classification report and a confusion matrix, take a look at the
    performance metrics of the random forest model with the count data on our test
    data:

```
print(classification_report(Y_test, rf_test_predicted_values))

target_names = ['Spam','Ham']

# Pass actual & predicted values to the confusion matrix()
cm = confusion_matrix(Y_test, rf_test_predicted_values)
plt.figure()
plot_confusion_matrix(cm,classes=target_names)
plt.show()
```

The report is shown in the following screenshot:

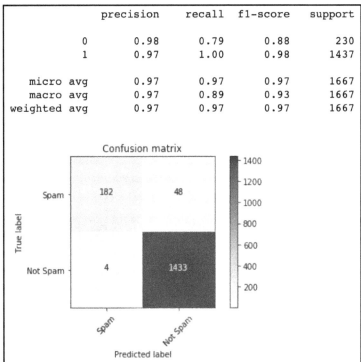

12. Build a model on a random forest with a grid-search on the TF-IDF data:

```
# Set the parameters for grid search
rf_params =
{"criterion":["gini","entropy"],"min_samples_split":[2,3],"max_dept
h":[None,2,3],"min_samples_leaf":[1,5],"max_leaf_nodes":[None],"oob
_score":[True]}

# Create an instance of the Random Forest Classifier()
rf = RandomForestClassifier()

# Use gridsearchCV(), pass the values you have set for grid search
rf_gcv = GridSearchCV(rf, rf_params, cv=5)

rf_gcv.fit(tfidf_train, Y_train)

rf_tfidf_train_predicted_values = rf_gcv.predict(tfidf_train)
rf_tfidf_test_predicted_values = rf_gcv.predict(tfidf_test)
```

```
rf_gcv_tfidf_pred_train_proba = rf_gcv.predict_proba(tfidf_train)
rf_gcv_tfidf_pred_test_proba = rf_gcv.predict_proba(tfidf_test)

print('The best parameters {}'.format(rf_gcv.best_params_))
print('The best score {}'.format(rf_gcv.best_score_))

print(classification_report(Y_test,
rf_tfidf_test_predicted_values))

target_names = ['Spam','Ham']
# Pass actual & predicted values to the confusion matrix()
cm = confusion_matrix(Y_test, rf_tfidf_test_predicted_values)
plt.figure()
plot_confusion_matrix(cm, classes=target_names)
plt.show()
```

13. Take the output of the `predict_proba()` methods to gather the predicted probabilities from each model to plot the ROC curves. The full code is provided in the code bundle.

    Here's a sample of the code to plot the ROC curve from the Naive Bayes model on the count data:

```
fpr, tpr, thresholds = roc_curve(Y_test, nb_pred_test_proba[:,1])
roc_auc = auc(Y_test,nb_pred_test_proba[:,1])

plt.title('ROC Naive Bayes (Count)')
plt.plot(fpr, tpr, 'b',label='AUC = %0.3f'% roc_auc)
plt.legend(loc='lower right')
plt.plot([0,1],[0,1],'r--')
plt.xlim([-0.1,1.0])
plt.ylim([-0.1,1.01])
plt.ylabel('True Positive Rate')
plt.xlabel('False Positive Rate')
```

With the complete code provided in the code bundle, we can view the ROC plot from all the models and compare them:

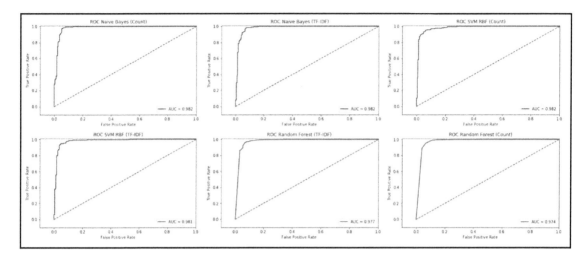

14. Average the probabilities from all the models and plot the ROC curves:

```
plt.subplot(4,3,7)

### Test Count Data
d = (nb_pred_test_proba + svc_gcv_test_proba_rbf +
rf_gcv_pred_test_proba)/4

fpr, tpr, thresholds = roc_curve(Y_test,d[:,1])
roc_auc = auc(Y_test,d[:,1])

plt.title('ROC Ensemble (Count)')
plt.plot(fpr, tpr, 'b',label='AUC = %0.3f'% roc_auc)
plt.legend(loc='lower right')
plt.plot([0,1],[0,1],'r--')
plt.xlim([-0.1,1.0])
plt.ylim([-0.1,1.01])
plt.ylabel('True Positive Rate')
plt.xlabel('False Positive Rate')

plt.subplot(4,3,8)

### Test TF-IDF Data
d = (nb_tfidf_pred_test_proba + svc_gcv_tfidf_test_proba_rbf +
rf_gcv_tfidf_pred_test_proba)/4

fpr, tpr, thresholds = roc_curve(Y_test,d[:,1])
```

```
roc_auc = auc(Y_test,d[:,1])

plt.title('ROC Ensemble (TF-IDF)')
plt.plot(fpr, tpr, 'b',label='AUC = %0.3f'% roc_auc)
plt.legend(loc='lower right')
plt.plot([0,1],[0,1],'r--')
plt.xlim([-0.1,1.0])
plt.ylim([-0.1,1.01])
plt.ylabel('True Positive Rate')
plt.xlabel('False Positive Rate')
#plt.show()

plt.tight_layout(pad=1,rect=(0, 0, 3.5, 4))
plt.show()
```

We can see the average result of the ROC and AUC scores in the following screenshot:

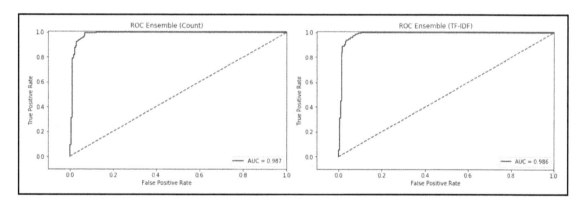

15. Check the accuracy of the ensemble result. Create an array of the predicted results, as follows:

```
predicted_array = np.array([nb_pred_test_tfidf,
svc_tfidf_rbd_test_predicted_values,
rf_tfidf_test_predicted_values])

print("Each array is the prediction of the respective models")
print(predicted_array)
```

16. Calculate the mode of the predicted values for the respective observations to perform max-voting in order to get the final predicted result:

```
# Using mode on the array, we get the max vote for each observation
predicted_array = mode(predicted_array)

# Check the array
print(predicted_array)

print("The accuracy for test")
accuracy_score(Y_test, predicted_array[0][0])
```

17. Plot the test accuracy for the models trained on the count data and TF-IDF data, respectively:

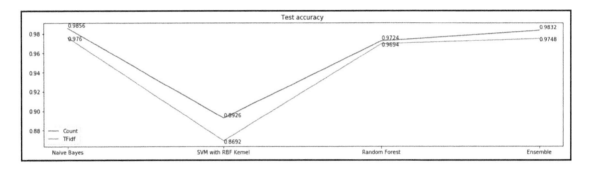

How it works...

In the *Getting ready* section, we imported all the required libraries and defined the function to plot the confusion matrix. We read our dataset, using UTF8 encoding. We checked the proportion of spam and ham messages in our dataset and used the `CountVectorizer` and `TfidfVectorizer` modules to convert the texts into vectors and TF-IDF vectors, respectively.

After that, we built multiple models using various algorithms. We also applied each algorithm on both the count data and the TF-IDF data.

The models need to be built in the following order:

1. Naive Bayes on count data
2. Naive Bayes on TF-IDF data
3. SVM with RBF kernel on count data
4. SVM with RBF kernel on TF-IDF data
5. Random forest on count data
6. Random forest on TF-IDF data

The Naive Bayes classifier is widely used for text classification in machine learning. The Naive Bayes algorithm is based on the conditional probability of features belonging to a class. In *Step 1*, we built our first model with the Naive Bayes algorithm on the count data. In *Step 2*, we checked the performance metrics using `classification_report()` to see the `precision`, `recall`, `f1-score`, and `support`. In *Step 3*, we called `plot_confusion_matrix()` to plot the confusion matrix.

Then, in *Step 4*, we built the Naive Bayes model on the TF-IDF data and evaluated the performance in *Step 5*. In *Step 6* and *Step 7*, we trained our model using the support vector machine on the count data, evaluated its performance using the output from `classification_report`, and plotted the confusion matrix. We trained our SVM model using the RBF kernel. We also showcased an example of using `GridSearchCV` to find the best parameters. In *Step 8* and *Step 9*, we repeated what we did in *Step 6* and *Step 7*, but this time, we trained the SVM on TF-IDF data.

In *Step 10*, we trained a random forest model using grid search on the count data. We set **gini** and **entropy** for the `criterion` hyperparameter. We also set multiple values for the parameters, such as `min_samples_split`, `max_depth`, and `min_samples_leaf`. In *Step 11*, we evaluated the model's performance.

We then trained another random forest model on the TF-IDF data in *Step 12*. Using the `predic_proba()` function, we got the class probabilities on our test data. We used the same in *Step 13* to plot the ROC curves with AUC scores annotated on the plots for each of the models. This helps us to compare the performance of the models.

In *Step 14*, we averaged the probabilities, which we got from the models for both the count and TF-IDF data. We then plotted the ROC curves for the ensemble results. From *Step 15* through to *Step 17*, we plotted the test accuracy for each of the models built on the count data as well as the TF-IDF data.

Sentiment analysis of movie reviews using an ensemble model

Sentiment analysis is another widely studied research area in **natural language processing** (**NLP**). It's a popular task performed on reviews to determine the sentiments of comments provided by reviewers. In this example, we'll focus on analyzing movie review data from the **Internet Movie Database** (**IMDb**) and classifying it according to whether it is positive or negative.

We have movie reviews in `.txt` files that are separated into two folders: negative and positive. There are 1,000 positive reviews and 1,000 negative reviews. These files can be retrieved from GitHub.

We have divided this case study into two parts:

- The first part is to prepare the dataset. We'll read the review files that are provided in the `.txt` format, append them, label them as positive or negative based on which folder they have been put in, and create a `.csv` file that contains the label and text.
- In the second part, we'll build multiple base learners on both the count data and on the TF-IDF data. We'll evaluate the performance of the base learners and then evaluate the ensemble of the predictions.

Getting ready

We start by importing the required libraries:

```
import os
import glob
import pandas as pd
```

We set our working folder as follows:

```
os.chdir("/.../Chapter 11/CS - IMDB Classification")
os.getcwd()
```

We set our path variable and iterate through the .txt files in the folders.

Note that we have a subfolder, /txt_sentoken/pos, which holds the TXT files for the positive reviews. Similarly, we have a subfolder, /txt_sentoken/neg, which holds the TXT files for the negative reviews.

The TXT files for the positive reviews are read and the reviews are appended in an array. We use the array to create a DataFrame, df_pos.

```
path="/.../Chapter 11/CS - IMDB Classification/txt_sentoken/pos/*.txt"

files = glob.glob(path)
text_pos = []

for p in files:
 file_read = open(p, "r")
 to_append_pos = file_read.read()
 text_pos.append(to_append_pos)
 file_read.close()

df_pos = pd.DataFrame({'text':text_pos,'label':'positive'})
df_pos.head()
```

With the head() method, we take a look at the positive reviews.

We also iterate through the TXT files in the negative folder to read the negative reviews and append them in an array. We use the array to create a DataFrame, df_neg:

```
path="/Users/Dippies/CODE PACKT - EML/Chapter 11/CS - IMDB
Classification/txt_sentoken/neg/*.txt"

files = glob.glob(path)
text_neg = []

for n in files:
    file_read = open(n, "r")
    to_append_neg = file_read.read()
    text_neg.append(to_append_neg)
    file_read.close()

df_neg = pd.DataFrame({'text':text_neg,'label':'negative'})
df_neg.head()
```

Finally, we merge the positive and negative DataFrames into a single DataFrame using the `concat()` method:

```
df_moviereviews=pd.concat([df_pos, df_neg])
```

We can take a look at the prepared DataFrame with the `head()` and `tail()` methods:

```
print(df_moviereviews.head())
print(df_moviereviews.tail())
```

The preceding code gives us the following output:

```
      label                                            text
0   positive  assume nothing . \nthe phrase is perhaps one o...
1   positive  plot : derek zoolander is a male model . \nhe ...
2   positive  i actually am a fan of the original 1961 or so...
3   positive  a movie that's been as highly built up as the ...
4   positive  " good will hunting " is two movies in one : ...
        label                                          text
995  negative  synopsis : when a meteorite crashlands in the ...
996  negative  it's now the anniversary of the slayings of ju...
997  negative  coinciding with the emerging popularity of mov...
998  negative  and now the high-flying hong kong style of fil...
999  negative  battlefield long , boring and just plain stupi...
```

From the preceding image, we notice that the positive and negative reviews have been added sequentially. The first half of the DataFrame holds the positive reviews, while the next half holds the negative reviews.

Let's shuffle the data so that it doesn't stay in sequential order:

```
from sklearn.utils import shuffle

df_moviereviews=shuffle(df_moviereviews)
df_moviereviews.head(10)
```

We can now see that the data in the DataFrame is shuffled:

	label	text
879	negative	capsule : the running gag pair of characters f...
310	positive	i rented this movie with very high hopes . \nt...
228	negative	the scene at the end of 1989's `dead poets soc...
891	negative	the makers of spawn have created something alm...
753	positive	robert benton has assembled a stellar , mature...
689	negative	tom dicillo directs this superficial comedy ab...
106	negative	another f txt_sentoken.zip quirky comedy from...
130	negative	five years after his directorial debut based o...
382	positive	another 'independent film' , this comedy , whi...
222	positive	after the average mouse hunt , the silly small...

We validate the dimensions of the merged DataFrame to see whether it holds 2,000 observations, which would be the result of combining the 1,000 negative and 1,000 positive reviews:

```
df_moviereviews.shape
```

From the preceding code, we notice that we have 2,000 observations and 2 columns.

We may also write the resulting DataFrame into another `.csv` file in order to avoid recreating the CSV file from the TXT files as we did in the preceding steps:

```
df_moviereviews.to_csv("/.../Chapter 11/CS - IMDB
Classification/Data_IMDB.csv")
```

Next, we'll define the `plot_confusion_matrix()` method that we have used earlier.

We can now see the share of the positive and negative reviews in our data. In our case, the proportion is exactly 50:50:

```
df_moviereviews["label"].value_counts().plot(kind='pie')
plt.tight_layout(pad=1,rect=(0, 0, 0.7, 1))

plt.text(x=-0.9,y=0.1, \
         s=(np.round(((df_moviereviews["label"].\
value_counts()[0])/(df_moviereviews["label"].value_counts()[0] + \
                 df_moviereviews["label"].value_counts()[1])),2)))
```

```
plt.text(x=0.4,y=-0.3, \
         s=(np.round(((df_moviereviews["label"].\
value_counts()[1])/(df_moviereviews["label"].value_counts()[0] + \
                  df_moviereviews["label"].value_counts()[1])),2)))

plt.title("% Share of the Positive and Negative reviews in the dataset")
```

The output of the preceding code can be seen in the following screenshot:

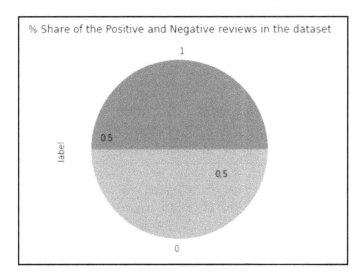

We will now replace the "positive" label with "1" and the "negative" label" with "0":

```
df_moviereviews.loc[df_moviereviews["label"]=='positive',"label",]=1
df_moviereviews.loc[df_moviereviews["label"]=='negative',"label",]=0
```

We prepare our data using various data-cleaning and preparation mechanisms. We'll follow the same sequence as we followed in the previous recipe to preprocess our data:

1. Convert all text to lowercase
2. Remove punctuation
3. Remove stop words
4. Perform stemming
5. Tokenize the data

Next, we'll define a function to perform the preceding clean-up steps:

```
lemmatizer = WordNetLemmatizer()
def process_text(text):
    nopunc = [char for char in text if char not in string.punctuation]
```

```
    nopunc = ''.join(nopunc)

    clean_words = [word.lower() for word in nopunc.split() if word.lower()
not in stopwords.words('english')]
    clean_words = [lemmatizer.lemmatize(lem) for lem in clean_words]
    clean_words = " ".join(clean_words)

    return clean_words
```

We call the preceding function to process our text data:

```
df_moviereviews['text'] = df_moviereviews['text'].apply(process_text)
```

We'll now build our base learners and evaluate the ensemble result.

How to do it...

We start by importing the remaining libraries we need:

1. Import the required libraries:

    ```
    import os
    import numpy as np
    import pandas as pd
    import itertools
    import warnings
    import string
    import matplotlib.pyplot as plt
    from nltk.corpus import stopwords
    from nltk.stem import WordNetLemmatizer
    from sklearn.feature_extraction.text import CountVectorizer
    from sklearn.feature_extraction.text import TfidfVectorizer
    from sklearn.model_selection import train_test_split
    from sklearn.naive_bayes import MultinomialNB
    from sklearn.metrics import confusion_matrix
    from sklearn.model_selection import GridSearchCV
    from sklearn.ensemble import RandomForestClassifier
    from sklearn.metrics import classification_report
    from sklearn.metrics import roc_auc_score as auc
    from sklearn.metrics import roc_curve
    from sklearn.metrics import accuracy_score
    from scipy.stats import mode
    ```

2. Separate the target and predictor variables:

```
X = df_moviereviews.loc[:,'text']
Y = df_moviereviews.loc[:,'label']
Y = Y.astype('int')
```

3. Perform the train-test split of the data:

```
X_train,X_test,y_train,y_test = train_test_split(X, Y,
test_size=.3, random_state=1)
```

4. Use `CountVectorizer()` to convert the text into vectors:

```
count_vectorizer = CountVectorizer()
count_train = count_vectorizer.fit_transform(X_train)
count_test = count_vectorizer.transform(X_test)
```

5. Use `TfidfVectorizer()` to convert the text into TF-IDF vectors:

```
tfidf = TfidfVectorizer()
tfidf_train = tfidf.fit_transform(X_train)
tfidf_test = tfidf.transform(X_test)
```

We proceed by training the base learners on the count data and on the TF-IDF data. We train the base learners with random forest models, Naive Bayes models, and the support-vector classifier models.

6. Train the random forest model using grid-search on the count data:

```
# Set the parameters for grid search
rf_params = {"criterion":["gini","entropy"],\
             "min_samples_split":[2,3],\
             "max_depth":[None,2,3],\
             "min_samples_leaf":[1,5],\
             "max_leaf_nodes":[None],\
             "oob_score":[True]}

# Create an instance of the RandomForestClassifier()
rf = RandomForestClassifier()
warnings.filterwarnings("ignore")

# Use gridsearchCV(), pass the values you have set for grid search
rf_count = GridSearchCV(rf, rf_params, cv=5)

rf_count.fit(count_train, Y_train)

# Predict class predictions & class probabilities with test data
rf_count_predicted_values = rf_count.predict(count_test)
```

```
rf_count_probabilities = rf_count.predict_proba(count_test)

rf_count_train_accuracy = rf_count.score(count_train, Y_train)
rf_count_test_accuracy = rf_count.score(count_test, Y_test)

print('The accuracy for the training data is {}'.\
    format(rf_count_train_accuracy))

print('The accuracy for the testing data is {}'.\
    format(rf_count_test_accuracy))
```

7. Evaluate precision, recall, f1-score, support, and accuracy:

```
print(classification_report(Y_test, rf_count_predicted_values))

# Pass actual & predicted values to the confusion_matrix()
cm = confusion_matrix(Y_test, rf_count_predicted_values)
plt.figure()
plot_confusion_matrix(cm, classes=target_names,normalize=False)
plt.show()
```

In the following screenshot, we can see the output of the preceding code:

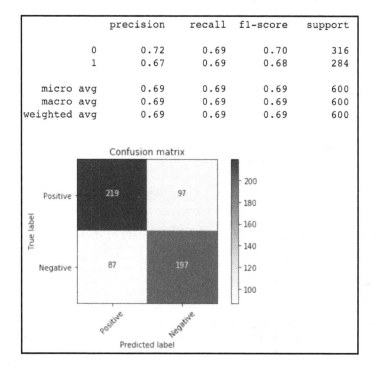

	precision	recall	f1-score	support
0	0.72	0.69	0.70	316
1	0.67	0.69	0.68	284
micro avg	0.69	0.69	0.69	600
macro avg	0.69	0.69	0.69	600
weighted avg	0.69	0.69	0.69	600

8. Train a random forest model on the TF-IDF data using grid-search:

```
# Set the parameters for grid search
rf_params =
{"criterion":["gini","entropy"],"min_samples_split":[2,3],"max_dept
h":[None,2,3],"min_samples_leaf":[1,5],"max_leaf_nodes":[None],"oob
_score":[True]}

# Create an instance of the RandomForestClassifier()
rf = RandomForestClassifier()
warnings.filterwarnings("ignore")

# Use gridsearchCV(), pass the values you have set for grid search
rf_tfidf = GridSearchCV(rf, rf_params, cv=5)

rf_tfidf.fit(tfidf_train, Y_train)
```

9. Evaluate the model's performance:

```
rf_tfidf_predicted_values = rf_tfidf.predict(tfidf_test)
rf_tfidf_probabilities = rf_tfidf.predict_proba(tfidf_test)

rf_train_accuracy = rf_tfidf.score(tfidf_train, Y_train)
rf_test_accuracy = rf_tfidf.score(tfidf_test, Y_test)

print('The accuracy for the training data is
{}'.format(rf_train_accuracy))
print('The accuracy for the testing data is
{}'.format(rf_test_accuracy))

print(classification_report(Y_test, rf_tfidf_predicted_values))

# Pass actual & predicted values to the confusion_matrix()
cm = confusion_matrix(Y_test, rf_tfidf_predicted_values)
plt.figure()
plot_confusion_matrix(cm, classes=target_names,normalize=False)
plt.show()
```

10. Train the Naive Bayes model on the count data and check the accuracy of the test data:

```
nb_count = MultinomialNB()
nb_count.fit(count_train, Y_train)

nb_count_predicted_values = nb_count.predict(count_test)
nb_count_probabilities = nb_count.predict_proba(count_test)

nb_train_accuracy = nb_count.score(count_train, Y_train)
```

```
nb_test_accuracy = nb_count.score(count_test, Y_test)

print('The accuracy for the training data is
{}'.format(nb_train_accuracy))
print('The accuracy for the testing data is
{}'.format(nb_test_accuracy))
```

11. Evaluate the other model's performance parameters
    with `classification_report()` and the confusion matrix:

    ```
    print(classification_report(Y_test, nb_predicted_values))

    # Pass actual & predicted values to the confusion matrix()
    cm = confusion_matrix(Y_test, nb_predicted_values)
    plt.figure()
    plot_confusion_matrix(cm, classes=target_names,normalize=False)
    plt.show()
    ```

12. Train the Naive Bayes model on the TF-IDF data and evaluate its performance
    the same way we did for earlier models:

    ```
    nb_tfidf = MultinomialNB()
    nb_tfidf.fit(count_train, Y_train)

    nb_tfidf_predicted_values = nb_tfidf.predict(tfidf_test)
    nb_tfidf_probabilities = nb_tfidf.predict_proba(tfidf_test)

    nb_train_accuracy = nb_tfidf.score(tfidf_train, Y_train)
    nb_test_accuracy = nb_tfidf.score(tfidf_test, Y_test)

    print('The accuracy for the training data is
    {}'.format(nb_train_accuracy))
    print('The accuracy for the testing data is
    {}'.format(nb_test_accuracy))

    print(classification_report(Y_test, nb_predicted_values))

    #Pass actual & predicted values to the confusion matrix()
    cm = confusion_matrix(Y_test, nb_predicted_values)
    plt.figure()
    plot_confusion_matrix(cm, classes=target_names,normalize=False)
    plt.show()
    ```

13. Train a model with a support vector classifier algorithm with the linear kernel on the count data. We also grid-search the C parameter for the SVC:

```
svc_count = SVC(kernel='linear',probability=True)
svc_params = {'C':[0.001, 0.01, 0.1, 1, 10]}

svc_gcv_count = GridSearchCV(svc_count, svc_params, cv=5)
svc_gcv_count.fit(count_train, Y_train)

svc_count_predicted_values = svc_gcv_count.predict(count_test)
svc_count_probabilities = svc_gcv_count.predict_proba(count_test)

svc_count_train_accuracy = svc_gcv_count.score(count_train,
Y_train)
svc_count_test_accuracy = svc_gcv_count.score(count_test, Y_test)

print('The accuracy for the training data is
{}'.format(svc_gcv_count.score(count_train, Y_train)))
print('The accuracy for the testing data is
{}'.format(svc_gcv_count.score(count_test, Y_test)))

print(classification_report(Y_test, svc_count_predicted_values))
# Pass actual & predicted values to the confusion_matrix()
cm = confusion_matrix(Y_test, svc_count_predicted_values)
plt.figure()
plot_confusion_matrix(cm, classes=target_names,normalize=False)
plt.show()
```

14. Train a model with the support vector classifier algorithm with the linear kernel on the TF-IDF data. We also grid-search the C parameter for the SVC:

```
svc_tfidf = SVC(kernel='linear',probability=True)
svc_params = {'C':[0.001, 0.01, 0.1, 1, 10]}

svc_gcv_tfidf = GridSearchCV(svc_tfidf, svc_params, cv=5)
svc_gcv_tfidf.fit(tfidf_train, Y_train)

svc_tfidf_predicted_values = svc_gcv_tfidf.predict(tfidf_test)
svc_tfidf_probabilities = svc_gcv_tfidf.predict_proba(tfidf_test)

svc_tfidf_train_accuracy = svc_gcv_count.score(tfidf_train,
Y_train)
svc_tfidf_test_accuracy = svc_gcv_count.score(tfidf_test, Y_test)

print('The accuracy for the training data is
{}'.format(svc_gcv_tfidf.score(count_train, Y_train)))
print('The accuracy for the testing data is
{}'.format(svc_gcv_tfidf.score(count_test, Y_test)))
```

```
print(classification_report(Y_test, svc_tfidf_predicted_values))
# Pass actual & predicted values to the confusion_matrix()
cm = confusion_matrix(Y_test, svc_tfidf_predicted_values)
plt.figure()
plot_confusion_matrix(cm, classes=target_names)
plt.show()
```

15. Plot the ROC curve for each of the models. The code for one of the plots is shown here (the complete code is provided in this book's code bundle):

```
fpr, tpr, thresholds = roc_curve(Y_test,
rf_count_probabilities[:,1])
roc_auc = auc(Y_test, rf_count_probabilities[:,1])

plt.title('ROC Random Forest Count Data')
plt.plot(fpr, tpr, 'b',label='AUC = %0.3f'% roc_auc)
plt.legend(loc='lower right')
plt.plot([0,1],[0,1],'r--')
plt.xlim([-0.1,1.0])
plt.ylim([-0.1,1.01])
plt.ylabel('True Positive Rate')
plt.xlabel('False Positive Rate')
```

In the following screenshot, we can compare the ROC curves of all the models we've trained:

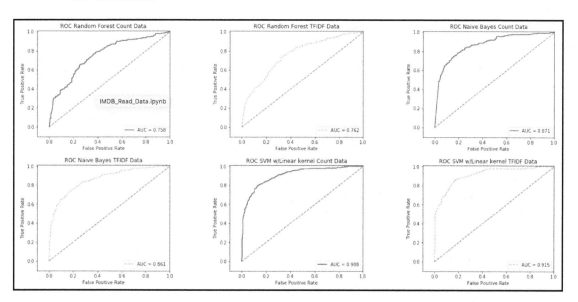

16. Plot the ROC curves for the ensemble results on the count and TF-IDF data:

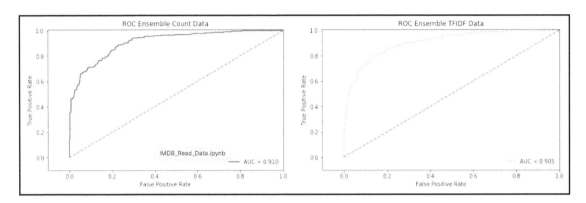

17. Calculate the accuracy of the ensemble with max-voting:

```
predicted_values_count = np.array([rf_count_predicted_values, \
                                   nb_count_predicted_values, \
                                   svc_count_predicted_values])

predicted_values_tfidf = np.array([rf_tfidf_predicted_values, \
                                   nb_tfidf_predicted_values, \
                                   svc_tfidf_predicted_values])

predicted_values_count = mode(predicted_values_count)
predicted_values_tfidf = mode(predicted_values_tfidf)
```

18. Plot the test accuracy for each of the models trained on the count data and the TF-IDF data:

```
count = np.array([rf_count_test_accuracy,\
                  nb_count_test_accuracy,\
                  svc_count_test_accuracy,\
                  accuracy_score(Y_test,
predicted_values_count[0][0])])

tfidf = np.array([rf_tfidf_test_accuracy,\
                  nb_tfidf_test_accuracy,\
                  svc_tfidf_test_accuracy,\
                  accuracy_score(Y_test,
predicted_values_tfidf[0][0])])

label_list = ["Random Forest", "Naive_Bayes", "SVM_Linear",
"Ensemble"]
plt.plot(count)
plt.plot(tfidf)
```

```
plt.xticks([0,1,2,3],label_list)

for i in range(4):
    plt.text(x=i,y=(count[i]+0.001), s=np.round(count[i],4))

for i in range(4):
    plt.text(x=i,y=tfidf[i]-0.003, s=np.round(tfidf[i],4))

plt.legend(["Count","TFIDF"])
plt.title("Test accuracy")

plt.tight_layout(pad=1,rect=(0, 0, 2.5, 2))
plt.show()
```

The following plot shows the accuracy comparison between the count data and the TF-IDF data across all models and the ensemble result:

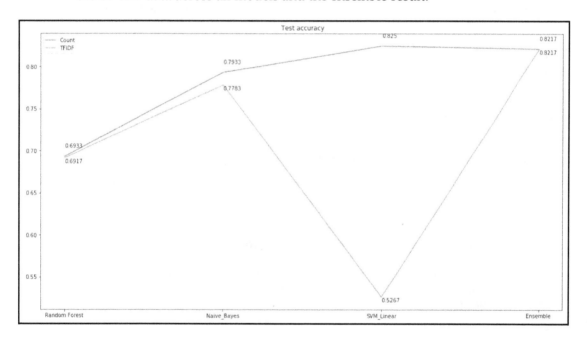

How it works...

We started by importing the required libraries. In this chapter, we used a module called glob. The glob module is used to define the techniques to match a specified pattern to a path, a directory, and a filename. We used the glob module to look for all the files in a specified path. After that, we used the open() method to open each file in read mode. We read each file and appended it to form a dataset with all the review comments. We also created a label column to tag each review with a positive or negative tag.

However, after we appended all the positive and negative reviews, we noticed that they were added sequentially, which means the first half held all the positive reviews and the second half contained the negative reviews. We shuffled the data using the shuffle() method.

We cleaned our data by converting it to lowercase, removing the punctuation and stop words, performing stemming, and tokenizing the texts to create feature vectors.

In the *How to do it...* section, we started by importing the libraries in *Step 1*. In *Step 2*, we separated our target and feature variables into X and Y.

We split our data into train and test subsets in *Step 3*. We used test_size=.3 to split the data into train and test subsets.

In *Step 4* and *Step 5*, we used CountVectorizer() and TfidfVectorizer() to convert the text into vectors and the text into TF-IDF vectors, respectively. Note that with CountVectorizer(), we generated the count_train and count_test datasets. With TfidfVectorizer(), we generated the tfidf_train and tfidf_test datasets.

In *Step 6*, we set our hyperparameters for grid-search to train a random forest model. We trained our random forest model on the count data and checked our train and test accuracy.

 We used the predict() and predict_proba() methods on our test data for all the models we built to predict the class as well as the class probabilities.

In *Step 7*, we generated the confusion matrix to evaluate the model's performance for the random forest model we built in the preceding step. In *Step 8* and *Step 9*, we repeated the training for another random forest model on the TF-IDF data and evaluated the performance. We trained the Naive Bayes model on the count data and the TF-IDF data from *Step 10* through to *Step 12*.

In *Step 13* and *Step 14*, we trained the support vector classifier algorithm with the linear kernel on the count data and the TF-IDF data, respectively. In *Step 15*, we plotted the ROC curves with the AUC score for each of the base learners we built. We also plotted the RUC curves for the ensemble in *Step 16* to compare the performance with the base learners. Finally, in *Step 17*, we plotted the test accuracy of each of the models on the count and TF-IDF data.

There's more...

In today's world, the availability and flow of textual information are limitless. This means we need various techniques to deal with these textual matters to extract meaningful information. For example, **parts-of-speech (POS) tagging** is one of the fundamental tasks in the NLP space. **POS tagging** is used to label words in a text with their respective parts of speech. These tags may then be used with more complex tasks, such as syntactic and semantic parsing, **machine translation** (**MT**), and question answering.

There are eight main parts of speech:

- Nouns
- Pronouns
- Adjectives
- Verbs
- Adverbs
- Prepositions
- Conjunctions
- Interjections:

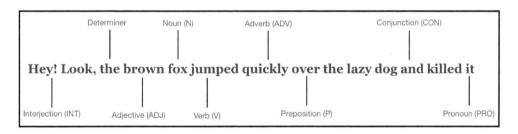

The NLTK library has functions to get POS tags that can be applied to texts after tokenization. Let's import the required libraries:

```
import os
import pandas as pd
import nltk
from nltk.tag import pos_tag
from nltk.corpus import stopwords
```

We take our previously created DataFrame `df_moviereviews`. We convert text into lowercase:

```
df_moviereviews['text'] =df_moviereviews['text'].apply(lambda x: "
".join(x.lower() for x in x.split()))
df_moviereviews['text'].head()
```

We preprocess the text by removing stop words, punctuation, lemmatization, and tokenization:

```
from nltk.stem.wordnet import WordNetLemmatizer
import string
stop = set(stopwords.words('english'))
exclude = set(string.punctuation)
lemma = WordNetLemmatizer()
def clean(doc):
    stop_free = " ".join([i for i in doc.lower().split() if i not in stop])
    stop_free = ''.join(ch for ch in stop_free if ch not in exclude)
    normalized = " ".join(lemma.lemmatize(word) for word in
stop_free.split())
    return normalized

tokenized_sent = [clean(doc).split() for doc in df_moviereviews["text"]]
```

We take a look at the list of the first 10 tokens from the first movie review:

```
tokenized_sent[0][0:10]
```

This generates the following output:

```
['star',
 'war',
 'came',
 'twenty',
 'year',
 'ago',
 'image',
 'traveling',
 'throughout',
 'star']
```

We perform POS tagging:

```
postag=[nltk.pos_tag(token) for token in tokenized_sent]
```

We print the first 10 POS tags for the first movie review:

```
postag[0][0:10]
```

We see the POS tagged words:

```
[('star', 'JJ'),
 ('war', 'NN'),
 ('came', 'VBD'),
 ('twenty', 'CD'),
 ('year', 'NN'),
 ('ago', 'RB'),
 ('image', 'NN'),
 ('traveling', 'VBG'),
 ('throughout', 'IN'),
 ('star', 'NN')]
```

Chunking is another process that can add more structure to POS tagging. Chunking is used for entity detection; it tags multiple tokens to recognize them as meaningful entities. There are various chunkers available; NLTK provides ne_chunk, which recognizes people (names), places, and organizations. Other frequently used chunkers include OpenNLP, Yamcha, and Lingpipe. It's also possible to use a combination of chunkers and apply max-voting on the results to improve the classification's performance.

12
Homogenous Ensemble for Multiclass Classification Using Keras

In this chapter, we'll cover the following recipe:

- An ensemble of homogeneous models to classify fashion products

Introduction

Many studies have been done in classification problems to find out how to obtain better classification accuracy. This problem tends to be more complex when there's a large number of classes on which to make a prediction. In the case of multiclass classification, it's assumed that each class in the target variable are independent of each other. A multiclass classification technique involves training one or more models to classify a target variable that can take more than two classes.

An ensemble of homogeneous models to classify fashion products

In this example, we'll use the Fashion-MNIST dataset. This dataset has 60,000 images of fashion products from ten categories. The target variable can be classified into ten classes:

- T-shirt/top
- Trouser
- Pullover

- Dress
- Coat
- Sandal
- Shirt
- Sneakers
- Bag
- Ankle boot

Each image is a 28 x 28 grayscale image. We will proceed by reading the data to build a few homogeneous models over a few iterations to see whether the ensemble can deliver a higher accuracy.

Getting ready

We'll use Google Colab to train our models. Google Colab comes with TensorFlow installed, so we don't have to install it separately in our system.

We import the required libraries as follows:

```
import numpy as np
import pandas as pd
import seaborn as sns
import matplotlib.pyplot as plt

import tensorflow as tf
from tensorflow import keras
from sklearn.utils import resample
from sklearn.metrics import accuracy_score
from sklearn.metrics import confusion_matrix
from sklearn.metrics import classification_report
from scipy import stats
```

We load our data from the datasets that come with `tf.keras`:

```
# Load the fashion-mnist pre-shuffled train data and test data
(x_train, y_train), (x_test, y_test) =
tf.keras.datasets.fashion_mnist.load_data()
```

We check the dimensions of the train and test subsets:

```
# Print training set shape
print("x_train shape:", x_train.shape, "y_train shape:", y_train.shape)
```

This gives us the following output:

```
x_train shape: (60000, 28, 28) /n y_train shape: (60000,)
```

We take note of the unique values in the target variable:

```
np.unique(y_train)
```

We can see that there are 10 classes labelled from 0 to 9:

```
array([0, 1, 2, 3, 4, 5, 6, 7, 8, 9], dtype=uint8)
```

We can take a quick glimpse at the first few observations as follows:

```
fig=plt.figure(figsize=(16,8))

# number of columns for images in plot
columns=5

# number of rows for images in plot
rows=3

for i in range (1,columns*rows+1):
        fig.add_subplot(rows,columns,i)
        plt.title("Actual Class: {}".\
                format((y_train[i])),color='r',fontsize=16)
        plt.imshow(x_train[i])
plt.show()
```

With the preceding code, we plot the first 15 images, along with the associated labels:

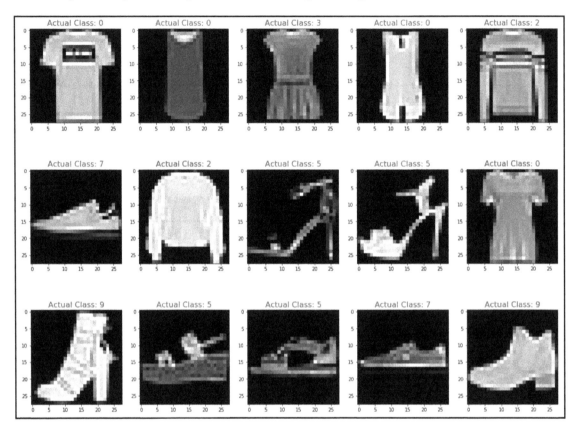

How to do it...

We'll now move on to training our models:

1. In the following code block, we'll create multiple homogeneous models over a few iterations using tf.keras:

```
accuracy = pd.DataFrame( columns=["Accuracy","Precision","Recall"])
predictions = np.zeros(shape=(10000,7))
row_index = 0
for i in range(7):
        # bootstrap sampling
        boot_train = resample(x_train,y_train,replace=True,
n_samples=40000, random_state=None)
        model = tf.keras.Sequential([
```

```
            tf.keras.layers.Flatten(input_shape=(28, 28)),
            tf.keras.layers.Dense(256, activation=tf.nn.relu),
            tf.keras.layers.Dense(128, activation=tf.nn.relu),
            tf.keras.layers.Dense(128, activation=tf.nn.relu),
            tf.keras.layers.Dense(128, activation=tf.nn.relu),
            tf.keras.layers.Dense(128, activation=tf.nn.relu),
            tf.keras.layers.Dense(128, activation=tf.nn.relu),
            tf.keras.layers.Dense(128, activation=tf.nn.relu),
            tf.keras.layers.Dense(128, activation=tf.nn.relu),
            tf.keras.layers.Dense(128, activation=tf.nn.relu),
            tf.keras.layers.Dense(128, activation=tf.nn.relu),
            tf.keras.layers.Dense(10, activation=tf.nn.softmax)])
    # compile the model
    model.compile(loss='sparse_categorical_crossentropy',
optimizer='adam', metrics=['accuracy'])
    # Train the model
    model.fit(x_train,y_train,epochs=10,batch_size=64)
    # Evaluate accuracy
    score = model.evaluate(x_test, y_test, batch_size=64)
    accuracy.loc[row_index,"Accuracy"]=score[1]
    # Make predictions
    model_pred= model.predict(x_test)
    pred_classes =model_pred.argmax(axis=-1)
    accuracy.loc[row_index, 'Precision'] =
precision_score(y_test, pred_classes, average='weighted')
    accuracy.loc[row_index, 'Recall'] = recall_score(y_test,
pred_classes,average='weighted')
    # Save predictions to predictions array
    predictions[:,i] = pred_classes
    print(score)
    row_index+=1

    print("Iteration " + str(i+1)+ " Accuracy : " +
"{0}".format(score[1]))
```

We mention seven iterations and 10 epochs in each iteration. In the following screenshot, we can see the progress as the model gets trained:

```
Epoch 1/10
60000/60000 [==============================] - 21s 351us/step - loss: 0.6613 - acc: 0.7526
Epoch 2/10
60000/60000 [==============================] - 13s 214us/step - loss: 0.4929 - acc: 0.8265
Epoch 3/10
60000/60000 [==============================] - 13s 213us/step - loss: 0.4746 - acc: 0.8398
Epoch 4/10
60000/60000 [==============================] - 13s 214us/step - loss: 0.4096 - acc: 0.8574
Epoch 5/10
60000/60000 [==============================] - 13s 213us/step - loss: 0.3872 - acc: 0.8656
Epoch 6/10
60000/60000 [==============================] - 13s 214us/step - loss: 0.3854 - acc: 0.8675
Epoch 7/10
60000/60000 [==============================] - 13s 213us/step - loss: 0.3710 - acc: 0.8718
Epoch 8/10
60000/60000 [==============================] - 13s 213us/step - loss: 0.3838 - acc: 0.8680
Epoch 9/10
60000/60000 [==============================] - 13s 213us/step - loss: 0.3645 - acc: 0.8743
Epoch 10/10
60000/60000 [==============================] - 13s 213us/step - loss: 0.3596 - acc: 0.8758
10000/10000 [==============================] - 4s 431us/step
[0.38200154910087586, 0.8627]
Epoch 1/10
60000/60000 [==============================] - 22s 359us/step - loss: 0.6461 - acc: 0.7645
Epoch 2/10
60000/60000 [==============================] - 13s 214us/step - loss: 0.4749 - acc: 0.8359
Epoch 3/10
60000/60000 [==============================] - 13s 214us/step - loss: 0.4325 - acc: 0.8506
Epoch 4/10
60000/60000 [==============================] - 13s 215us/step - loss: 0.4129 - acc: 0.8590
```

2. With the code in *Step 1*, we collate the accuracy, precision, and recall for every iteration on the test data:

```
accuracy
```

In the following screenshot, we can see how the preceding three metrics change in each iteration:

	Accuracy	Precision	Recall
0	0.8683	0.869687	0.8683
1	0.8435	0.849763	0.8435
2	0.8573	0.859797	0.8573
3	0.8654	0.867831	0.8654
4	0.8687	0.869421	0.8687
5	0.8453	0.859606	0.8453
6	0.8656	0.866652	0.8656

3. We'll form a DataFrame with the predictions that are returned by all of the models in each iteration:

```
# Create dataframe using prediction of each iteration
df_iteration = pd.DataFrame([predictions[:,0],\
                             predictions[:,1],\
                             predictions[:,2],\
                             predictions[:,3],\
                             predictions[:,4],\
                             predictions[:,5],\
                             predictions[:,6]])
```

4. We convert the type into an integer:

```
df_iteration = df_iteration.astype('int64')
```

5. We perform max-voting to identify the most predicted class for each observation. We simply use mode to find out which class was predicted the most times for an observation:

```
# find the mode for result
mode = stats.mode(df_iteration)
```

6. We calculate the accuracy of the test data:

```
# calculate the accuracy for test dataset
print(accuracy_score( y_test, mode[0].T))
```

7. We generate the confusion matrix with the required labels:

```
# confusion matrix
cm = confusion_matrix(y_test, mode[0].T, labels=[0, 1, 2, 3, 4, 5,
6, 7, 8])
```

8. We plot the confusion matrix:

```
ax= plt.subplot()

# annot=True to annotate cells
sns.heatmap(cm, annot=True, ax = ax, fmt='g', cmap='Blues')
```

The confusion matrix plot appears as follows:

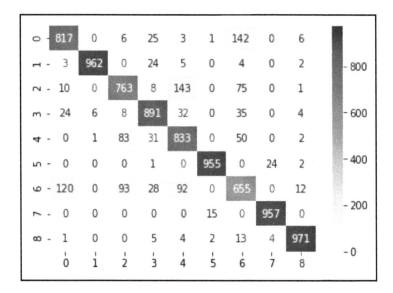

9. We create a DataFrame with all of the iteration numbers:

```
accuracy["Models"]=["Model 1",\
                    "Model 2",\
                    "Model 3",\
                    "Model 4",\
                    "Model 5",\
                    "Model 6",\
                    "Model 7"]
```

10. We then combine the accuracy, precision, and recall in one single table:

```
accuracy=accuracy.append(pd.DataFrame([[\
                                accuracy_score(y_test,\
                                mode[0].T),0,0,\
                                "Ensemble Model"]], \
                                columns=["Accuracy",\
                                "Precision","Recall",\
                                "Models"]))

accuracy.index=range(accuracy.shape[0])

accuracy.set_value(7, 'Precision', precision_score(y_test,
mode[0].T, average='micro'))
accuracy.set_value(7, 'Recall', recall_score(y_test, mode[0].T,
average='micro'))
```

In the following screenshot, we can see the structure that holds the metrics from each of the models and the ensemble model:

	Accuracy	Precision	Recall	Models
0	0.851	0.856075	0.851	Model 1
1	0.8601	0.861578	0.8601	Model 2
2	0.8531	0.855948	0.8531	Model 3
3	0.8331	0.843468	0.8331	Model 4
4	0.8467	0.846121	0.8467	Model 5
5	0.8523	0.85146	0.8523	Model 6
6	0.8353	0.837242	0.8353	Model 7
7	0.8675	0.8675	0.8675	Ensemble Model

11. We plot the accuracy returned by each iteration and the accuracy from max-voting:

```
plt.figure(figsize=(20,8))
plt.plot(accuracy.Models,accuracy.Accuracy)
plt.title("Accuracy across all Iterations and Ensemble")
plt.ylabel("Accuracy")
plt.show()
```

This gives us the following plot. We notice that the accuracy returned by the max-voting method is the highest compared to individual models:

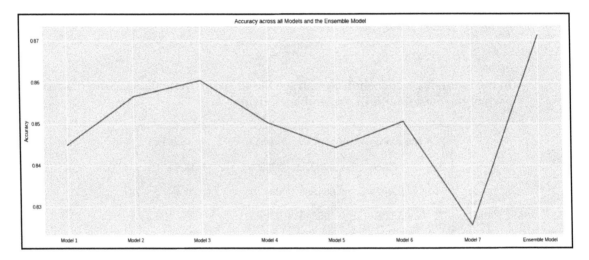

12. We also plot the precision and recall for each model and the ensemble:

```
plt.figure(figsize=(20,8))
plt.plot(accuracy.Models,accuracy.Accuracy,accuracy.Models,accuracy
.Precision)
plt.title("Metrics across all Iterations and models")
plt.legend(["Accuracy","Precision"])
plt.show()
```

This is shown in the following screenshot:

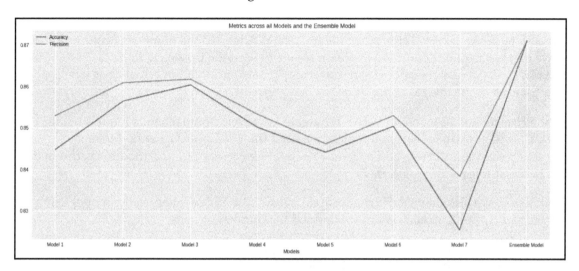

From the preceding screenshot, we notice that the precision and recall improve for an ensemble model.

How it works...

In the *Getting ready* section, we imported our required libraries. Note that we've imported the TensorFlow library. We can directly access the datasets by importing the tf.keras.datasets module. This module comes with various built-in datasets, including the following:

- boston_housing: Boston housing price regression dataset
- cifar10: CIFAR10 small images classification dataset
- fashion_mnist: Fashion-MNIST dataset
- imdb: IMDB sentiment classification dataset
- mnist: MNIST handwritten digits dataset
- reuters: Reuters topic classification dataset

We used the fashion_mnist dataset from this module. We loaded the pre-shuffled train and test data and checked the shape of the train and test subsets.

We noticed, in the *Getting ready* section, that the shape of the training subset is (60000, 28, 28), which means that we have 60,000 images that are of 28 X 28 pixel in size.

We checked the distinct levels in the target variable with the `unique()` method. We saw that there were 10 classes from 0 to 9.

We also took a quick look at some of the images. We defined the number of columns and rows that we required. Running an iteration, we plotted the images with `matplotlib.pyplot.imshow()` in grayscale. We also printed the actual class labels against each of the images using `matplotlib.pyplot.titlc()`.

In the *How to do it...* section, in *Step 1*, we created multiple homogeneous models using the `tf.keras` module. In each iteration, we used the `resample()` method to create bootstrap samples. We passed `replace=True` to the `resample()` method to ensure that we have samples with replacement.

In this step, we also defined the model architecture. We added layers to the model using `tf.keras.layers`. In each layer, we defined the number of units.

 "Model architecture" refers to the overall neural network structure, which includes groups of units called layers. These layers are arranged in a chain-like structure. Each layer is a function of its previous layer. Determining the model architecture is key to neural networks.

We ran through a few iterations in our example. We set the number of iterations. In each iteration, we compiled the model and fit it to our training data. We made predictions on our test data and captured the following metrics in a DataFrame:

- Accuracy
- Precision
- Recall

We've used `Rectified Linear Units (RELU)` as the activation function for the hidden layers. ReLU is represented by the `f(x) = max{0, x}`. In neural networks, ReLU is recommended as the default activation function.

 Note that, in the last layer of the model architecture, we've used softmax as the activation function. The softmax function can be considered a generalization of the sigmoid function. While the sigmoid function is used to represent a probability distribution of a dichotomous variable, the softmax function is used to represent a probability distribution of a target variable with more than two classes. When the softmax function is used for multi-class classification, it returns a probability value between 0 and 1 for each class. The sum of all probabilities will be equal to one.

In *Step 2*, we checked the structure of the accuracy DataFrame that we created in *Step 1*. We noticed that we had three columns for accuracy, precision, and recall and the metrics for each iteration were captured. In *Step 3*, we converted the datatypes in the DataFrame into an integer.

In *Step 4*, we performed max-voting using `stats.mode()` for each observation. Since we ran seven iterations, we had seven predictions for each observation. `stats.mode()` returned the prediction with the maximum occurrence.

In *Step 5*, we checked the accuracy of the model with the max-voted predictions. In *Step 6* and *Step 7*, we generated the confusion matrix to visualize the correct predictions. The diagonal elements in the plot were the correct predictions, while the off-diagonal elements were the misclassifications. We saw that there was a higher number of correct classifications compared to misclassifications.

In *Step 8* and *Step 9*, we proceeded to create a structure to hold the performance metrics (accuracy, precision, and recall), along with the labels for each iteration and the ensemble. We used this structure to plot our charts for the performance metrics.

In *Step 10*, we plotted the accuracy for each iteration and the max-voted predictions. Similarly, in *Step 11*, we plotted the precision and recall for each iteration and the max-voted predictions.

From the plots we generated in *Step 10* and *Step 11*, we noticed how the accuracy, precision, and recall improved for the max-voted predictions.

See also

The `tf.keras` module provides us with TensorFlow-specific functionality, such as eager-execution, data pipelines, and estimators. You can take a look at the various options the `tf.keras` module provides us.

In our example, we used the built-in optimizer classes provided by the `tf.keras.optimizer` module. We used the **Adam optimizer** in our example, but there are other optimizers you can use, such as Adadelta, Adagrad, Adamax, RMSprop, or SGD.

In the present day, the Adam optimizer is one of the best optimizers. It's an extension of **Stochastic Gradient Descent (SGD)**. SGD considers a single learning rate for all weight updates and the learning rate remains unchanged during the model training process. The Adam algorithm considers adaptive learning rates methods to compute individual learning rates for each parameter.

The `tf.keras.losses` module provides us with various options so that we can choose our loss function. We used `sparse_categorical_crossentropy`. Depending on your task, you might opt for other options, such as `binary_crossentropy`, `categorical_crossentropy`, `mean_squared_error`, and so on.

 In the case of multiclass classification, if the target variable is one-hot encoded, use `categorical_crossentropy`. If the classes in the target variable are represented as integers, use `sparse_categorical_crossentropy`.

You can get more detailed information about the other hyperparameters that can be used with `tf.keras` at `https://www.tensorflow.org/api_docs/python/tf/keras`.

Other Books You May Enjoy

If you enjoyed this book, you may be interested in these other books by Packt:

Building Machine Learning Systems with Python - Third Edition
Luis Pedro Coelho, Willi Richert, Willi Richert, Matthieu Brucher, Willi Richert, Matthieu Brucher, Recommended for You , Willi Richert, Matthieu Brucher

ISBN: 978-1-78862-322-3

- Build a classification system that can be applied to text, images, and sound
- Employ Amazon Web Services (AWS) to run analysis on the cloud
- Solve problems related to regression using scikit-learn and TensorFlow
- Recommend products to users based on their past purchases
- Understand different ways to apply deep neural networks on structured data
- Address recent developments in the field of computer vision and reinforcement learning

Machine Learning Algorithms - Second Edition

Giuseppe Bonaccorso, Recommended for You , Recommended for You , Learning, Recommended for You , Learning, Beginner's Guide

ISBN: 978-1-78934-799-9

- Study feature selection and the feature engineering process
- Assess performance and error trade-offs for linear regression
- Build a data model and understand how it works by using different types of algorithm
- Learn to tune the parameters of Support Vector Machines (SVM)
- Explore the concept of natural language processing (NLP) and recommendation systems
- Create a machine learning architecture from scratch

Leave a review - let other readers know what you think

Please share your thoughts on this book with others by leaving a review on the site that you bought it from. If you purchased the book from Amazon, please leave us an honest review on this book's Amazon page. This is vital so that other potential readers can see and use your unbiased opinion to make purchasing decisions, we can understand what our customers think about our products, and our authors can see your feedback on the title that they have worked with Packt to create. It will only take a few minutes of your time, but is valuable to other potential customers, our authors, and Packt. Thank you!

Index

F

false positive rate (FPR) 147
fashion products
  classifying, with ensemble of homogeneous
    models 293, 295, 296, 299, 302, 303, 305,
    306
feature engineering 11
feature scaling 85

G

Gaussian Multinomial Naive Bayes 102
Generalized Linear Model (GLM) 201, 241
ggplot
  working 35
glob 288
Gradient Boosting Machine (GBM) 188, 250
gradient boosting machine
  implementing, for disease risk prediction with
    scikit-learn 171, 173, 174, 176, 178

H

H2O
  used, for implementing stacked generalization for
    campaign outcome prediction 198, 200, 202,
    204, 205, 207
  used, for predicting credit card defaults by
    implementing random forest 151, 153, 154,
    156, 157, 158, 160
handwritten digit classification
  ensemble of homogeneous models 221, 223,
    225, 229, 231
hard-margin SVMs 114
heterogeneous ensemble classifiers
  used, for predicting credit card defaulters 233,
    235, 237, 240, 242, 245, 249, 252
heterogeneous ensemble method 209
heterogeneous ensemble model 39
homogeneous ensemble model 39, 209
hyperplane 112

I

iterative dichotomizer (ID3) 102

K

k-fold cross-validation (k-fold CV) 58, 60, 61, 63,
  65
kernel density estimation (KDE) 79
Kullback-Leibler divergence 104

L

L1 penalty and sparsity, logistic regression
  reference 93
learning rate 75
leave-one-out cross-validation (LOOCV) 58, 60,
  61, 63, 65
linear kernel 120
logistic regression
  about 87, 89, 93
  model, building 90, 91, 92
  working 92

M

machine translation (MT) 289
Matplotlib
  color map selection, reference 32
max-voting 42, 43, 45, 46
maximum regularization 242
maximum-margin hyperplane 113
mean square error (MSE) 41, 214
missing at random (MAR) 24
missing completely at random (MCAR) 24
missing not at random (MNAR) 25
missing values
  analyzing 12, 14, 16, 19, 22, 23, 25
  treating 12, 14, 16, 19, 22, 23, 25
  visualizing 12, 14, 16, 19, 22, 23, 25
model architecture 304
movie reviews, sentiment analysis
  with ensemble model 274, 276, 278, 281, 284,
    287, 288, 290
Multinomial Naive Bayes 102
multiple linear regression
  about 74, 75, 76, 86, 87
  model, building 76, 78, 80, 82, 84
  working 84, 85
Multivariate Bernoulli Naive Bayes 101

implementing, by combining predictions 191, 192, 194, 196, 197

implementing, for campaign outcome prediction with H2O 198, 200, 202, 204, 205, 207

Stochastic Gradient Descent (SGD) 216, 306

strata 53

stratified sampling 53

Street View House Numbers (SVHN) 221

support vector classifier (SVC) 168

support vector machine (SVM)
  about 39, 112, 114, 115, 116, 119, 121
  model, building 117, 118
  working 119

systematic sampling 54

T

term frequency-inverse data frequency (TF-IDF) 256

true positive rate (TPR) 147

types, missing values
  missing at random (MAR) 24
  missing completely at random (MCAR) 24
  missing not at random (MNAR) 25

types, Naive Bayes algorithm
  Gaussian Multinomial Naive Bayes 102
  Multinomial Naive Bayes 102
  Multivariate Bernoulli Naive Bayes 101

W

weighted averaging 49, 50, 52

winner-takes-all approach 191

X

XGBoost, with scikit-learn
  extreme gradient boosting method, implementing for glass identification 179, 180, 182, 184, 185, 188

www.ingramcontent.com/pod-product-compliance
Lightning Source LLC
Chambersburg PA
CBHW080621060326
40690CB00021B/4775